THE SILICON SYNDROME

THE SILICON SYNDROME

How to Survive a High-Tech Relationship

JEAN HOLLANDS

BANTAM BOOKS
TORONTO · NEW YORK · LONDON · SYDNEY · AUCKLAND

THE SILICON SYNDROME: HOW TO SURVIVE A HIGH-TECH RELATIONSHIP
A Bantam Book / August 1985

Library of Congress Cataloging in Publication Data

Hollands, Jean.
  The silicon syndrome.

  1. Marriage—Handbooks, manuals, etc.   2. Personality
assessment—Handbooks, manuals, etc.   3. Technology—
Social aspects.   I. Title.
HQ734.H777   1985   646.7'8   85-3995
                ISBN 0-553-05091-5

Published simultaneously in the United States and Canada

Bantam Books are published by Bantam Books, Inc. Its trademark, consisting
of the words "Bantam Books" and the portrayal of a rooster, is Registered in
the United States Patent and Trademark Office and in other countries.
Marca Registrada. Bantam Books, Inc., 666 Fifth Avenue, New York, New
York 10103.

To Don Wuerflein, my husband, my heart-help, who, in spite of thinking of me as "alien culture," is still smiling, negotiating, holding, and being next to me.

CONTENTS

ACKNOWLEDGMENTS

Thank you, Silicon Valley, your engineers and scientists, your partners and friends. Thank you, all those callers who have affirmed my work already, and those of you who have assured me that we have something important here.

Thanks to Mom, who taught me I can do anything I want to do, and to my brother and family, and to my children, Todd, Laura, Tom, Glenn, and their beloved ones, who have always encouraged me. Don's kids have helped too. My friends and motivators, Joan, Pam, and Monica, and my early inspiration, Trudy Duisenburg, have made this project fun and important. Jeanne Bernkopf, of Bantam Books, helped me in the last stages, and my clinic staff, by taking over for me and putting up with my valley fever, have assisted me too.

My most important inspiration and dedicated support has been my husband, Don Wuerflein, who has alternately loved and hated me throughout this delivery, and who is proud of the work. Don aided me with computer assistance right when we needed it, and he has given me the courage to start to talk about loving each other, by the scientific method.

INTRODUCTION

What Is the Silicon Syndrome?

The Silicon Syndrome is a cluster of symptoms that results when a scientifically oriented thinker mates, works with, or loves a more emotionally oriented person. These patterns are the consequence of the most complicated relationship combination: the union of an engineer/scientist with a nonscientific partner.

The major symptom is a crippling lack of communication caused by differing styles of thinking and feeling. He speaks Chinese; she speaks French. They do not know how to translate each other. They don't even know how to sell themselves or their ideas to their partners.

This couple has tasks to perform. To love. To survive. To bring children into the world, to feed them, teach them, and nurture them. Or to build empires, to solve world problems, to create a technology that enhances life. Or simply to build a nest. The major task is to satisfy themselves, challenge themselves, and nurture themselves—and herein lies the problem.

I came to know the Silicon Syndrome in the form of pain as couples shared their agony in my office. I conduct my practice as a licensed marriage and family therapist at the Growth and Leadership Consultants in Mountain View, California, in the heart of the Silicon Valley. Over a thousand electronics-related companies are located within ten miles of our clinic. The future of our world is created within minutes of my office. The word *communication* is spoken and printed and spotlighted and neon lighted in a thousand micro- and macrocomputers within easy reach of our clinic.

But we are also surrounded by houses, the homes in which our

1

technological geniuses eat and sleep and worry and feel joy. In these homes the communication does not match the promotion that this valley advertises.

I recognize the Silicon Syndrome whenever the wife says, "But he's always in front of the computer." Or, "He's more interested in printed circuit boards than he is in me."

I have learned to watch for this condition when the more serious symptoms appear, like alcoholism, depression, obesity, or other obsessive behaviors.

Another clue is the behavior of the children. When mother and father have distinctly different styles of reacting and responding to good news or bad news, and when they handle crises differently, the children automatically learn to use those differences. Drugs, sexual promiscuity or confusion, and all the acting out that a child can do may signify that mother and father are not communicating. If the parents cannot acknowledge a problem, their children will do it for them!

Now don't get me wrong. There are lots of successful relationships in the Silicon Valley. I am concerned with relationships that are affected by the inability of the engineer/scientist to relate to the emotional traumas that his partner is experiencing. All the couple knows is that their relationship hurts; it pulls from them. They are not really able to be independent; they are too enmeshed in the painful union. Corporately they can't get anything done. The drapes are only half-hung, the dinner parties turn sour, their lovemaking is stilted and sad, and all their accomplishments are tarnished by the lack of a cooperative relationship.

This condition is not limited to the Silicon Valley. If you live in Nebraska, or Georgia, or Connecticut, or any point in between, you may still need this book. "Scientific method" thinkers love and love all over the world. I guess that is why my work has attracted an international interest in the "thinker" and "feeler" syndrome. From Australia to France (the president of France) to China, I've been interviewed, called, and quizzed. Our clinic has had three hundred inquiries from *outside* the Silicon Valley about these differences in decision-making styles. When I lectured recently in Kansas, at Wichita State University, the audience knew just what I was talking about! Read this book if your approach to problems is different from your spouse's. That's reason enough.

I've been amazed at how many men are interested in my writing on this subject. Usually it is the women who gobble up "pop psych" literature. In this case, every newspaper article has attracted desperate men who want help in interpreting themselves to frustrated wives, colleagues, or employees. These men even drag their wives into therapy. What a switch!

The Growth and Leadership Consultants has had the opportunity to do management consulting and training within the electronics industry. We have had a two-dimensional look at the engineer/ scientist, at home and at work. We have advised and lectured and listened to the leaders of the Silicon Valley industrial community. But we have also had the privilege of studying the private family lives of these leaders because they have come to us for marriage counseling, or burn out, or stress symptoms. We can see both sides of their lives. Both sides are on the right track. Both sides count.

The purpose of this book is to mend relationships, to translate the engineers and scientists to their partners, and vice versa. I want to teach you how to live, work, and love together even when you are different and do things differently. I intend to charge you both with responsibility and to recharge your relationship—that is my goal. Roll up your sleeves. We have work to do.

The engineer/scientist picked you for valid reasons. He was smart enough to seduce you on your terms when he found you. In the first stages of love, he was practical enough to do what he had to do and love-struck enough to be almost as hysteric, romantic, and intense as any nonscientist lover. He used every resource to win you, promising to be your exciting, sexy, and romantic partner for the rest of your life. Then, when the complacency set in, he may have returned to the stereotypic "rational lover." He didn't lie. It's just that as he became secure in the relationship, his original sci-tech prototype personality began to surface.

That's not bad news. In order to reap the benefits of this sensible, stable personality, you will need to teach each other a few things. You will need to understand his personality and to translate his style so that you can tolerate it. Last, you will have to teach him about your style and needs. Maintaining a cozy connection when comfort differences and communication styles diverge is difficult, but not impossible. Learning to reframe your man's behavior into your own comfort level is the key. He's worth it. His logic and sense of responsibility will compensate for the work it takes to add to his state of the art.

If you, the reader, are a woman scientist—and there are increasingly more female engineer/scientists—forgive me for assigning that role to the male partner. It is just that here in Northern California where I live and work, 85 percent of the engineers are male. The interpersonal dynamics are the same no matter who is the sci-tech, so if you are a woman scientist, change my label of "man" to "woman" as you read. (This is good practice in translation, a valuable technique we all need in the field of communication.) Because you *do* have particular needs as a female scientist, I have devoted chapter 5 to those issues.

This book may itch, scratch, even hurt for a while, but it may save your relationship. Eventually the technical person will wear down his partner unless she offers a good fight. In this text I present some tools to make the match a fair one. For the engineer/scientist, I present ideas that will help explain you to others. I will also translate your partner's behavior for you. Again, the suggestions may be painful at first. But they get easier with practice. And they work!

1

How To Love Your Engineer/Scientist

RECOGNIZING THE SYNDROME

Twenty-five victims of the Silicon Syndrome gathered in our living room. We laughed, hugged, sipped coffee or wine, and wrestled with ideas for titles of a book about ourselves. Each person had been affected or had influenced this prospective book in some way. It looked like history in the making. We were embarking on the introduction of a new sociological understanding of our technological era. We were talking and writing about the pain and glory and complications of our era.

Jonathan and Linda had been clients of mine some seven years earlier. He was a chemist in one of our most exciting Silicon Valley companies. They talked about how they had come to me for marriage counseling earlier, and I talked about how Jonathan was the classic scientist who had never learned to share his feelings. Then they shared the reformation of their twenty-four-year marriage: how they have come to a new era and feel they are now in their second marriage to each other, and that it is wonderful! This couple was the perfect affirmation of my conclusions. They began their discussion by sharing what I had not even hoped they might reveal: the separation that they had imposed upon themselves, some years earlier, during their crisis period. Then they talked again about what they call their remarriage, or second marriage, and the profundity of that second phase of their commitment.

And then there was the new Silicon Syndrome couple. They

had been married less than a year. He was an executive searcher; she was a marketing manager in a manufacturing company. Jody and Bill had not yet completed their reformation period. They were still living in it, still suffering it.

Dr. Paul, a Ph.D. in electrical engineering, bounded in with his wife, Luanna, who taught yoga. They were a study in contrasts, but they were both feeling mellow and in the mood to share their experiences. Luanna said that she felt better just reading the few lines we had mailed to everyone in anticipation of the meeting. She was relieved "just to know that there is another couple out there like us, and that I have not been so thoroughly uncooperative in this relationship as I had been feeling."

There were two women scientists. One taught math and one was a computer programmer. They laughed at book-title proposals like "The Engineer and the Twit" (my husband's submittal). It was fascinating to listen to these women, who sounded so much like the men engineers and scientists at the party. When we took straw votes on various titles and subtitles, all the engineer/scientists, regardless of sex, voted together, even when the question at hand was not about technical issues. Very interesting . . .

There were three men (two bachelors and one engaged man) who claimed not to be scientists. Indeed, they voted with the women who were not technically oriented. These men seemed more sensitive, more group conscious and cooperative, and talked more in general, although each pointed out that he did have some technical expertise in his background. (Was this a rite of entry?) One of the men was a building contractor with a master's degree in marketing, another was a financial consultant, and the third was a salesman who had turned poet. All three men beamed throughout the discussion. I imagine they had been grappling with some of our problem-sets and had suffered through some of the predicaments we will discuss in this book.

And then there were Margaret and Harold, a beautiful, silver-haired couple who boasted a successful union because Harold had mastered some of the problems discussed in this book. Harold was an engineer for one of the "top ten" companies in the world, had worked for the company for twenty-five years, and was now a director, and his wife was in the field of counseling.

My husband, Don Wuerflien, was with us, taking credit for being the "subject" of the study. I reminded him that my first inspiration had come to me before I had even met him, at a retreat for ten couples. At that retreat, each male member of each couple team had periodically pulled back emotionally, and each female became more demanding emotionally. It struck me then, some twelve years ago—this strong tendency for woman to go "tiger" when man, no matter his mastery and aggressiveness in the professional world, goes passive in the emotional world.

Two more women joined our group, including my dearest friend, Joan, who has known me longer than anyone in the world except my mother. Although Joan is a drama teacher, not an engineer/scientist by profession, she is an engineer/scientist by personality. She thinks about things logically and rationally.

Last, there was Trudy, a woman who had confessed to being the unwilling and uninformed partner of a "classic case" and who now regretted that the communication gap had been so wide in her previous marriage. Trudy, the inspiration behind this publication, a publisher in her own right, reminds me daily that this is an important work, a gift to all the couples in the world who problem-solve and share feelings differently.

Well, we joked, played, strained our brains, laughed, cried, and finally a theme surfaced. It was the psychological phenomenon that happens when a scientist type meets and loves or works with someone who feels more quickly than she thinks!

Barbara, a teacher of right-brain/left-brain, continued to remind us what our brains were doing as we sought to find the perfect title for this book. She taught us how some of us ordered ourselves, and how some of us allowed our thoughts to "splay out" all over the floor, with random ideas, half-baked concepts, or half-finished words. Others created and tested theories, carefully interjecting ideas only after they had gone through some preliminary screening in their own heads. It was almost like watching the two brain processes working before us on my living-room floor. The syndrome was right there amid the onion dip and the salmon mousse.

When the title finally surfaced, we threw up our hands, glasses, and each other. Then began the rejoicing period. No one wanted to go home. I had told people when I called that we would end promptly at 10:00 P.M. (it was a week night) whether we had selected a title or not. Well, it was eleven o'clock, and not one person made a move to leave. It was as if we wanted to bond together, to treasure the moment when we had come to clarity about the way some of us lead and bleed our lives. We named ourselves the "Silicon Syndrome Society," toasted ourselves, and eventually filed home to our own sources of the syndrome, at whatever level it existed.

Wearily Don and I carried ourselves off to bed. We had delivered our baby. The birth was hard, the labor long, and the child was beautiful—truly a reflection of all of us, of our struggles, our confusions, and our relief!

I got up the next morning, grabbed the morning paper, and sat down to my poached egg. I was startled to see a Silicon Syndrome product right on the first page. The big photograph was of one of my clients, one of the victims of the syndrome—one who had not survived.

The newspaper story was about a brilliant entrepreneur who had designed a computer system for a major company. He and this company were merging, and he was being heralded as the brain trust of Company XYZ.

But I remembered the other story, the inside story of his marriage, his wife, his pain. Mostly I remembered his wife's story. It was about her birthday. He would not join her in going to her mother's house for her birthday dinner because he wanted to stay home and work on his computer concept—the one that revolutionized the computer business. A few months later she left him.

And a hundred faces appeared before me—all the engineers and scientists who thrive on their jobs, their inventions, their concepts, and who starve for their wives' understanding of the satisfaction they need at this particular moment in their lives. Other faces appeared—the tear-stained faces of the women who also starve, from lack of understanding of their needs, from lack of emotional content, from absence of discussion or affection, from emotional disconnection, and from too few gifts of empathy. All victims of the Silicon Syndrome.

The engineer/scientist personality is a man—or a woman—whose highly developed mental system works at all costs. He may be emotionally detached, allowing himself emotional release only in a safe form. The safe form may be his partner! Without her he may emotionally freeze to death or explode in a crazed state of pent-up yearnings, hysteric reactions, or wails from the past. His partner can bring psychic relief, because she can speak his emotion. Even if he consciously ridicules his undisciplined partner, or seems uncomfortable or embarrassed by her strong reactions, he will survive his own emotional life with more ease if he sometimes has her to mirror his hidden feelings. It is the balance of the two partners that keeps the couple alive and well.

His partner may actually need this logical and rational mate so that she can safely play out her own hystrionics. Consciously she may moan about his aloofness or his inability to communicate his pain, but her guarded unconscious keeps him around to protect her from being totally controlled by her emotions.

Witness a scene with me:

George sits quietly, drumming his fingers methodically on the kitchen table, avoiding the catsup spill and the unpaid bills that decorate the tablecloth.

MARTHA: Can't you say anything? [She throws her coffee cup at George.] I'm thinking about calling a lawyer.

GEORGE: No, I can't think of anything.

MARTHA: *George!* I said I'm thinking about calling a lawyer. And not about our wills, George. I want a divorce. I can't take it anymore. Say something!

GEORGE: I have nothing to say. I don't know what to say.

MARTHA: Your daughter has run away. You may lose your job. I've been diagnosed with a serious illness. And you just sit there reading the newspaper. [Martha crumbles.]

GEORGE: There is nothing to say. I've made the phone calls about Stephanie. I can't find her. I've read your biopsy. We don't know yet how serious it is. I've sent my report to my boss. I've done all I can.

Diagnosis: George: engineer/scientist
Martha: his partner choice

Prognosis: They can live happily ever after . . . in the Silicon Valley or anywhere else.

Explanation: George is the careful, scientific model, rational, cool under fire, who will be dependable, though rigid, and who will, by his stable nature, complement Martha. Martha is the verbal, emotional, social animal who will act out her feelings. She will even act out all of George's feelings, his fears, his need for emotional connection. She will, by her ability to communicate on an emotional level, compensate for the engineer/scientist personality when crises arise.

HE LOVES YOU BY THE SCIENTIFIC METHOD

It's hard to love an engineer/scientist. Sometimes it feels like trying to love your vacuum cleaner. It does the job. It is steady. It is reliable. It doesn't dazzle, polish, pet, or make you feel squishy.

The scientific method is to gather data, appraise the data, look for flaws, decide on a hypothesis, test it, and make conclusions. Scientists are not taught to feel, intuit, be spontaneous, or indulge in fantasy unless it can lead to a logical deduction.

So you fall in love with one of these machines. How do you survive? How does he survive your needing, nagging, crying, and begging for emotional connection and attention? And how do you plan, have fun, be sexual, spend your money, and parent your kids when your values about emotional expression are so different?

It starts with understanding your engineer/scientist. He is the perfect partner if you will take the time to translate his style and teach him how to listen to you, love you, and read you. That's all. And that is not impossible.

First, to begin to soften toward him, let's call him "sci-tech." That shortens it a little and makes it easier to read, say, and translate. Sci-tech is a person whose personality traits directed him to scientific and technological fields. More than that, though, he is a person who thinks with the scientific method, no matter his profession. If he went into the sciences, though, he did not turn robot just because he entered that field. He had learned to think that way long before he learned what the word *engineer* meant. He had already decided how to choose to be emotional before he was eight years old, long before he saw his first laboratory or computer.

This sci-tech person made discoveries as he was growing up. And then he made an unconscious decision to proceed with his life in a logical fashion, reading his environment and making choices that would effect the least emotional damage in him.

The professional direction toward science or engineering rein-forced the decision, of course, by continuing to teach him to be logical in his approach. It even gave him tricks, tables, formulas, and methods for developing a strategy for facing life. The profession also taught him efficiency, a critical eye, and a strong sense of responsibil-ity to the truth. Consciously, he made a decision to use the scientific method. He prided himself on grades, graphs, and absolutes. Con-sciously he also decided that he did indeed have feelings. He could feel them! Perhaps nobody else could feel them, but he could. So he concluded that he was, of course, a human being who had emotions that could be shared. He could be excited, sexually aroused, and have fun. The problem is that his unconscious decision to handle himself and his life by the scientific method wiped out his capacity to be available to his feelings!

Happily moving along, not knowing that his unconscious engineer/scientist personality cancels out his conscious decision to include feelings in his repertoire, he eventually finds a woman he wants to love. He thinks he can show her love because he feels it.

She will meet him in the blush of first love, when even the engineer/scientist can be romantic, passionate, and silly. She will, then, be fooled into thinking that he will always whisper while they are dancing, or even that they will always dance! Or that he will giggle in the park, write impassioned love letters, and show all the signs of the hysteric lovesick prisoner.

Sci-tech does not fool his love on purpose. He doesn't even know that this behavior is temporary. He feels it! The new love awakens neurons in his brain, new feelings in his groin, and he is happily and wildly in love. He does not expect that he will change. He doesn't know that this is Stage One in a relationship, available to all personalities. He has no idea that he will not be able to sustain the sense of romance and thrill once the first blush has been replaced by the security of the relationship. He will be as surprised as his partner when he no longer feels pain, joy, and ecstasy at the sight of his beloved.

In Stage Two a couple settles down, feels complacent in the relationship, and even begins the process of looking for differences. And, of course, they find them. In Stage Two the engineer/scientist personality returns in full measure. A flaw finder by nature and profession, he commences, then, to see the makeup spots on the pillow case, the bill for her mother's phone call, and he begins to "brittle up" in some of the critical areas of her life. This is not his fault. It is not her fault. It is human nature—no, natural—for him to return to his more comfortable form.

Stage Three is the decision stage. A couple will decide to split up because the differences are so enormous. Or they will decide to stay together and work on the differences, ideally finding a way to complement each other with their value disparities.

So you and your spouse have decided to stick it out, solve your differences, and make your marriage last forever. Well, dear partner choices and engineer/scientist types, I guess you have already discovered that there is no place to go to figure out how to do it! Yes, there are marriage counselors, "marriage encounters," entire book-shelves on relationships, and talk-show discussions from dawn to dusk. But you have found no concise formula to help you figure out your own relationship and make your differences balance each other rather than nibble away until you are a skeleton couple, bones stacked, flesh worn away by arguments, hurt feelings, and misunderstandings from Brillo pads to bladders.

By the way, I don't have the formula either! But I do have some comfort to offer, some ideas, exercises, and tests to share. In this book I will dissect the scientific personality so that you can understand it. Then your job is to translate *you*. It is a big job. Understanding ourselves is an enormous task. And encoding us to others multiplies the chance for error. But it is necessary.

Some of you who are interior designers or fitness teachers will find yourselves in the description of the engineer/scientist. There are thousands of men and women who are not in a technical field at all but who definitely fit the engineer/scientist personality. I want to address these people, no matter what their professions. I am studying the people who most generally act, think, and feel like the technical person, even if professionally they arrange flowers or teach English. It is the core personality that I will attend to in this book; the style of thinking, decision-making, and, most important, the style of feeling that most simulates that of the classic scientist or engineer. That is whom we will explore together in this book. You are going to grow to love him, if you don't already. You will also feel frustrated with him, if you don't already. But, most of all, you are going to understand him!

HOW TO READ YOUR "SCI-TECH" MAN

(He doesn't come with an instruction book!)

FIND THE ON BUTTON

First, find out what turns your sci-tech on—what gets him started. If you don't know where the power button is, your computer will sit there staring idly at you. So will he. Find the switch, the button, or the knob, and your computer will process, perform, and work for you. So will your beloved sci-tech man—when you find his source of power.

The on button for your sci-tech comes in all forms, shapes, and formulas. Just ask him. "Honey, if I were going to try to get your attention right now, what would I have to do?"

Or, "What would make you want to stop reading the paper or snoozing right now?" If he looks at you blankly or says, "Nothing!" don't get discouraged. He doesn't understand your language yet. He doesn't know what you are trying to do. He will probably even suspect your intentions. So don't feel despondent until you have tried every technique in this book. A reminder to console you in the dark recesses of your doubts: **He really wants to communicate; he just doesn't know how.**

The on button to your partner may be, "Guess what—I saved us forty-five dollars this month on the electric bill." Or, "Honey, the Forty-niners are playing the Raiders and I'm planning an early dinner so you can watch it from the beginning."

If your sci-tech is a "physical junkie," the way to find his power source is, naturally, to touch him. Touching is a very important sense. To fine-tune your touch you will have to learn exactly what kind of touching your spouse enjoys. You know about the kinds of touching you like, and the kinds you hate. Discover his favorite forms.

But even that is not foolproof. There are times when the favorite neck rub will not work. Learning to read your partner's response to your touch is essential. Find out just how and when it is appropriate. Sometimes the suggestion of a foot massage will be as big a turn-off as asking him to talk about how much he enjoys visits from your old sorority sisters.

On-button strategies may be suggesting a cup of coffee, or running a bath for him, or arranging some quiet time together. Tell the kids, "We all want to be quiet for the next half-hour because Daddy looks real tired and he probably has lots to think about."

Asking my husband if he would like to use the hot tub later on is a good starting place for us. From the suggestion, my husband concludes several facts: He knows that this is not my favorite activity, so he already suspects that I want to please him; he can feel my cooperative intentions. Second, since he enjoys that form of relaxation, he can begin to feel all warm and cozy just looking ahead to the soothing waters. With the suggestion, I have set in motion the beginnings of an opening toward the power switch.

RECOGNIZE THE OVERLOAD BUTTON
Learning what is too much is essential to a good relationship. If you can begin to anticipate your partner's mood swings from enjoying himself to being fed up, you will be able to prevent some ugly

scenes. Learn to spot the last straw for your sci-tech. Big, grown-up men (and women) can be like little kids who wrestle and tickle and play until they get dizzy and silly and overloaded with emotion, and become frantic and intense. You know how children end up crying over the tickling episode that started out so joyfully? Well, grown-ups get just as overloaded. They just don't cry. I wish they could sometimes. It would be helpful for your sci-tech to sit down and cry about the orders not being shipped, about the design that "won't go," about having too much work to do, or about feeling too much responsibility.

The overload does not have to be caused by too much activity or responsibility. Sometimes it is the result of depression or boredom, too much not going anywhere. The kind of overload that says he feels he cannot take one more dead evening, one more news show, one more conversation about Debbie's nursery-school class. Watch for that subtle, insidious overload. It is harder to spot. The anxiety that surrounds too much tension shows up dramatically. But the stress of too little emotional context or too little brain stimulation is more obscure. It is also more difficult to treat!

Coping levels, or stress levels, are different in each of us. Periods of our life affect our coping levels too. If your partner is in a major business crisis, he may be more prone to overload. If you, his partner, are in a physically or emotionally draining period in your life, you may spill over onto his coping breakpoint and both of you may reach disaster. Be as sensitive as you can to yourself and to your partner during high-stress passages in your lives. If he has a big work project, or business-partner difficulties, or if you have a big project or people problems coming up, watch out!

When you see your partner in overload, don't add to it. Back off on things about which you normally would not back off. Use discipline, patience, and all of your courage to hold back during this time, even when your partner is being difficult. The waiting could save your relationship.

The big problem for people who have to hold back their reactions to stress in their partners is that there is then no place to put their own emotions. It is vital, then, that you *find* another outlet for your frustrations. But choose your relief valve carefully. Often we use our kids for this sounding board. More dangerously, we choose a person of the opposite sex who can become such an important confidant that the "good listening ear" turns into a lover.

A relief or release person can be your neighbor, a friend who knows you and your partner, and, importantly, who knows your assets and liabilities as partners and who will not simply side with you, giving you biased encouragement about how awful your partner has been behaving!

Another very safe release person is a professional counselor who can be available to you when you hit your own overload button. If you establish a good relationship with your counselor and he/she has all the important data about you, then you can use him/her as a sounding board when the overload times appear. I suggest to my clients that they see me initially until we have a good working relationship, and then not return until a booster shot is needed (maintenance therapy), or until an emergency (like overload in either partner) occurs.

An excellent method of relief is to write down your feelings or complaints. Then save the document. You may want to show your partner the protestations at some point in the future, or you may eventually throw away the list. But the important thing is that you have been able to express your frustration in some way!

Talking into a tape recorder helps too. It is a marvelous way to play out your feelings, try on your monologue, and gather some insight without tormenting someone else. The tape usually does not have to be delivered.

Some couples communicate best on the telephone. Don't resist this method because it seems silly. Many couples can make soul-searching discoveries via the telephone. Without the face-to-face contact, you or your partner may finally say what is so hard to say in person.

Too many "stuffed feelings" get attended to by eating away your hurts or by drinking away the bad feelings. Washing away the frustration by eating or drinking them down has some serious side effects: obesity! alcoholism!

FIND THE RESTART BUTTON

When you have had an emotional estrangement because your partner is not available, because he is on overload, or because one or each of you has been upset, hurt, or ugly to the other, it's important to find a way to *reconnect* with your partner. What will get him started again? What will make him feel at ease with you, even loving toward you again? Or, more important, more available to you again?

Finding the restart button takes a thorough understanding of your partner, knowing how he feels his hurts, what he does about his disappointments. Does he sulk, take walks, stamp, sit, rant, rave?

How does your partner pull back and separate himself from you? If he yells, he may shout his feelings out. He may even have to have a final shouting session with you, one in which to let out the last vestiges of bad feelings. But most of our sci-tech men are not shouters. They are more quiet about their feelings. In fact, they usually withdraw, take unto themselves the pain, always attempting to build reason into their analysis of what happened.

With the sci-tech man who is a withholder, getting him started again may take two paths. You can prepare a way for him to digest his own analysis, then let him share it with you, and, finally, quietly ask him if he is ready to be with you again, or ready to hear your side of things now. Or you can present the facts of the disagreement to him in just the way he would do it himself, allowing for both sides of the argument (with his side presented first, of course!).

It is helpful to say something like this: "I wish the last hour [or day and a half] had never happened. I feel badly. You feel badly too, I know. I wish we could erase it from our slate. Let's just not compute the last episode. I want to be friends with you again. I have leftover feelings. You probably do too. But I'd like to start over again. Fresh. What can I do or say that would entice you into feeling ready to be with me again?"

Don't worry that you are giving yourself away. You too need a time and place to get your feelings resolved, to say your say! But the mending period, the time of reconstruction, must start *somewhere*. Since you are the one reading this book, I propose that it start with you!

Arguments or disagreements are funny. We can usually recall the pain. We cannot, however, generally recall the first move—who started the darned thing or how the fight really got going. So stop keeping track, or trying to. Because it won't matter in the last analysis. Get the **restart** started! You will both feel better.

As a counselor, I spend a great deal of time with couples who both try to convince me that they were right. Each lobbies for his or her position and attempts to persuade me to say that his or her partner was wrong. A waste of time, of course, because I can't find the truth. The truth lies somewhere between them both, between both stories, between both sides.

Concentrate on how to feel better, not on the initiating incident. It's often frustrating to couples who come to me because I won't allow the blow-by-blow recounting of the incident. What these partners want from the retelling is to blame. To that I say "no thanks."

Blame is wasteful and time-consuming. "What will make you feel better?" is the key to reconciliation.

I understand that we learn from history. Sometimes we do have to go back over events to check out the anatomy of a disagreement. Don't go back over, though, seeking the guilty party! Assume you both are guilty; each has a part in the incident, and what you are looking for is *understanding,* not guilt!

When you see your sci-tech man in gear again (mended), you will know he is back on target, available to you. If you are not sure that he has restarted, try something like, "Are you okay now? You still look a little annoyed. Is there more I can say, more you need to say?"

There was no instruction book that accompanied your partner. There was no owner's manual for you to read to help you start your own life. Learning to cope with your differing styles and decision-making methods and your communication tactics will help you both cope with the big and little problems of your complicated life.

The partner of the sci-tech person often gives up if she can't quite easily find the restart button. She will join tennis clubs or women's organizations, go back to school, or find her own career path.

She does not, however, work to reconnect in her marriage. It seems too difficult. After years of frustration, she attempts a parallel course, with each partner doing his/her own thing! Eventually the system breaks down, caving in because one partner becomes top-heavy with the responsibility of the relationship.

All too late the sci-tech realizes that his marriage was worth saving, and he begins the process of reconstruction of the marital contract. By that time his mate has already divorced him emotionally.

So, couples in the Silicon Syndrome exist in three states:

1. Parallel course, both unconscious of the widening gaps.
2. One or both parties realize the gaps are too wide; the separation is imminent.
3. One or both parties begin the reconstruction of the relationship.

THE DIFFERENCE BETWEEN MANIPULATION AND STRAIGHT COMMUNICATION

A manipulator tries to get what he wants without letting the other person know what he is after. He tries to sneak it in on you. A straight communicator tells his partner the goal he is working toward and tells his listener exactly what he is willing to do to get it. People are so fearful of manipulation that they shy away from basic bargaining tools! The truth is that we are all manipulators or are being manipulated most of our lives. Manipulation can be very subtle (the teacher's nod of appreciation when a student gives the right response, or the subliminal brainwashing techniques used on television).

It is fair to let your partner know that what you want may inconvenience him, but that you are willing to perform some compensating behavior, just because you want it so very much! That's honest.

Engineer/scientists are, indeed, wary of too much manipulation. They are truly not very good at it themselves. They then protect themselves against others who are better at it than they are. They want to know what is going on all the time. They are very concerned about looking foolish, naive, or gullible. That is because the scientist inside of them is supposed to be completely foolproof. That scientist checks things out so well that he would never be taken in. So be prepared for your partner's wariness of your methods if you seem to be asking something of him in a roundabout way. He will also be nervous if you put it out too straight, if you don't throw curves or camouflage what you want. "This seems too simple," the detective inside of him says. He doesn't trust his partner's intentions. He believes she is still angry. He knows he is. He knows that she was wrong, dead wrong. "She just wants us to make up. She is sorry. She wants us to be in the good shape we were in before all this happened," he worries. "But what else? What else does she want? What is she not telling me? Or, what am I so stupid about that I am missing?" Nothing, darling . . . nothing.

It seems that you are damned if you do (talk straight) and damned if you don't! Yes, in the beginning this will feel true. Eventually, though, when your sci-tech begins to trust you, trust his own translation of you and your relationship, he will settle into looking for the straight message: "I feel; I want; I will!"

WHAT TO DO IN EMERGENCIES

You can plan on crises; they do appear. In Silicon Valley. In other valleys. And in other hills. In every home. Even yours. But what do you do when these emergencies arise? If you are in the Silicon

Syndrome, it is probable that you have two differing emergency styles. I believe these crises styles are the most important thing I can point out to you in this book.

I'm not talking about the life-threatening crises. Strangely, most of us can handle the big problems. I am talking about the little things: the car transmission, the lost promotion, vacation plans, the burned roast, a rejected application, a child suspended from school.

How do you generally react to stress? How does your partner generally react to bad news?

In general, when there is a crisis, the sci-tech goes into his head, to think. And in general, his partner goes to her internal microphone, to talk. And, in general, the result is misconnection and emotional isolation. He is trying to think to himself . . . she is trying to talk to him. . . .

THE THINKER (THE "TREE PERSON")

Let's imagine that our sci-tech man has a big crisis at home or work. It is an awful mess. A really dreadful thing has happened. What does sci-tech do?

He runs up to his brain . . . to think.

And there he sits, in his little "tree house" in his brain, looking down on the big mess. But he is safe, having climbed the rickety little stairs to his brain tree house, or having taken the instant elevator. He has arrived.

While he is sitting up there in his tree house, he can look down at the situation, the crisis, thinking about what to do about it. And he is alone! There is room for only one person in this safe space. The stairs or the elevator permit only him. He will not be disturbed.

Here sci-tech will ponder, analyze, wonder, and debate with himself, not taking in any ideas that could confuse, distract, or sorrow him. He will deal with the problem in his own orderly fashion, taking one part of the problem at a time, in any fashion that his brain is programmed to address.

Well, there he sits, resting, getting away from the immediate crisis, but still able to look down and see it. While he is sitting there, he nurtures himself, just a little, petting away the frustration, the disappointment, the fear.

And, as time goes by, he is able to come up with some conclusions. The confusion has given way to rational decision. "Here's what I did. Here's what I should have done. Here's what John should have done. Here's what I can do. Here's what Mr. Wilheim can do.

This may be a way to solve the problem. Move this to here. Fire up this. Or promise her that. This move may be a way to solve the problem, to dismiss the error, to turn the thing around."

So sci-tech sits in his tree house, thinking, and analyzing, and planning, and developing new tactics for when he will come down from his brain. He can see the problem very well from up there! He can spot all the imperfections; he can draw logical conclusions.

When he feels safe enough, he can come down, well petted, safe, nurtured, and with a plan, an action plan for making it better.

THE TALKER (THE "TELEPHONE PERSON")
Now the talker has a problem. A horrible crisis has occurred, at home or at work. What does our talker personality do? She rushes out to tell someone!

And with her loudspeaker, or her telephone, she talks, or yells. She tells the problem to anyone who will listen. And she pets herself as her listeners respond to her with, "Oh dear . . . isn't that awful?"

Each time she tells the problem to someone, she gets an idea about it, some clarification, an answer, some comfort. "Why don't you do this?" they say. With each comforting statement or suggestion, she feels a little less frightened, a little more capable of handling the problem, a little more okay.

As time goes by, she is able to come up with some conclusions. She feels healed, better about the crisis, the awful mess, ready to deal with the problem.

THE "TREE" AND THE "TELEPHONE" PERSONALITIES
Now, if the thinker and the talker personalities share the awful crisis, you know how each is going to handle it. He will be up in his brain and she will be reaching for the telephone. She can't see him; he can't hear her!

This, in the main, is the Silicon Syndrome dilemma. I have exaggerated the positions a little. But the direction our couples take is usually as I've suggested. Sometimes the positions are reversed. And sometimes, heaven help them, both partners go to their brains. Oh, it is quite all right to be in your brain. But when a crisis hits and you have to make a decision, or if there is a great deal of sorrow connected to the event, it is hard on the couple when they cannot connect until each has done his "solo" mind-searching.

The problem is timing. If you are both up in your brain, one of you will ultimately come down. If you come down simultaneously, you are lucky. Those simultaneous departures are about as frequent as the simultaneous orgasms that couples long for. So, usually, someone is waiting for the other to return, waiting, feeling lonely, wondering, perhaps judging, or feeling judged.

The thinker wants so much to have his "alone" time; to be able to digest the problem, to have an objective look at it. The talker wants so much to talk about it, to have someone with whom to share her reactions and feelings.

The problem for the talker is that she does not get her problem-solving needs met at all because her partner is up in his brain, getting his work done up there. Even if he did stay down with her, or came down prematurely, he would not be at full power; he would be missing that cultivation work that he needs when he takes problems to his brain!

So, if the talker wants to talk to her partner and he is up in his brain, she has to shout to try to get him down. If he comes down too soon, he is groggy and lifeless; and if she waits too long, she will pop with emotion. Herein lies the tragedy.

IS THERE A SOLUTION?

What can you, a Silicon Syndrome couple, do when your crisis behaviors are so different? The most important thing you can do is to know that you are different, to label those differences, and to expect your partner's behavior patterns in crisis. Don't disappoint yourself with anticipating that "this time he will be different," or "this time she will rise to the occasion." Plan on the thinker and plan on the talker. Expect your differences!

And, before the next crisis, contract for some compromise crisis action that can take care of both partners' needs. I suggest the 1/3, 1/3, 1/3 method.

One-third of the time, contract that the thinker will go immediately to his brain, allowing himself to digest the problem alone. During this time, the talker must be quiet around him; provide him that time for himself. You may talk to friends, to yourself, or to a counselor, but don't talk to your partner! Until he is ready to come down from his brain and talk to you.

Another third of the time you both will do it the talker's way. Old brain will not go up! He will experience the crisis, will catch himself as he begins to journey upstairs, and will stop himself (or, more likely, his partner will catch him). Then you will say, "Honey, this is my time. You promised to stay with me in this, talking to me, even if it is hard for you."

Now, the last third of the time will be a real compromise. Each of you will be creative and think of a way in which you can use both of your emergency styles at the same time. Let me give you some examples: Use a teletype machine so you can SOS messages to him and he can answer as soon as he is ready. Then you are at least in some form of communication. The teletype machine may simply be handwritten notes. But you know that you have some means of communication available to you; sci-tech knows that his reveries will be disturbed during some of his quiet time but that he can choose when to answer the notes.

Another way to do this compromise is to set precise limits on "what is enough." Plan for twenty minutes for the alone time and twenty minutes for the talk time. And do not exceed your boundaries. Even the talker can wait twenty minutes, no matter what the crisis is, and even the thinker can endure twenty minutes of discussion if he knows that there is a cut-off point!

Sometimes a couple simply needs to set up a system for signaling each other. It is okay for the thinker to have to endure the talker if he knows that there is a way to shut her up, a signal, a soft method that will not hurt her feelings but will let her know that he has had enough. The "time out" signal works for some people. Some couples use a kiss or a tap on the shoulder, and one couple uses the words "I will eat" or "Aunt Mary" to signal that the thinker is reaching the end of his ability to cope. The talker needs a signal that she can use to awaken her brain man. A word, a gesture, which both of you agree on, can bring him back, ready or not, to cooperate with your needs!

Find a way to use your emergency kit! Have your tools ready. There will be crises. When a crisis arises we generally go into our most exaggerated behaviors. The brain person thinks harder, longer, more deeply. The talker talks louder, longer, more passionately.

You will see these differences in handling problems in your workplace too. Contrasting personalities do not appear just in love relationships. Two business partners fall into the two divergent camps. Just when Bob wants to shout with Roger about the problem, Roger is up in his brain tower. Wilbur and Orville may have had the same problem. Hewlett and Packard, Procter and Gamble may have been thinker-and-talker combos. You can be sure that they all found a scheme to be together in those emergency times. That scheme will make the difference.

You will have different crisis styles. Plan on that. And then work up your contract so that some of the time your partner will be totally cooperative with your problem-solving style, and some of the time you will be patient while adjusting to his style. And some of the time, come up with a creative compromise that gives each of you a little relief.

Don't expect perfection. The first time you try this, you may both feel frustrated. The contract may bomb. It may take months to perfect your system.

Some helpful hints: You can decide that if the crisis is actually one that affects one partner more than the other (it is his job, his mother, his car), you will use his crisis style to handle it. Eventually he will come down from his brain. You just have to wait until he is ready. Sometimes it takes three hours, sometimes three minutes, and sometimes it may take three days. Another hint: Plan your outer-limit boundaries. "Three days is too long for me; let's maximize your 'away position' to two days; that is all I can handle without contact."

Don't be discouraged. Even if it goes badly, you are beginning a system of working together. Since we are in air-raid status, of course your most primal operating style will come into play, and it will take all your strength and patience to cooperate with your partner. It gets better. You will be amazed at how creative you can get when both of you set your minds to this solution. The alternative is awful; it is loneliness, misunderstandings, and alienation. Choose your "emergency plan." It's easier! On you . . . on the relationship. . . .

"YES" AND "NO" MEAN "MAYBE"

The engineer/scientist is very slow to say "yes." He is much safer saying "no" to things. If he is always having to check for flaws and failures, he is then very careful to use reservations about almost anything. He will say things like, "Well, if I get home early enough . . ." or, "If there is enough money to do that, then . . ." Our "no" man is known to change his mind. His partner may even decide that his "no" means "maybe."

I learned that about my husband. After I was married for about a year, I began to feel depressed. I started counting up all the times Don seemed negative about my wonderful ideas. Since I have so many wonderful ideas, poor Don has had lots of opportunities to say "no."

I thought of the times I had begged him to go dancing with me, and he always replied, "Oh, I sweat too much when I dance."

Then I recalled how I had asked Don to learn to play tennis. "Oh, I'm allergic to sun," he replied.

And I yearned for Don and me to play bridge together. It was my favorite game, and I just knew that he would make a great bridge player. So I bought him books and urged him to learn the game. Still he said "no." He claimed he had to work too hard at his designing table and that his power-supply engineering business required too much daytime brain power for him to want to invest in more brain strain in the evenings.

I was depressed. I actually wondered if maybe I had selected the wrong person, since he was becoming so negative about trying new things. At that point I decided that I had married a "no" man.

When we had been married about two years, I was driving home from work one evening reviewing my life with Don again. I was thinking about how depressed I was becoming because of Don's inability to say "yes." And then I thought about dancing. . . .

Well, I had to admit that Don had, in fact, taken up dancing. To be sure, he had taken eleven dancing lessons that same fall. Yes, he did sweat. But he did continue to dance. I had somehow forgotten that when I was adding up my Bad-Don list.

Then I thought about tennis. Last summer he had, indeed, played tennis with me. He wasn't too bad, either. He had even suggested we try it again sometime. Wow! What was I thinking of when I fantasized that Don was someone who wouldn't try anything?

And last, I remembered bridge! The many nights we had been playing with Lee and Clarke and Mary Ellen and Ivan. And the times he had listened to me and tried to read the bridge column in the newspaper. Hmmm . . .

So on the way home that day I made my miraculous discovery. I decided that Don wasn't really a "no" person after all. He was a "maybe" person. When he said "no" the first time to tennis, or dancing, or bridge, he meant "no" at the time, until he reconsidered it! Eventually he said "yes." He had to register his reservations first, though. It was very important for me to learn that. *His registering the reservations actually allowed him to then consider the possibility of the "yes"!*

So when I got home that night, I announced to Don that I had finally figured him out! Smugly I readied him for my major pronouncement. "Don," I said, "I finally have you figured out. When you say 'no,' you mean 'maybe'!"

"Yes, you're right," he said quite willingly. I was dumbfounded. But then he made his profound pronouncement. And he did it without years of agony or analysis. "Jean," he said, "and when you say 'yes,' you mean 'maybe'!" And we both brought to mind the many times I'd promised something earlier in the evening and changed my mind later, or when I would say "yes" to two sets of friends for the same evening and overbook myself. That's how I had ended up with two housecleaners on the same day! I felt sorry for each of them, and then I couldn't get out of it.

Don was right. For me, "yes" means "maybe." It means my intention is to do it. It means I want to. And it also means I could change my mind.

For Don, "no" means he is not eager to do it; that he immediately needs to demonstrate precaution about it. But it also means that he could change his mind!

Watch out, then, for preconceived notions that your sci-tech man is so rigid that he can't make a reverse turn just when you least expect it!

THERE IS A HEART INSIDE THE TIN MAN

The hearts of sci-tech people are the same shapes as ours. Remember, they actually even feel things. It's just that they have such a hard time showing those feelings and talking about them. Their difficulty is allowing themselves to express the misty and suggestive feelings that could help their partners uncover the emotions within.

Let's take a look at some of the more classic sci-tech stereotypes.

Dr. Peterson: He is president of the BBI Corporation. He is tall, intellectual, and precise. Vice-presidents fear him, secretaries quiver in his presence, and his family thinks he has no vulnerable spots at all.

The truth is that Peter Peterson is actually a bundle of feelings. He feels inferior to his chairman of the board. "I'm too intellectual for John. He thinks I'm a stuffed shirt, and I feel like one in front of John, too! He always has funny things to say and I always feel like such a boring dullard around him."

Peter also feels fragile around his senior vice-president. He feels like a little boy sometimes, asking the senior vice-president to do things that Peter feels he ought to do. At other times he feels that he is whining and complaining too much. These feelings have nothing to do with the truth. But the feelings are Peter's truth. And sometimes he feels darned insecure.

With his secretaries he feels that he is not friendly or charming enough. He often wishes that he could tell jokes or something. It would help if he could write funny memos sometimes. But, no, "I'm just plain stodgy," he confessed to me.

With his family, Peter Peterson is also afraid to show his real feelings. He often fears that he might cry. If he really looked at his thirteen-year-old son and let himself feel the compassion he experiences when the lad can't make the team, or do well in school, or talk to girls, Peter would feel dreadful! Instead, he looks away, not letting himself take in all the pain around his son.

He keeps the damper on. Tightly!

And with his wife, Martha, he keeps the damper on too, because he fears telling her how dependent on her he feels. He wishes he could just lie with his head in her lap, and have her pet his hair and say that everything is going to be all right. Peter has so little experience telling people he feels vulnerable that to tell it even to Martha is too much. The secret lies between them.

And now about David Heller. David looks like the independent type who takes life as it comes. He doesn't seem to get ruffled, and he doesn't seem to need anybody. The David everybody knows would not get jealous, feel lonely, or be worried about abandonment at all.

The inside David is fighting to stay emotionally alive. He is deeply frightened of abandonment. At some primary time in his life he probably experienced a sense of abandonment (Mother lost him in the supermarket, or he was left at Grandma's house too long), and his deep emotion is the worry of a repeat performance.

"Oh, come on," you say. "My David is afraid I will leave him? Are you kidding? He doesn't even know if I've left the house for hours at a time. I don't think he would miss me at breakfast except for wondering where the toast was."

Yes, David does have feelings of worry over being rejected and alone. But those feelings are so well hidden that there is little chance David will tell you about them. Most of the time he does not even feel them. Those deep feelings surface only when David is truly threatened. A David will come to my office because his wife seems to be leaving him, and then give way to the surprising worry of loss. His wife and family become startled by David's strong reaction to a possible separation. They expected him just to be grumpy or, in fact, complacent. But finally the chains to David's heart have been jiggled. And he becomes highly emotional, frightening himself and everyone else. Yes, it takes a big tug with men like David. The feelings are there, though, deeply recessed, and available when the going gets rough.

WHY DO SCI-TECHS SNOOZE OFF ON YOU?

A person whose deep feelings are available only when they are in fear of death of the relationship has to work very hard to continue to keep those scary feelings under wraps. When an interpersonal relationship gets "heavy," he wants to get away, not touch those major and overwhelming feelings. So he nods off!

Yes, he does. To escape contact with his emotions he will go to sleep. I see that happen weekly in therapy groups. The very people who need to get in touch with themselves will nod off when the emotions get to a high level. They can't seem to take in the strong feelings. So, in protection, they wander off to sleep, not allowing themselves the possibility of feeling what the other group members are feeling.

• *Your sci-tech fears contact.* He doesn't want to "get into it with you" because he is not adequate in emotional debates. He is afraid he will cry, or worse, lose control and kill you. The hidden, stuffed-down rage in an emotionally detached person is amazing! Keeping all those feelings tucked under results in a big pile of them. So your man is like a teapot, ready to bubble up, whistle, and explode. But he is really afraid to make any bubbling sounds. Still, it gets hard to stifle the sounds. Very hard. Better just to get away, distract himself, remove himself from the possibility of letting off steam!

• *Your sci-tech fears performance.* He is afraid that if you go into a nice, intimate little chat, you will end up asking him to do something he cannot do. He is basically a pleaser, you know, one who wants to accommodate. So if you ask him for something, he is going to want to oblige. Better just not to hear the request than to try to do it and fail. He does not want to fail! The fear of performance failure comes in all kinds of packages: the fear that he won't say the right thing; the fear of sexual expectations; the fear that you will want to be

closer to him than he wants; the fear that you will demand promises
of chores from him.

• *Your sci-tech fears complaints.* Oh, he really knows that he is not
perfect. He is as sure of this as anyone is. But he does not want to
hear about his failings from you or from anyone. **Engineer/scientists
take critical evaluations very badly.** They do not like reviews;
they do not take criticism or suggestions well. They wish they could
be right about everything, and it is so hard to have their failings
pointed out to them. Their egos are so bound up in performance that
it is very hard for them to distinguish their chores or tasks from
themselves. So they shy away from complaints, withdraw, find a
book or a computer to crawl into, and escape the onslaught they
fear.

HOW CAN YOU WAKE HIM UP?

Let your partner know that you are *not* going to overwhelm him
with all the possible emotions he could feel about a single topic. Just
say, "Phil, I want to talk about Charlie. I don't want to talk about
every aspect of Charlie; just about the way he seems to separate us,
put us into two camps."

In that way you have given Phil the meeting agenda. You have
shared with him the range that the topic will cover. Then, in order
to reassure Phil about how the discussion will proceed, you set up
the parameters. Remember how engineer/scientists love structure
and rules?

"I will talk to you about this for only thirty minutes. If we
haven't resolved this by then, I will put it away and we can talk
about it next week. Could we start in a few moments?"

In this message you have told him exactly how long he will be
beleaguered by the painful topic. He knows the limits. He will be
very cooperative. I promise!

Last, you will need to tell him the boundaries you will keep
about the discussion. "I won't throw anything at you. I will not be
physical! If I cry too much, just signal for time out and I will back off
for a bit. And I will try not to shout. I will sit right here and you can
sit there. I won't get out of my chair."

Now this may all be very difficult for the emotional woman who
has been stifling her feelings for a hundred years with Phil. It is a
place to start, though. The hardest lesson for a hysteric partner is
to begin to be disciplined. **But he won't hear a thing if you are
shouting!** Closing him down with feelings that are too strong for

him to bear will net you nothing. You will have to learn to approach your partner in stages, giving him only what he can bear and allowing him time for digestion. He needs an incubation time to take in your feelings.

All this takes patience. In other parts of the book I will equip you to keep your guard up while you wait for your partner to come around. Be prepared to wait . . . and wait . . . and wait. He will be worth the wait. I will also give you things to do that will allow you to express your own feelings. Again, it will be worth the wait. . . .

WHAT IF YOU THINK THIS IS ALL TOO MUCH WORK?

Some of you readers are about to get angry with me. You will say, "This is too hard. Why do I have to do all the work? Why are relationships so much trouble? How come he never has to do any of the initiating?"

Let's liken a relationship to a Frisbee game. In order to have a game, somebody has to get the Frisbee. You may be wishing he would get it, and he may be wishing you would get it. Wishing will not start the game. He may bemoan that he *always* has to get the Frisbee. Or she may complain that he never makes attempts to find one. And they never have a game. . . .

Since *you* are reading this book, you are all I've got. It's like the person who comes to my office for therapy; that person is all I've got. If I'm lucky enough to have the couple together, I can assign some special work for each member of the team. I can say, "Both of you go out and find or buy a Frisbee. Then if both come back with a Frisbee, you will have a second game later."

So, because you are my reader, it is up to you to save your relationship. But you don't have to do all the work. You have to do the *first* work—make the first move. Maybe he/she will make another first move at another time. Maybe she/he has already made a lot of first moves in your relationship. It doesn't matter. Keeping score in a relationship is not important. It is like the informal Frisbee game. What counts is the throw, the run, the catch, the feeling of play, the interaction between two people.

Making the first move, then, is vital to your relationship. The next thing that is essential is that you begin to have faith that you can teach your partner how to make the *second move*. And that will take time. You can make lots of mistakes in your teaching. You will probably slip, and get mad or complain the first time you try to teach. And then it won't work. But you've got lots of time to get this second move going! Take your time, allow for mistakes, for your own backsliding, for the sabotaging that you alone will do, despite your good intentions to make this relationship well again.

The first move may take several false starts. It's all right to go back the next day and say, "You know, honey, I tried to tell you something pretty important yesterday. And I blew it. It did not come out right and I screamed the same old thing I always scream. But I am beginning to trust my own good intentions, and I think today I will be able to say it all a little better."

Another complaint you will give me while you are reading this book is: "Why do I have to change to accommodate my partner?" The answer to this is the same as the answer I gave earlier in this section. But, believe me, it bears repeating: You are all I've got! You can make the first move. And I will teach you how to teach your partner to make the second move. And I will help you to decide when your partner is uncooperative enough to cause you to give up. I will assist you in making new moves on your partner, some he will not even notice, some he will suspect you of, but all designed to get your partner to want to catch the Frisbee.

Some of you will say, "Why bother?" Or, "Why not give up right now? If the relationship is so bad already, why give it another effort?" It *is* hard work, just as parenting, or being on the city council, or starting a mail-order business is hard work. But being in a productive relationship in which both partners get most of their needs met is worth the effort. You may discover, despite your fears of having to give too much, that things will begin to fall into place. You will be able to choose the new car together, your old friends will start coming around again, and there may even be some laughter in the room occupied by the two of you at the same time. Find the key, the magic key, to turn your partner on, to turn him around, to turn him in your direction. Let me help you find the formula. Then, if it is still too much work, we'll look at separation alternatives.

I am not asking you to take poison! I am urging you to incorporate some skills that can work in any relationship. Whether you use these tools to get cooperation from your hospital nurse some twenty years from now, or from your landlord, or your boss, you will acquire some tactics that I guarantee will get the job done, no matter what the dilemma. And you don't have to live in California to enjoy these techniques.

There are long-suffering couples who will never give up on a relationship but who have given up on a potential for happiness.

Take a new start; it is never too late. Yes, it's harder when the scar tissue is deeper, but not impossible. Breathing fresh air into a dying relationship is actually vitalizing to each member of the team. The bonus, of course, is that the team also benefits. The point of this book is to give you the courage, the motivation, to translate your partner again, or maybe for the first time, and to teach your partner more about you.

2

Silicon Syndrome Couples

PARTNER CHOICES

How the sci-tech shops for a partner depends on his personality type. A very rational type will make lists of characteristics he wants in a partner, and then he will proceed to shop for her. In his approach he will be practical and methodical. If he wants an outdoor woman he will look for her in state parks and outdoor activities. If he wants an intellectual partner he will look for her in university libraries or intellectual social activities.

However, the problem for most technical men is that, even if they are very organized in collecting data about things and systems, they are not able to be as pragmatic and methodical about finding a partner. Robert may research for years for the proper stereo, computer, or automobile equipment. But when women are the search subject, the equipment seems to shop back, fight back, and throw all kinds of surprises into the shopping trip not listed in consumer manuals. Shopping for a woman is confusing, confounding, and downright disarming.

Most people, men and women, make first-level decisions about a partner based strictly on physical attraction. We search for the perfect-looking person. We want and expect a chemical attraction to a candidate who looks a certain way. We do not listen or touch. We simply look, checking out our possible partner on what we see.

The second-level decisions are made up of considerations beyond the physicality of our candidate. At this point we are looking for what is inside that beautiful or handsome head. At this point we are looking for what is beyond the surface. This is an important decision-level point, but it still is often covered by the physical attraction we spot at the first level, which keeps interfering, coloring our judgment because he or she looks so right to us.

Third-level decisions concern our emotional compatibility. This is such an important level for consideration that it is too bad that the first two levels have already influenced us so. Unfortunately, we don't make any of the levels of decisions based on a conscious level. Our unconscious is doing most of this initial screening for us. Eventually our conscious mind does address the problem of emotional compatibility, but usually not until we have encountered some major communication barrier.

It is sad that we spend so much time discovering the physical and internal attractions instead of looking for a form of "coupling quotient" from our partners. I had one client, a woman who had been disappointed with many relationships, who actually gave her prospective partners a compatibility test on the first date. It was a four-hundred-question test she had developed herself. That was the right idea, but the wrong method, and much too early to be testing each other.

There are indicators for problems available to us, though. Usually, we just don't want to see them!

The first-level search demands most of our time and attention. At this first level we all too often make major commitments to each other, usually before we are ready really to test the relationship. Poor sci-tech usually has little reference for understanding the second- and third-level decisions, so he is at a disadvantage when shopping for a partner.

And so the student of science becomes the slave to passion. An MIT graduate with a fellowship at Stanford, and the fair-haired boy at the research agency, Paul is really an emotional adolescent about women. He doesn't know how to approach them, to evaluate them, or how to look for the perfect complementary partner. All he knows is that she looks good and he feels a surge of passion when he thinks about her!

Women seem more sophisticated about relationships and partnering. They appear to be more selective about finding the appropriate partner. Indeed, they are not. Often they too base partner choices on physical appearance and initial good feelings, rather than on a more long-term compatibility system. Yes, as much as they talk about coupling, marriage, and love, they are still pretty naive about which prerequisites in a potential partner will carry over to lifelong partnership material.

Why are we all so dumb? Because of the movies, the love songs, the commercials, and the "tinselization of romance." We are all committed to the notion that love should be exciting, perfect, and last forever. There are few classes in building or maintaining relationships. The first effort close to that is the famous premarital counseling. And that is offered too late!

By the time a couple decides they want (or the church imposes) premarital counseling, most couples are already committed to each other, to the date, and to all the paraphernalia of the wedding. There is more attention given to the wedding invitations and favors than to the understanding of the differences between the two intended partners. By the time the date is set, the partnership is set! At that point, the couple, I'm sorry to say, usually just goes through the motions of counseling because there is no question of whether or not to marry. That decision is firm. The rest is routine. "Listen, pledge, explore, but what does it matter? We are going through with it anyway."

Sadly, I see many couples who enter premarital counseling and end up knowing, somewhere along the way, that the relationship is not good. But the wedding has been set, if the reception has been arranged, the bridesmaids have already ordered their dresses. Men are better at calling off weddings because they are not as caught up in the wedding planning as the brides.

Putting the marriage into motion hastens the *commitment phase.* A couple came in to see me with serious problems. They did not seem compatible; there were problems of possessiveness and jealousy. Then one day, to my surprise, they came in with the news that the wedding date was set. They had discovered that the church of their choice had but two dates left for weddings—June 3 and September 18. It was then April. They chose June 3, because September seemed too far away. Had they waited until they were ready to decide *if* they should marry, they might have been able to choose better *when* they should marry!

The day before the wedding they both came to me in tears, wanting to cancel the plans. They had had the most frightening fight just the night before. But both had been highly involved in wedding planning. The groom had driven to the wine country to pick out special cases of wine for the ceremony. The bride's mother was flying out from Detroit; she had already boarded the plane. The caterer had a no-refund policy on the two-thousand-dollar luncheon he had prepared. So the wedding proceeded. Two months later, the couple dissolved their marriage.

The point is that we don't get to really shop around. That wonderful glow of a new person who seems so adoring often is enough. Partners who appear to be different in the beginning (she is a ballet dancer, he is a biochemist) need to take time to look at their differences and to integrate their styles long before the passionate first period has died down.

I will present some prototype sample couples for your consideration. They are made up from the types of couples I work with every day in my office. Since I've seen over three thousand couples in my practice, I believe I have experienced most of the complementary personality styles that Silicon Syndrome couples choose to adapt. I hope that you will find yourself listed here. Even if you are not the classic couple, or do not live in Silicon Valley, try looking for yourself in this list.

Actually, it's easier to find a mate among the models given, or a boss, or a bothersome colleague. It is much harder to find ourselves. We seem to do a better job of hiding us from us. This comes from years of self-rationalization, protection, and defensiveness. "No, I couldn't be that bad! . . . But my husband fits that description to a T!"

Don't be offended by the seemingly light way in which I approach your differences. I *know* that the problems are heavy. I know that some of you reading this book are on the edge of marital disaster, and others have already passed the turning point and are feeling vulnerable and weary.

The saddest of all the calls I receive are from the sci-tech whose mate has left him, and when I ask him why, he says, "I haven't the slightest notion." If you can't understand what your partner is talking about, if you really don't have the slightest notion why both of you, or either of you, feel so bad, join in this exploration of your interactional process, of all the ways you show or hide yourself from others.

I have witnessed your pain, been sprinkled by your tears in my office, and have seen the great sorrow that comes from years of being misunderstood. Sometimes it is more than misunderstanding. Sometimes it is actually a sort of "crazy-making" process that sours a relationship, but it can be impossible to spot on your own.

There are tears that never get shed, inner tears that block or clog up inside one's body, preventing that good relief that comes when we can release the pain. Inner tears are as valid as those that flow, but they get less attention. And less compassion from others!

The engineer/scientist personality often chooses a complementary partner who compensates for his personality deficits. I have specialized in translating engineers to their colleagues. Through marriage counseling, I have learned to translate them to their partners and to themselves:

"It is possible that we may want to choose to spend the rest of our time on this planet in a committed form"
may mean:
"I want to marry you, baby!"

"Leave me alone. I can't deal with you and all your noise and silly wailings"
may mean:
"Honey, it is hard for me right now to take in all you have to say. Can we postpone your important feelings until I am more available to them and to you?"

"I don't care about the vacation. I don't care if we never go away again! Planning something with you is too much work"
may mean:
"I haven't any ideas right now. I am dry creatively. In fact, planning vacations is not much fun for me. You are better at it than I am, and I feel inadequate when you want me to try to plan with you."

I have learned that in order to survive in the Silicon Syndrome you will have to do the following:

1. Translate your partner or colleague into your own language in order to understand him.
2. Translate *you* to your partner. Speak *you* in his language so that he can begin to hear or see you.
3. When talking to each other, use your partner's vocabulary and feeling intonations, not your own.
4. Listen to your partner from his perspective, not your own. (I know. It's hard.)

5. Problem-solve using the scientific method! And share feelings using the emotional method!

Assessment tests, the Strong/Campbell Vocational Test, the Self-Directed Search, and other career-inventory tools describe the engineer/scientist as a person, man or woman, whose work and personality habits exhibit attention to detail, concern for perfection, and a rational approach to all things. Most scientists and engineers have a high I.Q., even though I have discovered them to be a little slower street-wise or relationship-wise.

My understanding of the forthcoming couples has come from living with my husband the last seven years. Don and I have groaned, sweated, and plowed through the difficult interactional process.

We started out attempting to please each other in all ways. That is a wonderful time. We both seem to like the same things. We are feverish to be together. You have probably all experienced it: the honeymoon period, when everything the other one does is charming and wonderful and adorable. Unfortunately, this period usually precedes the *real* honeymoon. It usually occurs in the "falling-in-love" period.

It happens in the first sweet taste of a relationship when the couple has not had to make too many major decisions together. Anyway, after Don and I had passed the initial stages we began to realize that we were different about almost everything. He likes to be alone, I love to be around people; he is a night person, I am a morning person; he studies and researches, I jump into things; he believes in planning and saving, I like to buy now. And about emotional things: Don likes to think about what he feels, digest it, test it, and then share it. I like to pop my feelings out the minute I experience them. Then I like to talk about them, analyze, and digest the analysis. The major pain is that the more needy I feel, the more frightened Don becomes, and the less well he can handle my emotions. And the more he pulls away from me, the more I want from him, and the needier I feel.

Don't be discouraged. I'm not. I was not, even as Don and I negotiated our relationship. Because I know something you may not know. Being a team player is an acquired skill. It does not come naturally. And it is possible to learn. Don and I had lots to learn, lots to negotiate, but I knew that it was possible. I have seen too many miracles in my office not to believe that with time and patience, if you both are motivated, two personality styles can gel and integrate and use each other to the couple's best advantage.

The problem for most of you readers out there is that you will want to believe it is possible to persuade your partner to be just like you—to change, to grow, to love all the things and people ou love. I have that hope too. But, on the way to that illusionary hypothesis, how about simply negotiating for what you want? I am fearful that your dream of the perfect mate may keep you from knowing and enjoying the one you have.

THE PERFECTIONIST AND THE "EASY DOES IT" PERSONALITY

The scientist needs to be right. The research, the life, depends on it. In engineering, one megasecond or one joule can make the difference in the launch, the project, the decision. His quest for accuracy, his need for precision, carries over into his emotional and interactional life. His partner may be looking for the big picture, but this perfect man may be frustratingly eager for the complete details. His deductive reasoning prevents him from expressing an opinion or a reaction until he has the full complement of information. The exacting details are tiresome, though, sometimes even for him.

So he tends to pick a mate who can bring some relief to his routine. His "dingbat" partner is comic relief when this pair presents itself to others, even though the frivolous partner bears the major ridicule in the relationship. The easy-does-it personality can relax with her own mistakes, can even tolerate his, and can really enjoy life even when the ship is stuck on the sand bar or the bridge cards have jelly on the edges. This partner will teach him that it is okay to be wrong sometimes, that it can even reduce his chances for ulcers, hypertension, and the other body-threatening results of living on a tight string.

The relationship problem for this couple is that they will have to adjust continually to each other's style. The problem comes when he is faced with trauma—the income tax auditor, or the wall that is short three inches of wallpaper.

Prescription: Take turns doing it each way. Decide which are the appropriate items for the perfect style and which are the times that can safely take a more laid-back, imperfect approach. The sci-tech might need to be in charge of the budgeting preparations (leaving room for errors by his mate, knowing that she will make some!), while vacations may need to be under the supervision of his mate because she can allow for the imperfections of timing, arrangements, and schedules.

Sample couple: Paul and Lisa have been married ten years. He remembers their anniversary with ease; his appointment book is always carefully attended. He buys gifts on a schedule and always remembers to buy the precise gift according to whether it is a wood or a tin or a gold anniversary. For ten years (tin) he bought complete camping utensils and other tin appurtenances for the big camping trip planned for that summer. They were to meet at Original Joe's at 8:00 P.M. for dinner. The gifts, perfectly wrapped, were on her side of the table. But Lisa, never mindful of the time, did not show up until 8:35, a little disheveled, a little tired, and forgetting that it was their tenth anniversary. She did bring a package, though. A Hawaiian floral-print shirt with shorts to match. Of course, the evening was a disaster. . . .

Paul needs to learn that Lisa does not enjoy his precision timing of their anniversary. She wanted a more frivolous gift, not so utilitarian. She could have survived the evening if he had not pounced on her for being late. Paul probably needed to give Lisa the gift of an extra thirty minutes without consequences on their anniversary.

Lisa must learn that flowers are just not Paul's choice of design. If she really wants to please him and not herself, her gift to him needs to be more defined, perhaps stripes or squares. And being late on their anniversary is in poor taste on Lisa's part because she knows how much Paul values being on time.

Compromise is required for this couple. He needs to provide for a margin of error for his wife. She needs to make a concerted effort on the major occasions of their life. To give a gift, each needs to consider the other's value system, not his own. If you want to give something to your partner to please yourself, for heaven's sake do it, but not under the guise of "I thought you would enjoy French aftershave for a change."

Lisa will have to be prepared for the fact that although Paul may wish for perfection at all times, he may not always be the example of it!

THE CAUTIOUS AND THE RISK TAKER

The engineer/scientist personality is highly sensitive to criticism. He will sacrifice success if the chance for error is too great. A partner who can field criticism well is a complement to this cautious person who runs from attack. His guard is always up. He is interested in proceeding slowly, especially in expressing his feelings. Always looking for flaws, he is not interested in jumping into error-producing events or expressions.

To provide relief to himself, though, the cautious sci-tech chooses a risk taker who will stick her neck out to be experimental. The risk taker will complement her partner's caution because she is not afraid to push him beyond his proscribed boundaries. She is success oriented and will try new things or take a prominent position in the community or in political arenas. The experimenter will assist the cautious one in bringing some excitement to his structured existence. She actually rounds out her partner's portfolio.

Prescription: He may need to tone down his critical evaluations a little. He may need to think: "Why not?" instead of "Why?" But she will need to be particularly discreet about *when* she will experiment. He needs preparation for most surprises. In dividing responsibility again, this couple can assign "safe" decisions depending on the nature of the possible consequences. In financial issues they may need an arbiter because their differences are too wide.

Sample couple: Carl and Rita are planning their daughter's graduation party. Carl really wants to get involved this time. He is proud of his daughter's standing in her graduating class. He wants to plan a party for forty kids, hire a guard to watch for intruders, and to inform his daughter of the time, menu, guest list, and all precautions. Rita is disgusted by his approach, berates him for not knowing kids at all, and makes him feel inadequate as a father. Rita then jumps up and calls her mother to urge her to invite their daughter to Arizona, suggesting a plane that leaves immediately after graduation exercises.

Rita needs to be more delicate with Carl's feelings. She could give Carl credit for wanting to have the party in the first place. That is really out of character for him, and he needs reinforcement for taking the risk at all. To surprise Carl by making other plans spontaneously is the worst thing she can do for Carl's already damaged ego.

Carl has to look at the kind of party he was planning. Was it to suit his needs or his daughter's? Too much planning may destroy the intention. Can he learn to say something like, "Rita, I really want this to be an event that will please the kids, and I want your help."

THE ASSERTIVE AND THE PASSIVE

The skilled scientist or engineer is often promoted to a managerial position. Sometimes he is assertive to begin with. Often he is not. I have taught many new directors and vice-presidents how to say no, how to delegate, and how to be emphatic. But there are still some sci-techs who are naturally assertive, who want to be in charge, who want to have control. This personality will pick a passive partner who expects to be directed and who wants to feel dependent.

The partner will know when her mate goes too far (she has experienced it often enough), and so she will "soften" things out with others for her bossy mate. But between the two of them she usually comes out feeling resentment. She doormats herself into his heart, and then pays the price by not getting what she wants.

Prescription: Assertiveness training for the passive mate. She needs to learn how to take care of herself when her sci-tech wants to be in control. He is used to pushing colleagues and secretaries or nurses around all day. He is good at making decisions, but when he comes home he forgets that this is a *co-equal* relationship. He will need to step back, give up some of the control, and let her practice some new responsibility of her own. This is hard to do. She will slip and want to be dependent. He will forget and try to take over. Worrying primarily about issues of control, and fearing it in others, this sci-tech believes that someone has to be in charge at all times.

He translates "Let's make love, honey" into "Perform, dummy!" Phobic that he will be called on to do something on command, or that he may have to relinquish control to others, he will often assume the dominant position, even when an authoritarian position is foreign to his nature.

Sample couple: Al is so comfortable being in charge that it is hard to handle having Patsy take over, even in making love or designing the kitchen. Each partner will have to move over to mid-court a little, with Patsy practicing making decisions and Al stepping back. The key here is that Patsy will make mistakes. Without practice she is going to goof up on some things. This couple will spend too much time defending themselves if they can't decide that each is allowed plenty of errors in life. It is not *that there is a problem* (for there will always be problems), but *what will we do about the problem?* that matters.

THE INDIVIDUALIST AND THE JOINER

Doing it all alone is his style of working. If it weren't for his wife, who can't stay away from people, he would be a hermit. He is the perfect project man at work, as long as he doesn't have to integrate any of his project with that of another human being. The problem is that he continues this solo workmanship at home, choosing to do dishes alone, declaring that he gardens better without chattering, and never really integrates into the household.

His partner, of course, has to be a social being or they would never have gotten together in the first place. She probably made the first move, and has probably been making the rest of the moves ever since. In the beginning, though, this bothered neither partner. They were just pleased with being together, never minding how. As time wears on, she wears thin. Because the individualist is unwilling to provide boundaries for others, his lack of limits can be interpreted as indifference. He does want a social life, in some form, and thus he chooses a partner who can create parties, friends, and company activities for him. The problem is that her greatest strength becomes her greatest weakness when he gets fed up with her socializing style.

Prescription: The individualist needs lots of time and space alone. He is actually invaded by people. They bore in on him and make him uneasy. He becomes anxious when he feels bombarded by too many people contacts. His joiner mate, on the other hand, will shrivel up and die if she does not have the social interactions that feed her soul. Compromise is in order. Spend part of the time attending to him, protecting him from too many people-events, and spend another part of the time feeding her with the connections she needs to survive. Group therapy would be appropriate for him, but, of course, it is she who is dying to try it!

Sample couple: Irvin did not want to go to the company Christmas party. "Everybody just gets drunk and sloppy," he said, "and in between you have to make small talk with people you don't even know or like."

Julie, naturally, wanted to go. When Irv announced that he would not go (and it did not matter whose company party it was—hers or his), Julie attacked him with all the antisocial labels she could summon.

What she could have done, however, was to make him an offer something like this:

"I know you won't enjoy this party much. I'd like to help make it easier for you to tolerate, though. Because I really *need* to have this kind of social activity once in a while. And you happen to be part of my need. My 'neurotic me' needs to have my husband with me during these social occasions. So I'll make you a bargain: We can skip the cocktail party at Mark's before the dinner. I will arrange for several of our friends and people whom you enjoy to be sitting near us. I will urge you to dance only three of the dances. And I promise to leave with you at ten-thirty P.M.

"In exchange for this, I will plan Sunday for us to be completely alone. I'll bring you breakfast in bed and let you read the paper until noon, without disturbance. I will plan projects for myself all day and through the evening, so that when you want to check in and be with me you can. I know that you need times to be alone, and I will not let people intrude on your solo time if you will give me this opportunity to have fun for a few hours."

THE HIGH PROFILE AND THE LOW PROFILE

This MIT grad, high-jump star, Ph.D., and president of Super-Tek, has done it all. And he continues to do so. An amazing man who can combine his calculating mind with high-tech politics, he keeps his image high profile. And he likes it that way. He really enjoys being on the front line, the front page, and the battlefront. His only problem is that it is difficult for him to be really intimate or to show vulnerability. No matter, he says. He has very little to be vulnerable about. He creates images. He creates his own press with his work, his family, and his wife. But with his wife, or his vice-president, his secretary, and most of his board of directors, *he* needs to be the star! So he has picked a low-profile mate who can be the counterpoint to his bigger-than-life approach.

She is the perfect complement for the "Man of the Year." She doesn't mind the background spot—even prefers it. She can give her mate the adoring look whenever it is needed. She means it too. She does adore her husband. She admires his outgoing, bold approach and feels that she is getting close enough to that style by being next to him. She does not want it for herself. Once in a while she gets a peek at the inside man, and that intimacy is enough, especially because she knows that nobody else gets to see that aspect of him at all. Problems arise for this couple when she doesn't get that chance for intimacy with him. Then she feels bombarded by the outside world and jealous of his time with others.

He may feel discouraged when he wants his mate to entertain without him, or when he sees her "wallflowering" at a company party. He wants her to be interesting to others; he actually wants a social extension of himself. At the same time, and this is the tricky part, he needs her quiet, reserved nature to be there for him. It is a fine line this lady has to walk, being mindful not to steal her husband's show while being available for him socially in just the way he expects. She must never compete for attention, yet be social enough to please him.

Prescription: Find a way to sort out the "outside times" and the "inside times." He will rarely initiate the quiet visits, and she must not take that personally. The woman who believes she is not enough for a husband like this is in trouble. Not because she is not okay, but because she thinks she is not okay! I tell such a client that if she were Sophia Loren or Brooke Shields, he would still reach outside the relationship for contact, strokes, and social interaction.

Sample couple: Sampson worked every night until eight or nine o'clock. He also traveled a lot and spent many weekends in the plant. Lynn also had a demanding, high-level job, but she needed Sampson for sustenance much more than he needed her. When he did come home, he liked to invite the neighbors over. He even talked on the phone a lot.

Each partner needs to look at his/her own priorities and then make the negotiation that will give him more of what he wants from a relationship. Sampson needs to be in Lynn's presence when he is entertaining. He wants that "host couple" feeling. And he needs to trade that for some of the simple, intimate time (although quite boring to him) that Lynn requires.

Lynn will probably be content with the background spot if she reminds herself that Sampson is also the key to her social connections, those precious ties that she would have difficulty cultivating on her own.

THE GENIUS AND THE RELIEF

The genius can solve every technical problem he encounters! Just ask him and he will come up with the answer. Except the answers about people—here his computer tilts. He can't figure out people.

Usually alone, always quiet, poor Genius never learned the art of small talk. He is comfortable fixing things. He loves to stretch his brain. But he is lost when it comes to just being there. If there is no task at hand, he feels useless and foolish—just like the gangly kid he was in high school. Here's where the cheerleader comes in.

The genius picks a partner who will offer him some psychic relief. She doesn't look for problems. She just wants her team to win. No matter what the difficulty (20 to zip), she will keep on cheering. She is not interested in her man's special skills, his technical know-how, or his ability to solve what no one else at Megaconomics can! She will encourage her man to be as relaxed as he can be.

His brain works overtime and hers takes frequent vacations. Together they can solve any dilemma because she will prescribe the mental-health breaks. The problem they encounter is that sometimes he grows despondent because she rarely wants to compete with him on an academic level. He can get disgusted, too, when she yearns for the superficial, even the supernatural, above the rational approach to problem-solving.

Her complaint with him is that he is always responding with a "How can I fix it?" mentality, which precludes the reflective listening response that she needs. It is easier for Genius to solve a complicated issue than to sound empathic. He has little patience with "Ah, there, there" responses, even though such a response would push his partner more quickly into a problem-solving mode.

Prescription: Genius must learn reflective listening. He needs to be able to respond as though he really could put himself in his partner's position. This couple will probably do a lot of lobbying for their separate positions. But what each needs to do is put himself in the other's place, saying inside, "Well, if I were she now, I would be feeling pretty sad."

The cheerleader has to learn to present information to her man in as logical a manner as she possibly can. She can even urge him to consider her emotional needs from a problem-puzzle viewpoint. "What can you do, dear heart, to convince me that you love me when you stand there sternly tapping your foot?" Given a problem to solve, Genius may respond.

Sample couple: Gerald and Cherie are going steady. He is terribly impressed with his high-level, exciting position at the company. At home he has a new computer, and that challenges him too. He would like to share the technical issues both of home and of work, but Cherie is not at all interested. She, on the other hand, is depressed because Gerald never seems interested in sharing his emotional reactions with her. She has to break down and create a great emotional scene before she can get his attention. Then he looks hopeless and forlorn, wondering if there is anything in the world he can do to get back his cheerful woman. Of course there is! But not by *fixing* it. Not by suggesting different options or by denying her reality. He can help her out simply by listening with his most empathic ear. "Damn, it must be hard for you to sit here while I go on and on and on about my computer as if it is some kind of new lover!"

THE DEPENDABLE AND THE FLAMBOYANT

You can set your watch by this sci-tech. He is predictable. He makes a stable boss, partner, and colleague. Always on time for meetings, he remembers everything from the top secret to the trivial, and besides that, he will bring home the bacon! He will stray only short distances from the house (maybe to the computer store or the hardware store). He plays by the rules, and he will find out exactly what the rules are. He is not interested in gray areas; he wants to know what to expect and plans to do the job on time, in form, and without hoopla. He is a company man; he dresses, plays, and works by the company rules.

For a change of pace, he tends to pick a flamboyant wife, partner, or even secretary. Because he has no sense of the ridiculous, he seems to appreciate it in those who are close to him. His wife is the cut-up, the practical joker and light touch that such a starchy person needs. Although he will wear the standard company costume, she will show up at functions in the most inappropriate, but still suitable to her, attire. "Only she could get away with something like that," they mutter. He agrees.

The problem for this couple occurs when they are both in their respective corners, poles apart, and feeling in need of understanding. He wants the peace of some security and stability, and she wants a playmate who will tease and clown for her.

Prescription: Both partners have some work to do. Alone, he would bomb, except in the laboratory. He needs the charm of his creative wife; yet he also needs to know that there are boundaries for her behavior. While they can both give her permission to wear battery-operated flashing earrings at home, she must draw the line at flights of fantasy at his office parties or when his family visits from Wisconsin, and at times when he wants to rest from the excitement. He, on the other hand, must sometimes enter into the spirit of things. Although she desperately needs "old faithful" for balance, she also needs someone who will humor her antics and let her play straight once in a while.

Sample couple: Dan and Fanny came to my office when there seemed to be little hope. Dan was worn out; she was gone every night, delivering singing tele-cookie-grams. He complained of a messy house, bills overdue, and no money in the checking account. Although Dan earned a very good salary, Fanny tended to surprise Dan with tickets to Europe, new saunas, and lots of luxury items well beyond Dan's CPA mentality. Fanny complained too. Their life was drab; Dan was always depressed. Even the surprise pornographic video cassettes did not awaken poor Dan. "She couldn't rent the damned things, like ordinary folks," he growled. "She had to buy them, at eighty-nine dollars each!"

Dan and Fanny needed a break from their positions. I suggested a nice, structured, predictable environment for three weeks, so that Dan could feel grounded again. During that time, they were to devote every other weeknight to their individual priority pastimes. After a month they came upon the perfect recreational activity for them: square dancing. Sci-techs love square dancing, if they have to dance at all, because the caller tells you what to do, there are no required spontaneous moves. Dependable Don can learn the calls, not make mistakes, and feel secure as soon as he learns the dances. Fanny, in the meantime, can enjoy the atmosphere and the moves while she laughs and plays and sings with the caller. I also prescribed a housekeeper, some budgeting for Fanny, and a whole lot of "letting go" exercises for Dan.

THE DATA SEEKER AND THE BEHAVIORIST

This sci-tech is in his glory when four or five people are sitting around sharing information about the latest technology. Always involved in research, even if it is about lawn sprinklers or the latest food processor, data seekers revel in finding information. They are especially eager to seek information about things, processes, or systems. The human system, unless it is physical, is less interesting to them. Humans are not as easy to study; they are not predictable.

The data-seeker's partner will be the psychotherapist in the family. She will explain the kids to him. And him to the kids!

Humans are not a safe model for a man who is more comfortable with data. He shies away from emotional interchange because he knows that he will be shortchanged. He cannot compete with his partner's ability to understand those around her. So he sticks his head in the sand or in the computer or in the book, and lets his spouse take on the full-time counseling for the household and, surely, for the problems of the two of them.

Again, the dilemma for this couple is timing. When he most wants to talk about widgets and gadgets, she most wants to talk about her feelings. Her feelings go on forever; there is nothing concrete that he can get his hands or brain on, and he loses patience with the psychological approach to everything from peeling apples to lovemaking.

Prescription: Encourage this man to gather information about relationships, team playing, and all the aspects of family interaction. Actually, he will be a great psychology student if he is given the logical theories behind the science of psychology. Always a practical man who can be pragmatic about what he wants, this partner will yield to long discussions if they are approached in a businesslike, structured manner. Discussions need to conclude with action items, plans for future agendas, and the sense of organization that his encyclopedic mind demands.

Sample couple: Doug let his wife, Bertha, handle all the emotional traumas until she seemed to disappear one day. Oh, she still lived at home, but she began acting ill around the house. She was not sick. She simply overdosed on her own analysis and decided to leave him. She fell in love with the marketing manager who loved to talk about emotional things with her.

Doug was urged to study the parameters of their disengagement. Being the good student, and being motivated at last, he began to delve into the holes in their relationship. Bertha shared her needs with Doug, told him in what ways the marketing manager stimulated her, soothed her, and made her feel that her emotional life was a valid one, and even one that another human being was interested in sharing. Luckily, Doug and Bertha discovered their abyss soon enough, went to a marriage encounter and classes on communication, and put the needed spark back just in time for Bertha to decide to market herself to good old Doug again.

THE RATIONAL AND THE HYSTERIC

The engineer/scientist, with a highly developed brain, seeks rest from his brainy struggles within. If called on to demonstrate emotion, he hides, deflecting attention away from himself and onto his more hysteric partner. If tears are in order, he will downright refuse to participate. His beloved can cry for both of them, and, indeed, she does. Deeply sensitive inside, with a heart of gold but little resource to express himself, he needs his emotional partner to scream out for him. This sci-tech works overtime to protect his own vulnerability, to keep from exposing his responsive or sensory self to others. Besides, his partner does it better!

The rational scientist rarely makes mistakes. His logic will win in any argument, but when he pushes too far, his family and friends and even colleagues back away. The more he stiffens and goes tight, the more his mate begins to unwind. At this point she is an emotional drain to him. He does not know how to handle her, and he is humiliated and feels disgusted with such a bizarre range of emotion, completely unavailable to him should he try for it.

Prescription: It's simple. We just teach him that feelings are a state of the ego, like the child state, that do not adhere to thinking. When we convince him that feelings are not logical, never will be, and never can be, he can stop trying to make sense out of reactions, his own or his mate's, and then he can try for some empathy. She also has some tools to use. She needs to use the rational approach whenever she can. Like the sci-techs who come to my office with the problems of their lives outlined on yellow legal-size paper or sometimes chronicled by computer, she needs to present him with some rational homework once in a while. It is not beyond her. She usually just chooses not to. When I can convince her, though, that this approach will get her an ear, an opening to the heart of her partner, she will make some efforts. Actually it is rather a kick to put down in logical fashion everything that bothers her, and, of course, he is very impressed.

He responds by remembering that feelings are not rational, so that when she begins to emote, he does not rush to tell her that she doesn't make sense. Instead, he listens with his most compassionate ear, and, with fine tuning, he even begins to hear some things.

Sample couple: Helen is always calling ultimatums, threatening everything in the book. The ultimate ultimatum is her own death. One day, if she gets desperate enough, she might try that. It is so hard to get Robert's attention. Tears won't do. Screaming won't do. So each time she has one of these attacks of "No Robert"—when Robert isn't there for her—she has to deepen her offense, use stronger tactics. It doesn't work, of course.

Helen will have to sit down very quietly with Robert *when there is no immediate crisis,* so he won't be on his guard. Then her approach needs to be something like this:

"Robert, I've turned over a new leaf. I want to be able to receive your attention, and what I have been doing certainly isn't getting me that. Therefore, I have decided to be systematic. I promise you that I will reduce my 'show biz,' completely stop the ultimatums, and appeal to you in a low and quiet voice, hoping that you can hear my wishes and will attempt to respond to me with your understanding of my dilemma. Then I will promise a problem-solving session within twenty-four hours so that we can alleviate any potential problems."

Everybody except Robert knows that problems are always potential. But he does want an intention of peace and of peacemaking. He can be available to Helen if he does not fear the emotional scenes that have taken their toll on him. He will probably agree to this suggestion.

It will take a few tries. They will not achieve success the first time. Robert will argue, he will protest, and Helen may fall back into old, undisciplined ways. The important word here is not *position.* It does not matter what their positions have been. Spouting those leads only to lobbying for them, and that does not work. The important word is *intention.* Their intention is toward harmony. With two styles of handling crises and problems in general, they will have to begin to integrate both systems, allowing the rational approach as well as the feeling approach, perhaps not simultaneously, but inevitably.

SILICON PARTNERS COME WITH DIFFERENT SHAPES BUT SIMILAR PROBLEMS

All Silicon Syndrome women seem to feel the same pain. Their partners are not completely available to them. It may be because their mates are totally preoccupied with business, projects, or goals. Or it may be that they simply are unavailable to their partners' feelings.

Why suffer? Why don't more women get out of these stifling relationships? Many do. Silicon Valley leads the nation in divorce rates.

Yes, women are leaving. But before *you* leave, let's see if there is anything you can do to save your relationship. That may take some figuring out—about you! We will take a look at your personality, your dependencies and insecurities, and your fragile parts.

First, though, a few words about your men. They don't really want you to leave their homes. They don't even want to be bad partners. Many are completely unaware of how unhappy their partners are. Oh, yes, you have given them complaints. They knew you didn't like this or that, but they honestly didn't know it was *that* bad.

"Well, he is unconscious, then!" you say. You are right. He is. He is unconscious about your pain and his own inadequacy and emotional famine.

He is unconscious, period, about feelings. He does not really experience his emotions, such as his disappointments, frustration, or loneliness. You may have notions that it is you with whom he does not want to communicate. Yet another part of you knows that he does not, in fact, communicate well at any level about emotions.

So stop taking his detachment personally! You need to learn how to raise his consciousness. I will teach you to do that. Then you will have a fair chance to evaluate your relationship. You may still want to leave after you have given him the information he needs, but at least you will have given both of you all the opportunity you need to assess your relationship.

Let's talk about you. What is your personality like? Your sci-tech partner probably looked for some compensating qualities in you. Maybe he needed your vulnerabilities, your inefficiencies, and your playfulness. But you have other wonderful qualities that your sci-tech may or may not need as much.

I'd like to tell you about my own transformations in some areas. In my first marriage I assumed the responsible role. Although I was married to an engineer, he was not the classic engineer. He did not have those rigid qualities or a sense of duty to perform. And so I seemed to be in charge of many aspects of our life. I was the worrier, the controller, the serious-minded parent.

But we got a divorce. I noticed, by the way, that after our separation my former husband seemed to take on a great deal more responsibility for his life. Who was holding up whom?

When I met and later married Don, I was impressed with his enormous sense of obligation. He was answerable in every area of his life. Of course, I was greatly relieved. Here was a man who would do it all! And, of course, he was greatly relieved. When he met me, he saw a woman who was willing to do it all! I was always on time and always calculating the efficiency of a decision. And so two super-responsibles married; both were relieved that they no longer would have to carry the entire burden.

Something very surprising happened. I soon discovered that Don was even more serious about things than I was. And I was used to having a relationship dynamic in which one person was more responsible than the other. Front court or back court, it didn't seem to matter which side I played. So, especially because it seemed so appealing to me, I found myself, for the first time in my life, playing the irresponsible role. I actually heard Don saying the same sentences I had screamed a thousand times at my former spouse. "Why are you late this time? Why have you overbooked your schedule again and gotten us into this terrible muddle? Why are your bank accounts overdrawn? How could you forget?"

I was completely startled one day when I realized that within a matter of one short year I had changed myself to the irresponsible position. I liked it too! It was very freeing. I had few cares, lots of fun and frolic, and little to worry about, because I knew that someone (poor Don) would attend to things.

But I did not want my husband to feel the same way about me that I had felt in my previous marriage. So eventually I stopped doing that. I wanted to do my part. In the second year, then, we began to reassign responsibilities. Gloriously, we have divided them in half. I take charge of the food, utilities, clothes, my career, my children, the inside of the house, and our social life. Don is responsible for the mortgage payments, the loan payments, his business, the pool, the cars, the yard, and major vacations. I am in charge of insurance and tax filing, and he is in charge of the house and business taxes. It works out perfectly. If I want to spend all my money having the house cleaned, Don does not complain. If Don pays for a pool service, I do not complain.

Now, I know that it is easier not to complain when there is enough money to go around for everything. No matter what the amount of income, though, it is priority-setting that makes the difference! The point is that I did make changes that actually compensated for Don's style of coping. Although my natural inclination might have been to complete the seesaw, with one up and one down, I was willing to play either side of the game. To continue that position was dangerous to our marriage.

Back to you. Do you have some compensating behaviors that complement your partner? Maybe you aren't so silly when you are with your friends. Maybe you seem like the frugal and stable one when you work on a committee or at your own job. Which are the qualities you like about yourself, and which are the qualities you want to give up? If you are a risk taker, does that serve you? Does it get you in trouble, or does it keep your life from being boring? If you are a doormat, does it help you to avoid confrontation, or are you getting tired of being walked on?

Warning: Your partner may sabotage you if you try to change something. Not because he is a terrible person, but because he wishes to maintain the equilibrium of the relationship. If you change, he will be frightened, unsure of his position, and unsure of you. Why would he want to change from being a serious-minded person if your giddiness has served him so well all these years? So you will have lots of work to do to remind him that this is a change you opted for and that you want his cooperation.

You will both slip, although he may do so more often than you! He is not eager to give up his "dingbat," even if he made lots of noise about you throughout your marriage. So be patient with each other as you both make the changes necessary to allow your growth.

If you take assertiveness training and start talking like you know what you want, your partner may call you anything from a women's libber to a selfish bitch. He may not understand your motivation, and he certainly won't understand if you compensate in the wrong direction and actually become aggressive for a while.

If you have been the behaviorist, always smoothing out your life for your partner, and you no longer wish to do that, he will be like a lost puppy. "But I don't know how to talk to your mother," he will wail. The lament of an abandoned husband who has finally been given the responsibility for talking to his own children can be devastating. "What will I say?" he shrills.

Don't completely abandon him. Lead him to the nearest parenting class, give him psychology books, or sign him up for a consciousness-raising retreat. He will need some guidelines. Many women make appointments with me for their husbands. They leave their men at the door, just like a child whom they leave at the teacher's door, and then they say, "Fix him." Sometimes I do!

If he is motivated, that husband and I together figure out what to do. If he is secretly plotting the end of the relationship but is too passive to make that happen, he will surely not cooperate by learning how to be more strategic at home.

Take a long look at yourself. Are there things you want to change in your life? How much do you want that kind of change? If you are sure of your own motivation, then do it.

Here is a list of proposals for you. Choose what fits for you. You will know the prescription when you see it listed below.

1. Take assertiveness training.
2. Take a business course or home-finance course.
3. Take a career-analysis course.
4. Give yourself some personal therapy to check your self-esteem.
5. Join a women's group, or, better, join a mixed group to hear how other men talk!
6. Take a time-management course. Learn to be more cost efficient.
7. Read about procrastination, learning disorders (you may have one), and other inhibitors to solid functioning.
8. Have a physical checkup. Plan a new health regimen for yourself.
9. Check your weight problem. Do something about it!
10. Other health issues? Drinking or smoking? Fix them. It will be a real boost to your ego.
11. Check out your friends. Are they going anywhere? Stick close to those who are on improvement campaigns. Drop the others.
12. Evaluate your complaints. Are you merely accumulating resentments about your mate because you are no longer interested in doing your share?

WHY CAN'T I CHANGE?

Some of us are deeply afraid to make the moves we need to make. If we give up our current position, no matter how painful it is, we will be stepping onto new ground, trying new behaviors. That new ground is full of tremors! The problem with change is that we have to traverse the bridge from the old behavior to the new place.

THE BRIDGE OF CHANGE

Old Behavior	*New Behavior*
I'm used to this place.	I've never been here before.
It is warm and cozy.	It is cold and different here.
I am used to this position.	I feel itchy!
I feel safe here.	I feel uncomfortable.
People treat me the same.	People treat me differently.
I know what to expect here.	I am afraid of the future.

Even if you were a victim wife and you are now free, you may miss the security of the situation you knew. Even if you were disappointed a lot and mistreated, you could expect the eventual apology, the final remorse.

Bridging to the new behavior feels strange. When people treat you well, you may feel a little odd. You are not sure what will come next. Maybe you could find someone like old Mike who would treat you badly again! Then at least you would know what to expect!

I am amazed at how uncomfortable people feel with their new behavior, even if it is exactly what they have been fantasizing about. Why can't we enjoy the new position? Simply because it is *different.*

Risk takers learn that new adventures don't have to feel worse than the old trips. They can anticipate success or good feelings. An insecure partner will imagine that if she starts standing up to her husband he will treat her badly. She cannot allow herself the luxury of anticipating gentle and kind treatment from her mate.

My friend says I have a "loving eye." That means that I can see the good in everyone. It means that I do not expect bad treatment. And then I usually don't get bad treatment. People read my trust, my good spirits about them, and they don't want to disappoint me. If you can begin to adopt that philosophy about your mate, you may be surprised that he actually may want to treat you better!

THE DEPENDENCY TRAP

Some women put up with the Silicon Syndrome because they do not think they have another option. "Oh, I couldn't support myself now, after thirty-five years of being a housewife." They don't realize that they may not need to support themselves financially. (There must be some reward for thirty-five years of service!) But even if they do, they might actually feel better using their own talents and trying on the world, instead of staying at home in a bad marriage.

A woman client came bounding into my office one day. She looked twenty years younger than when I had last seen her. "I left him," she sang. "After forty years of marriage, we are going to be separated. And I am going to be free!"

This was a woman trapped in her own home, trapped by rules and prohibitions from which she was unable to unchain herself. She had lost so much love for her husband that she could not consider asking him to cooperate in changing the system. It was easier for her just to leave him, scattering all the old patterns, miseries, and habits behind them.

A possessive man who is unable to let his wife grow and change creates a dried-up system for the couple. The husband eventually may want to remodel the marriage, but his wife may be beyond the point of listening by then.

Being dependent is a result of the symbiotic attachment. But the possibility of total dependence really stems from the low self-confidence of at least one member of the party! If a woman feels chained to a man, it is often because of an early emotional bondage that fixed her in the needing position. Perhaps her father abandoned her, or she had an alcoholic father, or she learned to depend completely on a father figure (in the absence of a woman nurturer), and so she ended up completely hooked on needing a male figure, *no matter how badly he treats her.*

THE JEALOUSY GAME

What is jealousy? Jealousy is the uncomfortable state in which we experience others having a joyful action, or being the recipient of action, that we are not having.

We need to learn to accept jealousy as a real and human emotion. It is not always possible to eradicate or diminish it when we experience others having what it is not possible for us to have. Jealousy is a feeling, just as legitimate and just as profound as sadness, joy, or fear.

Jealousy is not sex-determined. It is possible on both sides of the relationship. But it is an insidious and poisonous emotion that affects the whole relationship even if only one person is infected. It is even a little contagious if the afflicted partner chooses a mate with low self-esteem.

Jealousy does not have to be about another lover in your life; it can be about work, your mother, or your vegetable garden. First let's talk about the sci-tech who is jealous, though this is a rarer emotion in sci-tech personalities than in more hysteric persons.

When the sci-tech member of the team is possessive and jealous and his partner buys into that dynamic, we've got a mess. It is hard to step back out of such a relationship "fix" if each of you becomes entrenched in an offense-defense relationship.

The jealous sci-tech may believe:

1. That his woman has only a limited supply of love to give. If she uses it all up on the children or her friends, there may not be enough left for him.
2. That he is not as adequate as the next person who may come along to win the attentions of his beloved one. He worries that he will come in second in any comparison.
3. That somehow it helps to be obsessed by worry. Because he gets so hooked on his compulsive behavior, he builds in protective measures to ease his anxiety. They don't work, though, because his head, full of negative scenarios, works faster than his reality-testing.
4. That he has to get all of his needs met by one person. Therefore, he is powerless when the one who fills his needs is not always available. He doesn't know how to resource for himself.

Now, all of the above can apply as well to the jealous woman. Let's add some traits to her behavior (knowing that, again, the pronouns may be interchanged).

The jealous partner of a sci-tech often does the following:

1. Tortures herself with boundless schemes about how her mate could cheat on her. This obsessive worrying causes strained behavior and defensiveness from the poor guy who, perhaps, simply likes to spend time at the computer store!
2. Retreats back to the beginning of their relationship when he seemed more attentive. Then she lives in the past, wishing it would return, or in the future, expecting that behavior to reappear in some miraculous new form.
3. Finds fault in her partner to put him on his guard so that he won't think he is attractive to anyone else.

4. Peeks, listens, follows, spies, and questions every moment of his behavior, almost prophesying disaster.

Even if the green-eyed monster has never hit your relationship overtly, take a look at some of the danger signs and the prevention work that is possible regarding this highly charged emotional condition.

Being run by jealousy, just like being run by any other single emotion, is wasteful, time-consuming, and unhealthy. To come to a state of maturity, you must first decide to understand your dilemma. The next step is to correct it or contract to reduce your anxiety, by asking your partner to cooperate with your neurotic thoughts or behavior.

Jealousy is the response to an illusion. The illusion is that your relationship, or your job, or your family life will always be secure. The illusion is of security—that there will be no change in your status with another. We expect that no external will alter the state of security we once had, or that we may have now.

Popular love songs exacerbate our pain and pathos about jealousy. They try to convince us that love is here to stay, promising eternal security. Poetry and prose assist us in imagining that should our loved one desert us, or reach for someone else, there is no hope; we must consider dying of a broken heart.

In jealous states we generally externalize the problem to something that *someone else is doing.* "You made me feel this way. You made me jealous by what you did."

This fault-finding trait keeps us from looking at the possibility that there may be another way of handling the facts so that we can be more comfortable, without controlling or changing our partner. This is hard to do. It is much easier to insist, to beg, to frighten, to demand the partner do whatever it will take to bring us out of the jealous state.

The jealous person usually puts the objects of his/her affections on a very high perch. This pedestal does not allow for mistakes, for the imperfections of being a human being. We attribute superhuman traits to our beloved one: "He will love me forever, no matter how pathetic or demanding I become."

Making our loved one into an idol can create great disappointments when later we discover that he/she is as human and frail and suggestible as all of us. Reality about our lover is different. It calls on us to attribute mature understandings and mature feelings to the actions of others.

I will now define two personality styles. We will call one "Mature" and one "Jealous."

Mature	Jealous
Present-oriented	Past- or future-oriented
Uses partner for a mirror	Needs partner to satisfy ego
Realistic about partner	Attributes superhuman qualities
Commitment to authenticity	Believes others cause pain
Uses union for growth	Wants things to stay the same
Shares adventures	Gives to get
Believes in sharing	Believes in sacrifice
Wants the relationship	Needs partner to survive!
Finds relationships easy	Works at the relationship
Knows there is enough affection	Feels love is limited
Understands partner's limits	High expectations
Accepts partner's mistakes	Wants retribution, reprisal
Explains his/her anxieties	Withdraws or retaliates
Enjoys partner	Possessive of partner
Gives partner room	Oppressive
Accepts own feelings	Sees the problem as partner's
Understands partner's errors	Expects perfection in partner
Understands love as a journey	Wants it as in the beginning
Thinks positively	Imagines the worst
"I know I am a good partner"	Fears others are better
Shares, contracts to reduce anxiety	Obsessive, compulsive worrying
Wants to be there	Always evaluating partner
Takes what he/she gets	Finds faults in partner

When you discover that you have strong feelings of jealousy that seem out of proportion, take a look at earlier experiences that placed you in the same predicament. Find a way to explain this insight to yourself and to your partner. Inform your partner that you are going to attempt to overcome your current dilemma by resolving past pain or at least by understanding possible overreactions.

All of us will have anxious states now and again. Ask your partner to help you with your discomfort by cooperating as much as it is comfortable for him/her to do.

Here is an example:

Lucy and Bill had just started a relationship. Bill's job required his attendance at many office and company social events. Bill always brought Lucy along. But Lucy did not know all of the customers, nor did she really enjoy all of Bill's colleagues. She realized that he needed to attend these functions at this stage of his professional career. But every time they attended a function, they came home and had a fight. Lucy felt left out, neglected, and lonely. She did not think that Bill treated her very well. Yet he always seemed to have a good time, to enjoy everyone at the party, picnic, or social event. When there was dancing he danced with as many other women as Lucy thought he could squeeze in. Bill complained that Lucy was a grouch before, during, and after these functions. He was baffled and miserable.

The solution was really quite simple. We asked Lucy to come up with a signal to Bill whenever she began to feel left out, or lonely, or jealous at those times. The signal was negotiated; it was one that Lucy could tolerate saying or using, and it was also one that Bill could tolerate seeing or receiving. They decided that she would come over and rub Bill's neck whenever she had those feelings—provided she did so *within limits.*

The limits were: 1) not more often than every twenty minutes; 2) not while Bill was deeply engrossed; 3) in a subtle way so that neither would be embarrassed.

What is important is that at the times when Lucy was feeling jealous, Bill agreed to *make an effort to demonstrate his affection or respect for her in the presence of others whenever possible.* It was not enough for Bill to take Lucy to a quiet corner and remind her that she was his wonderful partner. She needed the public affirmation of their relationship.

At the given times Bill would simply say something to others about Lucy's projects, talents, or events. He was acknowledging that Lucy was an important person and that she had interests of her own. Or Bill would acknowledge their relationship by sharing something they had recently done together, or something they planned to do.

Last, Bill would publicly demonstrate his partnership ties with Lucy by grabbing her hand, asking her to dance, putting his arm around her, or by *rubbing her neck!* This miraculous little maneuver saved their relationship, *and* Bill's job, and they learned they could contract in other ways to assist each other when either had a neurotic approach to a situation. For instance, whenever Bill called his father back east, Lucy would refrain from judgments about Bill for the next four hours. She knew that Bill needed a gentle approach after a discussion with his judgmental father. This helped again when it was important to Bill to make good impressions on the boss who insisted on the social entertaining.

Jealousy is a state of mind. We can learn to discipline ourselves when possessive feelings overtake us. A good, strong ego cannot generate ongoing jealous attacks for long. If a partner is a woman-izer or a philandering flirt, or is maliciously and intentionally trying to create a situation, a mature person will choose either to negotiate for change or to end the relationship. A mature individual will not stay in a masochistic relationship if he/she continues to have anxious feelings because a partner is pathologically unfaithful.

The mature person wants a relationship *with* his partner. The jealous person *needs* it!

The mature person realizes there is enough love and affection to ·go around. He/she realizes there is an endless supply, like the ocean, to be dipped into with a teaspoon or a bucket. He/she will know how to bargain to get more if the partner is not hearing his/her wishes. The jealous person worries that the supply is limited. He/she gives to get, always manipulating, always fearing the supply is running out. Love, good, pure love, does not run out. It comes in like the tide . . . sometimes high, sometimes low . . . but . . . **always.** . . .

JEALOUSY IS NOT THE SAME AS CARING

We often confuse jealousy with caring. If we want a specific caring style we may imagine that jealousy will satisfy that wish. Forget it. Jealousy, as we have seen, is dangerous, unhealthy, and often discovered in immature people.

If you want a special intensity from your partner, you may need to ask him for it. It is not too much to ask a partner to treat you in a very special way. Explain that you need to know that you are very precious to him. This special request is safer and healthier than asking him to show you the neurotic display of jealousy that is always fostered by personal insecurity.

Beware of the jealousy games that many couples exchange for whole marriage lifetimes! These games are usually created to sus-tain a state of chaos in the marriage. The constant uproar causes excitement. The relationship is not boring, but this is a terrible price for a little excitement. Try asking for what you want instead. Request special demonstrations of love. Tell your partner that you know he may think this is silly, that surely he would never want such antics, but that you want this behavior to satisfy your longing for approval or acceptance. Remind him that you will not abuse the request, and that you know it is difficult for him to comply, but that it really is important for your relationship!

COUPLE COUNSELING

I am willing to strategize with any wife to get her husband to come for therapy. I have had only a few men refuse to continue after they finally did come in. This is because I am able to talk the language of doctors, lawyers, and scientists. These men talk in terms of logic and treatment, and I can field their questions and their distractions. I would like to share with you some expertise.

Here is how I talk: "Yes, I can see that you believe you have a very good marriage; that you have given your wife everything. I even understand what you mean when you say she seems to be very neurotic, never satisfied, and quite immature." Meet your man on his own field! Talk as he talks.

All of this is warmup to get him to realize that I do see his perspective on things. (And I do!) I believe that, from his looking glass, his wife appears the way she does. Now, my job is to get him to take a look into her mirror. This is no small task.

THE TISSUE BOX TRICK!

The first thing I do in couple counseling is teach the "tissue box" trick. I pick up the box, examine it, and explain to the husband: "This side of the box is your wife [the side with the tissue dangling out]. It is her perception of things, made up of her experiences, her chemistry, her psychological makeup, and the cognitive translations of her life."

Then I turn the box over and show both of them the bottom side of the box. On it is usually some printed material, sometimes a picture of a flower or something, a trademark, and the computer language—black narrow lines.

When I show the other side of the box, I begin to prove to the husband that I understand there are two sides to every story. And then I gently stroke his side of the box, telling them both: "This is Tom's side of everything. It is made up of every experience he has ever had, his chemistry, his psychological makeup, and his cognitive translation of all the facets of his life." Tom begins to relax.

Then I say the magic words. "You see, Dorothy, Tom sees no little pink tissue hanging out of his side. He can stretch and stretch himself, but for all his deep concentration, he cannot see that tissue hanging out. Instead, he sees only the printed material, the trademark, and the computer lines."

Then I turn the box over again to show Dorothy's side and comment to Tom, "And you see that from her side she cannot see those computer lines or the trademark. All she sees is the little pink tissue hanging out."

To me this is the perfect scientific and clinical description of two people and their perceptions, and usually these wonderful, logical men get my point.

Then I ask them for their views of the relationship. I let them talk. I don't interrupt, roll back my eyes, or snort. I listen. I empathize with their pain, even if the pain does not appear in the form of tears, body language, or anxious talk. The pain is often very quiet, hidden below the words, or the body talk, or the content of the complaints.

And mostly I know what the partner does not know or no longer can let herself know: that, in fact, this man really does want to be a good partner. But he has protected himself so well from feelings that he is not available to his partner's suffering, and even less so to his own.

And I know that he does not know how to listen, how to talk, how to make the sounds of love even though he feels it. I have seen too many conscientious men who want to respond and who fail the test because they are so inexperienced in passion, unless it is sexual passion, or in intensity, unless it is intensity about *Sky Lab*! I am confident that they want to learn.

Wives, though, who have suffered the pain of husbands who rage and rave, strike back and use subterfuge instead of direct statements, but give up more quickly when the husband waivers a little in my office. These wives are freaky, timid about being vulnerable, and frightened of being disappointed again. But I help. I push the husbands on through; sometimes I have to bolt the door, listen through deep primal wailings, and keep the couple there in my office until they are ready to listen to each other.

When the husband knows that I can listen and that I believe in the two-points-of-view system, he is then ready to listen to me. Then I can speak for his wife, plead her case, open him to the possibility that both have some responsibility for the mess in their marriage. I can urge him to be patient with his partner, to allow her to scream and cry a little, even if he is uncomfortable with that kind of behavior. I begin the process of trust, teaching him to give her the benefit of the doubt. I urge him to consider her *intentions* of goodwill, even when the contests sound like hateful or ugly accusations.

Last, I remind the husband that I need his input about his wife so that I can understand her and begin to help her. This is what finally gets him. He learns that I want to help his wife, with all those beastly problems she has, and that he does have some information that can aid in my work with her.

He also learns that I don't bite, that I seem able to comprehend his needs, too, and that I am a very logical and rational woman. Bingo!

Now, can you do that for yourself? Can you plead your case, hear your man's pain, be patient, allow him to rant and rave, and know that you want to trust his intentions? The job is yours. Trust the relationship. Be political with him. Be rational and logical. You have that capacity!

SILICON SYNDROME PRESCRIPTIONS

If you are stuck in the Silicon Syndrome and see no way to relate to your husband, let me give you some other things to do. By the way, reading this book is already freeing up your relationship, giving you a new mindset about possibilities, raising your consciousness and, I hope, your faith in your partner's cope-ability!

• *Join some activities.* Don't stay home and brood, drink, sleep, or cry. Get someone to talk to. Other women feel as you do. You are not alone. The silicon valleys all over the world are sprinkled with frustrated women who do not understand the technology of their partners' work or emotional lives. We are actually blanketed with every symptom of this condition. Find an ear for yourself. . . .

• *Create a project to feel intense about.* The happiest, most productive women, whether they are working inside or outside of their households, have a cause they are *passionate* about. Find the kind of project that feeds your soul, one that is so exciting to you that even if your husband has to go to Japan for weeks you can be content, busy, and satisfied. Join a political campaign, establish a home for unwed mothers, develop an art association, or run for the planning commission. Do something that is a lot bigger than you are. That is the key! And if the first project fizzles, doesn't hold your attention, or doesn't even feel good at all, look again. Sometimes it takes a year to develop your passion project.

• *Get involved in your husband's company if you can.* Find out what makes the company work. Go to the stockholders' meetings even if you don't have any stock. Read the prospectus on the company. Check the stock market. Follow the company's growth. Being informed about your husband's company will serve you well when you want to have an intelligent conversation about the status of the company.

By the way, if your partner objects with: "What's all this sudden interest and snooping around?" he may be confused and scared. Respond with: "I am going to elevate my interest in my source of income. I do not intend to interfere, but I want to be more informed." Husbands may worry about their wives' new interest, but they also worry about wives who get drunk at the office Christmas dinner and begin "popping off" about what pitiful husbands they have!

I am amazed at how often the wives of company presidents are not even on speaking terms with their husbands' secretaries. The two women who serve a man's life ought to be on the same team. Instead there is often jealousy, misunderstanding, and hurt feelings, which burn the telephone lines between them. Many times wives don't call their husbands at work at all because of a secretarial miff! Pity!

• *Perform at your highest level in your own profession if you are interested in developing your career.* If you are not interested in a career, enjoy your grandchildren, your jazzercise classes, or your tennis team, but for goodness' sake, enjoy something!

If you are interested in career goals, don't let your husband's involvement be a barrier to your growth. Dual-career marriages can be highly successful and satisfying.

I am delighted that my husband, Don, and I both work so hard and are so enthusiastic about our two corporations. We are each on both corporations' boards of directors, and we each take an active interest in our partner's pursuits.

Give yourself the opportunity to use your best talents. If this means more education or retraining, do it. The excitement you bring home to your marriage because you are content and motivated will be an enhancement to your relationship. Happy independence!

• *Last, plan some mutual activity that both of you can enjoy.* Learn dominoes and get a tournament going between the two of you. I have friends who take watercoloring classes together and love it. They even went on an art-appreciation cruise last year. If you both enjoy dogs, training or raising them, or just watching dog shows, add this important activity to your life.

Work to put these or other joint activities high on your priority list. It is important that the two of you feel like a team, even if it is the community high school's volleyball team. Find a mutual love: maybe it's a sports-car club, square dancing, church, or a country club. Build this social contact into your life. Your relationship needs the support of a community bigger than you are.

• *If you really cannot generate any ideas, at least implement this one:* Both of you read this book, consider applying some of the principles, use a few of the exercises, and together commit to the task of new understanding for your relationship. Cheers! You are on the way!

• *If you are sour on your husband's company, if it has caused you much pain and suffering and you just can't stomach the possibility of interaction about it yet, give it and yourself a rest.* Then take the two of you to an outside source so that you can begin to mend the difference. At the very least, acknowledge to each other how hard this position is for you. Husband wants support and comfort about the workings of his company; wife wants to participate but is broken about the whole thing, feels alienated and without loyalty, and wishes it had not happened. Speak to each other about how hard this is for *both* of you.

LOVE SCHOOL

No matter what your degree, you probably didn't get a love class. My fellow psychotherapists do teach love school in our therapy groups, but there is usually nothing offered to someone until after he/she has made an attempt at *love*. There is a plethora of relationship seminars available these days, but people still don't get taught about relationships in the early, formative years of their lives. We still don't even agree about what love means.

"He won't say he loves me." I've heard that hundreds of times in my office. And yet the man is spending every waking moment with this woman, he has pledged his life, his work, his mortgage, and he never looks at another woman. But he chokes on the word *love*. He thinks it means "I can't live without you." Or he thinks it means "mushy-goo-goo," or that if he says the word it diminishes his actions of love.

In my opinion, love is sharing, being vulnerable, and being enhanced by the sight or thought of your partner. Love means, "I like you so much that I have to find something, a word, that means you are more special to me than all the other people I also really like."

The definitions of love are as long as the history of civilization. Find your own definition and see if you can convince your partner that it could be a valid definition for both of you. If it is not, keep talking until you both agree on an appropriate phrase, sentence, or word. Don't give up until you have settled on a definition both of you believe.

RESPONSE SCHOOL

Instead of trying to let our partner know that we hear him, we often try to convince him/her that what he/she said was wrong. We attempt to convince or dissuade our partners with one of the following tactics:

Distracting Statements: "Well, isn't that a funny thing to say? By the way, did you think that movie last night was funny?"

Attorney Statements: "No, it definitely was not on our anniversary. Your uncle Fred was here that day, and that was in November."

Give-up Statements: "You are so right. I am a bastard. It's all my fault."

Defense Statements: "Well, I only do it because you talk so much."

Offense Statements: "How can you talk about my weight when you drink like a fish!"

Denial Statements: "Now, honey, you know that's not true. You must be tired."

Persuasive Statements: "I should know something about this. I've done a lot of research on this subject."

More Persuasive Statements: "Well, the neighbors and the children all agree with me about you."

When the same tired subjects come up, the same tired responses come up too. Thus, the arguments go on into the night, with neither party making ground, and ending with both of you feeling frustrated.

THE ONE-TO-FIVE METHOD

It is important before trying to make a decision together to know whether you are deadlocked. And, if so, how badly. If one partner convinces the other that the particular issue is important to him, the second partner may simply acquiesce because the issue is not a high-priority item to her.

If it seems like one partner is always getting his/her way about things, the one-to-five method should be employed. Again, you need to look at the priority items before assigning a valence to your desires. Don't get caught assuming you know what is important to your partner. And don't make the mistake of assuming that things you don't care about are not important to your partner.

My value system gives high priority to all matters about people, feelings, fun, and enjoyment. My husband's priority is focused on things, order, efficiency, and peace. You can see where we would have problems if I did not give priority to things that my husband thinks are important, and vice versa. Frankly, I am quite messy around the house, compared to Don, but I have learned that keeping things neat has a big impact on my husband. Don has also learned that what happens emotionally to my friends has a strong impression on me.

Assign a number to your desires. "One" is the slightest desire, while "Five" is very strong. "Bob, it is a number Four to me that you go with me to the party tonight and act like you are having a good time." You have a right to ask Bob for the gift of going to the party even if he is not eager to do so.

The notion of gift-giving will help. About sex, for instance, we need to think of giving gifts to each other. "No, Harry, I am not really interested tonight, but I would like to be there for you anyway. I love you and I would like to give you the gift of my attention, even if the idea doesn't really excite me tonight."

Don't worry that your partner will abuse the system with too many Fives. People don't do that. Calling wolf with all Fives is a stupid thing to do. Some of us are more intense than others; the sci-tech usually has a flatter range of emotional desires and may use more Twos and Threes than you do. Eventually you will both begin to adjust your rating system so that the values are comparable, and you will standardize your responses so that you can easily read each other's desire level.

"WE DON'T HAVE FRIENDS ANYMORE"

If your relationship isn't working very well, you will experience a kind of isolation more deadly than a tax audit. A dysfunctioning couple pushes people away with their petty arguments and general morose state. A powerless couple can't cooperate to make a social activity, such as a bridge game or a picnic, work without getting upset or creating depression. Thus, friends shy away.

You will notice that neurotic couples cluster together. That is · why you will eventually hear: "All of our friends seem to be getting divorced."

Another reason that couples finally discover they have no friends may be because they have been symbiotic partners, depending completely on each other. Possessive and jealous partners need exclusive rights to their partners. Their mates may be so insecure that they cling to the demands of the obsessive partner, obeying stupid rules because their tyrannical partners are so demanding.

When one of these parties requests some "space," the demanding partner will surely object. "I am suffocating," the stifled partner cries, but the relationship thrives while balanced on the leaning states, the places both partners had depended on. No outside friends are needed. Friends only complicate the symbiosis.

WHEN YOU START TO GET HEALTHY

When a couple starts to get better, they will often drop their former, unhealthy couple friends. Most dysfunctional couples, frustrated with their pain, will not even seek friends, settling down in their own isolation wards with statements like, "You see, how could we give a dinner party together? We can't even make toast together without the toast or one of us burning!"

The complementary couple will handle the same issues differently. Let's say that David hates cocktail parties because he is awkward about making small talk. Daphne, though, loves parties. David will agree to go to important parties with Daphne (like the condo party), and Daphne will agree not to harass David into being the life of the party. She realizes that David does not enjoy social events but will accompany her as a gift to her. Daphne believes that she is worth the gift—this is the key! David also knows that Daphne will accompany him to the birdwatching meeting the following week, even though Daphne finds those lectures boring. She will give David the gift when he calls on her to join him. Each is willing to do something special for his/her partner, and each feels confident that he/she *deserves* the partner's cooperation. The pay-off is that the indulging partner can feel good about himself in this ultimate gift-giving ritual.

At another time, Daphne might decide to go to the party by herself, leaving David at home with a good book, knowing he is happy and not recriminating himself for balking about the party. I like to remind couples that enjoying activities such as parties or birdwatching is usually a learned behavior and not a characterological disorder.

Find friends who will complement your relationship. If you are lucky enough to find a couple in which the wife is the sci-tech personality, you will really get a bonus. She can help translate your sci-tech partner to you. Hearing the same words coming out of her mouth will not be as painful as when you hear them from your spouse. If the man in the other relationship has more of the intuitive, emotional qualities that you might wish for in your husband, he can help your mate learn some of those qualities. He can tell your mate, "Oh, come on, Bill, let's give the gals a break and treat them to the romantic dinner they deserve!"

When a couple like David and Daphne begin to acquire healthy communication habits, they will also begin to acquire healthier friends. A more open attitude emerges. New friends open up new possibilities for the couple who may have been stuck for years. Daphne may even hear David say, "Well, I've never enjoyed parties before, but maybe I just haven't ever been to a good one. I'll give it another try!"

3

Tools for Successful Coupling

This chapter will give you tools for making your relationship work. The exercises require perseverance along with the knowledge that the first time you try something there may be no immediate improvement. You have probably mastered your bad habits over the years, so it may take a while to implant some new thinking or behavioral change. There is one important requirement for making these tools successful—motivation. If you are both motivated to make the relationship better, you have already started the journey.

ABOUT MOTIVATION

But what if you are not both motivated? Does the one motivated party work at it anyway? Of course! There *is* hope for a relationship when only one person is carrying the weight or rowing the boat. It is easier when both want to make it work. Easier, but not completely necessary.

You see, if one of you begins to make some changes, the other sometimes responds with changes of his/her own. Usually it does not take much inspiration to draw out the disinterested party to begin at least to look at cooperating! Here's why:

Sometimes one of the partners is simply tired of making all the effort. He may see himself as the one who has done all the work, made all the adjustments. It does not matter what the truth is. *His* truth is that he has been doing all the work. So listening to some new tactics can be just enough to prime his emotional connection pump again, starting the renewed commitment to health.

Sometimes just finding a new way to say the same old thing is enough to rejuvenate a tired couple. Even if your relationship is a little sour at this moment, it may be possible to bring it back. I have been dumbfounded at how little it takes to nourish a dying relationship. Sometimes couples come to me who have been married and miserable for twenty-seven years. The divorce lawyers are in place, and papers have been filed. On a whim sometimes, or on advice from the courts, friends, or one of the partners themselves, they come for a "last ditch" counseling session. If I can get them to do just a few of the exercises listed in this chapter, they will sometimes decide to reconnect, and run happily out of the office, tearing up divorce papers on the way.

Now, I don't think that one visit was magic. In fact, they will probably start bickering and arguing again on the ride home. But sometimes we want so much to believe it is possible to save the relationship that we jump at any little hope of rejuvenation.

Or take the couple who has been living together for five to seven years. Suddenly they decide to come to counseling. The appointment decision seems almost accidental. "Oh, we just heard about you and decided to try a session or two," they mumble. Closer to the truth may be their unconscious need for some status change. Usually one wants to deepen the commitment toward marriage, and the other wants to widen the gap, perhaps toward separation.

After a session or two I may get a cancellation. Then they appear a few weeks later, beaming. "We decided to get married," they gleefully announce. "It was just time, and we each had some vacation coming, so we did it." They are holding hands and looking like the appropriate newlyweds.

But the next visit or two brings back the old patterns of pain. What happened is that as the result of a few positive conversations, they were fooled into thinking that they were whole again, and that they would make it after all! Had they shared with me their plans to marry, I would have suggested postponing the vows until they had gotten some more tools under their belts. Then they could have assessed the advisability of the permanent union.

I guess I am delivering this as a warning to those who may be in this situation. After some easy conversations, a premature hope may invade the relationship. Usually the eager partner is ready to pounce on the idea of marriage anyway, the moment the reluctant partner weakens. This is the same prompting that sometimes occurs when there has been a shock in the life of one of the partners. When a parent or loved one dies, or is desperately ill, suddenly a profound desire for marriage pours in upon the heretofore reluctant partner.

Sometimes it takes just a few good emotional interchanges for a couple to feel all too hopeful again. Wait to test your newfound relationship before you decide it is permanently cured. The slightest improvement can tease you into a false security. By waiting, by testing out your transformed relationship, you will have the opportunity of *deciding to marry* instead of *deciding not to put it off any longer*.

Let's get back to my original statement. If you are both motivated, you will have a better chance of making the following techniques work for you. If at least one of you is open to change, you will raise your odds in favor of the partnership. Try some of these tools and wait for transformation. But change is slow; it will not happen overnight or within a month. Give yourself six months to adopt some behavioral changes in your relationship, and you may experience some fresh hope for the perhaps now dreary partnership.

There are two ways to get closer, to feel more understood, and to be a more productive team:

1. Share your feelings
2. Problem-solve

I want to take those two areas and give you exercises for each. I know that sometimes these experiences overlap, but I want you to consider that the dynamics really are different. One is the expression of what you are or have been going through. The other is an action mentality in which the two of you try to make some decisions that will enhance your life.

You may find some of these tools pretty simple. They are. It's just that when you are on a downward trail, falling into abusive habits, it is hard to recall the simple touches that could pull you back to safety.

ABOUT SHARING FEELINGS

(When they get too intense too long . . .)

"Pete, I resent that you look bored when I try to tell you about my day when I come home from work," Lydia opens.

"Oh, hell, can't you ever say anything nice?" Pete replies. "You are always nagging or complaining." (This is a close-down process that intimidates Lydia and makes her worry that she might be a habitual complainer. She will then feel hesitant about saying anything more.)

But Pete goes on with, "I'm not a good listener, and I never will be." (Proclaiming no possibility for change.)

And then he might get in a little deeper, cementing his refusal to change with, "If you'd wanted one of the sweet, goody-two-shoes listener types, you should have married Willy. He would have listened to your drivel all night long." (Pete, eager to go on, throws in one of his own old resentments with that one.)

Last, Pete finishes with his defense: "I can't listen to anyone when I first get home because I'm too tired."

Now Lydia can continue the argument with, "Well, nobody tells you to work so hard. If you wouldn't spend so much time on that stupid secret computer project, you wouldn't be such a mess when you get home."

"Well, if you weren't so extravagant with money and would budget better, I wouldn't have to have such a gigantic income."

Now Lydia has the great comeback. "What do you mean, extravagant? What about the five-hundred-dollar suit you just bought? And the golf clubs, when you already had two sets?"

"You know I bought that suit for the convention. And the doctor said I needed to exercise," he continues to persuade.

And finally, Pete makes his major offensive statement so that Lydia can start all over again to defend herself. Pete says, "God, I have to play golf! It's the only exciting thing left in my life! Certainly our sex life isn't. You've said no to me the last four times I've approached you."

Lydia can now start again with her original statement: "Well, Pete, why would I want to make love to someone who won't even talk to me when he comes home at night?"

Our couple has now come full circle, back to the complaint about Pete not listening. Lydia's initial resentment was not acknowledged, nor will the final one be heard.

Usually the initial complaint is lost in the acceleration of the discussion, often with both partners unable to recall what the original resentment was. Pete will go away feeling that Lydia doesn't care about how hard he works and that she is sexually frigid; Lydia will feel that he will never listen to her!

THE "TIME-OUT" SIGNAL

When one person is on "overload" about any aspect of the relationship, he needs to give a signal to let the other one know that he will "pop" if he has to hang in there another moment. Some people become overwhelmed when a partner cries for more than five minutes. Others become depressed with a lover who rants or raves or raises his voice, while still others become overburdened when a partner talks in a depressed style about work, family, or the world. Do not put a value on what your partner chooses to balk at. Each of us has a different tolerance level for different forms of communication or action or behavior. Don't judge your partner's intolerances. Accept that he/she has some; just as you do.

The time-out signal takes a negotiated contract between two people. I'm not suggesting that it has to be notarized, or even that it has to be written down, but I am suggesting that you must both agree to the terms of the signal format for it to work permanently.

First, decide which kinds of action can call for "time out" by your partner. Spell out each one of those possibilities. The more of those situations you can anticipate before the fact, the better your chance for success. Planning in advance for explosions and unhappy dialogues will reduce the pain if they actually do occur later. We do so much prevention work in the field of health and medicine—we even floss our teeth to prevent gum disease. Yet, it has been hard to get across the idea that prevention work in relationships can alleviate disease too. Taking as much time as teeth flossing takes can actually improve the life of your relationship. Those minutes can be spent in sharing beautiful sentiments, but they can also be spent in planning some prevention work for when you will next hurt each other's feelings.

It took Don and me two and one-half years to debug our prevention work. It was worth the effort, though.

Both being very opinionated and sensitive people, my husband and I would now and then get into an awful fight about something. I would cry and go on and on. Don would feel terrible. As time wore on, it seemed to get worse. Don would get very tired when we argued so long. Actually, after fifteen minutes he has exhausted his patience with emotional conversations. His tolerance level for pro-longed discussions is low. He wants to get it out, talk about it, and put it away. I, on the other hand, enjoy discussing something from every angle. I especially want to share feelings about every nuance if there is a problem between the two of us.

Often those discussions would go on for two, three, four hours, sometimes on into the night. I actually love those marathons. I've learned that when people get tired, they let their defenses down, and some new information surfaces. But Don hates those long sessions. Yet, sometimes the topic is too heated, the issues are too long overdue, and even he knows that it may be time for one of these prolonged talks.

But eventually Don wears out, or down, or something. Anyway, before we had this plan, Don would eventually give out. After hours of going backward, as Don thought, he would storm out of the room, yelling, "I'm going to sleep on the couch. This conversation could go on all night, and I need to be on time for an early meeting tomorrow."

Some folks get so frustrated that they leave the house over one of these midnight matches. Others just fall asleep on their partners. Maddening! Still others get so frustrated that they get drunk or violent, or both.

None of these solutions to the dilemma seemed right for either Don or me. I would feel nervous or interrupted because I would never know when Don would reach his boiling point and quit. It could be in the middle of the sentence. Worse, I would know that I could not follow him to the living room to continue the discussion, because he would go right outside to go to sleep on the backyard lawn. There was no way to continue the discussion when Don had reached *maximum tolerance* level.

So we came up with the time-out signal. He simply says, "That's it. I can't take any more." The difference between now and before we began using the signal is that now I am absolutely assured that the discussion will resume sometime soon!

Our rules are that if the discussion happens in the middle of the night, we must continue the discussion in the morning—*the very next morning*—even if it means setting the alarm early to avoid being late to work.

If the problem arises during the day and Don still gets tired or disgusted, at any point he can call "time out." This means he gets one and a half hours off from the discussion. He can leave, go for a walk, or get back to his own projects. He need not talk to me about anything for one and a half hours.

I am okay with this plan because I know that we are going to continue the discussion later. What if he calls "time out" in the second discussion? That's fine. Then we have another cooling-off period in which each of us has an opportunity to assess the situation and take a look at our positions. It is difficult to continue a position when you have the opportunity to get some distance. On the second or third round, people get more articulate and actually present their feelings with more clarity. I assure you that usually only one "time out" is necessary!

At first we used only one hour for the relief period. But then we found that a funny thing was happening. Fifty-nine minutes from the time-out signal, I would be poised at the door, waiting to resume the hot discussion. And Don would crawl in, really quite unready to continue, but being an honorable man, he would fulfill his part of the contract, hesitantly.

What Don really wanted to do, and sometimes got away with if I wasn't poised in the doorway, was to come in, take a cup of coffee, pat me on the head, and wander about for a little while, glancing at the newspaper or petting the dog. . . . He seemed to be waiting, stalling. He was getting ready to work *up* to it. If I could have relaxed and stopped worrying that he would *never* continue the discussion, I could have patiently waited for his return to me. Sometimes that would take five minutes, sometimes three hours.

That is why we built in the extra thirty minutes. The first hour is the prescribed time for Don to get back to me, physically, but the thirty minutes following that hour became very important to our reconciliation. Don calls this period the Neutral Zone, or the "Entering Jean's Atmosphere" Time.

I don't care what you call it. It works! For the sci-tech, or the person who has difficulty with emotional scenes, who feels that it is foreign for him to whine or fret or cry or share hard feelings, this getting-ready period is really important. It is the time to prepare for the being together again, perhaps in a hard way.

Negotiate for the perfect signal for each of you. Both of you must agree on the signal. Then set your own time arrangements. Both of you need to agree on the length of the time out and to the important "neutral zone" time. This system may mean the end of your drawn-out, no-win marathons. It may also mean the end of your partner's escape-artist moves.

Each of you will get his needs met. He will have his boundaries. You will know that there is a time set aside to finish the discussion if he should want an escape route. No matter the pain that may surface during the conversations, both partners will be spared resentments and will no longer be robbed of the precious time that must precede a real problem-solving time. Remember, this first period is *simply a time to share feelings. No problem-solving yet, please.*

SAYING THE MAGIC WORDS

Saying the magic words can bring peace and repair to a damaged relationship. The magic words are not: *I love you.* People who beat each other up, who manipulate or torture their partners say "I love you." Even people who steal, cheat on, and belittle their mates say "I love you."

No, "I love you" is not enough, because, you see, loving is not enough. You have to be comfortable with your loved one. You also have to feel safe. I love many of my friends, but would not want to live with them. I even have grown children, whom I love, but I no longer want to live with them. I also love some public figures, and ice-cream sodas, and Liza Minnelli, but I do not choose to live with them. To me, the most important issue is that I want to be with my husband the rest of my life. I feel comfortable with him and I choose to live with him. *Choose to!*

Here are the words that get more work done than "I love you." They explain your differences and heal when rote adorations are not enough.

Sit facing each other. There is nothing as profound as eye contact. Now, one of you say the following sentence. Then the other say the same sentence.

The magic words are: *"I know that my personality is hard on you."*

I ask a couple (or colleagues, in the case of my management consultations) to say the following to each other:

"I have faith that I will be able to teach you how to meet most of my needs."

If I am with two managers from a company, I have them say to each other:

"I trust that I can teach you how to be able to work best with me."

If I am with two lovers, I have them say to each other:

"I trust that I will teach you how to love me in my form of love." (We assume that the partner wants to learn this. Sometimes we need to say this assumption too.)

And now something about the words "I love you." These words mean different things to different people. Some people have been so traumatized by the emptiness or the lies behind the words that they no longer use them. How sad for the partner who needs the words!

Each of us, of course, attributes different meanings to the

words. Check out your meanings with each other. To me they are expressions of affection, adoration, and admiration. To someone else they may mean dependency, weakness, or pain. I enjoy Sondra Ray's definition of love: "I am enhanced by your presence. I feel better about my self when you are in my life."

Don and I learned that we had different capacities for words of love. The words, that is. I am not talking about the deeds of love; only the words. I enjoy words, even like to repeat words, as you may discover in this book, and love the sounds of words. I am an auditory person who uses love words long before love touches. But Don is much more conservative with his love words. He does not give them away easily. He never says anything as rash as "I love Paul Newman," yet I say something as committal as that several times a day.

What we have learned is that because I give love words away so easily, I need a bunch of them to feel loved. So "I love you, I love you, I love you" feels better than one lonely, almost unheard "I love you."

Now Don, who is careful, precise with his words, wants and needs one simple "I love you." If he hears more than one set from me, he thinks it is simply an exaggeration and that I am *protesting too much*! Thus, the second "I love you" sounds less well to Don than the first one, and with the third I am losing ground.

I shared this conclusion with my women's group. They were astonished to discover that they all wanted more than one "I love you," while all of their men seemed to feel more trusting if there was only one. At that meeting we decided, though, that we would all go home and teach our men to say "I love you, I love you, I love you."

The next week Lucy came in beaming. She shared that she had told her husband about our discovery and had asked him to give her three in a row sometime, but he had just shrugged and sighed. Then, on her way out to group that night, he had walked her to the car. After he tucked her into the car, she had rolled down the window to remind him to turn off the sprinkler in the backyard, and he had reached down and shouted, *"I love you, I love you, I love you!"*

Lucy was delighted. She proclaimed, her eyes brimming with tears, "That was the first time I ever really felt my husband loved me."

You see, he was conforming to her love needs. He was giving her a gift of the way she likes to receive love. Later we learned that he had intended to be funny, maybe even sarcastic, but when he saw the look on her face, he knew that he was doing something pretty profound. It does not matter that he did not start out to be completely honorable. What does matter is that he got a glimpse of the kind of response he could get by giving Lucy her kind of "I love you."

Now Lucy, and I, and perhaps some of you have another important fact to learn. If we want to give our partners their kind of love talk, it might require saying but one "I love you."

MIXING SHARING FEELINGS WITH PROBLEM-SOLVING

The biggest communication barrier for couples is the mixing of problem-solving and the sharing of feelings. Even psychotherapists confuse us with the introduction of both of these communication methods at one time. You may be right in the middle of solving a problem with specific and concrete methods when your therapist will stop you with, "And how do you feel about that?"

Couples do this to themselves all the time. It is pretty hard to have a pure communication process going on at all times. But it is important to be able to differentiate the two processes and then to slip back and forth between them as you need to.

On the other hand, sci-techs hate mixing sharing of feelings with problem-solving. They are so much more comfortable when they can divide the two reactions. Their partners hate that the sci-techs don't want to combine these two methods of communication. Of course, in the main, sci-techs like to stay away from the feelings sessions altogether. "Let's just decide what to do!" they plead.

To have your sci-tech attend to you, you can use certain preliminary styles to get his ear. Air your complaints before they become mountains. Sci-techs hate those loaded, skyrocketing talks that seem to build up to, "And while I'm at it, I may as well tell you that I have never liked the way you kiss. . . ."

So that you won't put him off guard, and so that he won't put you off, just give him the simple, unemotional facts about the topic you wish to discuss with him. Your complaints don't have to make sense or be rational, but your approach to them does. Remind him that these are your perceptions based on your set of experiences. Many conversations are stymied with, "But, Susie, that doesn't make any sense."

Just inform him that you know it does not make any sense to him, but that you do think the topic is worthy of discussion. Then suggest that he let you know when he is ready to have a talk with you that will not sound orderly or rational. Tell him that you want to share your feelings and that you will be available for him to share his. Although most of us don't usually prelabel our intentions, give him parameters around the discussion, like, "I'll share my feelings on this subject for only ten minutes."

You will have to teach your sci-tech that feelings are really our *child states* of being. When children (and adults) have feelings, they really do not have to pass critical analysis or validity scrutiny. When the child cries out for something in the store, he does not rationally decide that his mother can't afford it. It does not matter; he just wants it! And being disappointed or sad does not depend on whether we deserve it or whether it is fair that we get it!

The feelings, though, are valid. They are legitimate! We feel what we feel. Period. They are the declarations of our emotional life, without justification.

When we share our feelings we often hurt our listener or accuse him/her without good cause. We tend to polarize our partners, startle them, and catch them off guard.

Conscientious couples jump back and forth between problem-solving and sharing feelings. When your partner begins to problem-solve, you may get caught in an emotional reaction. It takes great discipline to hold back the feelings until the problem is resolved. Often a good conceptual blockbusting session will exacerbate (or degenerate) into emotional sparring that touches every "energy button" your relationship has ever known.

When I ask clients to share feelings, I also ask them not to expect promises of behavioral change from the partner just because they have squeezed out a painful reaction!

So, dividing your two communication sessions will take discipline. I suggest that you do the sharing-of-feelings part first. But put parameters around the session. We don't need anything as long as a "time out" here, since neither of the parties is on overload. Plan on a five-minute monologue for each of you during a particular session. And set the clock! Sci-techs are always afraid that the five minutes will turn into the all-night marathons that almost every couple eventually endures. Then plan on another five-minute response time for each of you. So far you've only used up twenty minutes!

There may be some unfinished business or some rebuttal time

needed, so plan to use the last five minutes for each of you as a wrap-up time.

Make some rules about how feelings will be presented. Here are my suggestions:

1. No physical abuse. Each must remain in his/her chair. You can even decide on the decibel level that each of you can tolerate.
2. Don't hedge or go overtime, or else you will lose credibility.
3. Listen as well as you can, with eye contact and appropriate body language. Give your partner the benefit of your full attention.
4. Always use a clock. You will be amazed at how long five minutes can be when you have your partner's undivided attention and know that he/she will not bolt out of the room over touchy subjects.

This form of planning will save you lots of heartaches and heartburn. Your sci-tech will love all the preplanning and the protection of the structured exercise. The more *protection* you can offer him, the better. Emotionally, he is just not as equipped for histrionics as you are.

His worst fear is that you will lose control. No, even worse than that, that he will lose control! These rules ensure that the odds for control loss are reduced. Therefore, he can concentrate on your feelings and the content of those feelings.

THE "I RESENT THAT YOU . . ." EXERCISE

Each partner starts with *"I resent that you . . ."* and completes the statement. One sentence only! The other partner responds with three statements. These three statements are the magic to this process. The receiving partner answers with:

"Thank you for sharing that."

"Your saying so may not change my behavior."

"I'm not going to defend myself."

This may seem like a very simple exercise. It is. And it incorporates all of the important aspects of communication. I have used this technique with over two thousand couples, and it is foolproof. Sci-techs love it!

Partner One starts with an "I resent . . ." statement, followed by Partner Two's three responses to the statement. Partner Two then presents his "I resent . . ." statement, followed by Partner One's three response statements. Do several rounds of this process, alternating who begins with the "I resent . . ." statement.

I have discovered that each of the three responses really demonstrates a point. The process begins to set in motion the underlying theory I am trying to impart. The theory is: You don't have to do anything about what your partner does not like. But you do have to let your partner know that you *hear that it is a problem* for your partner!

The second part of this exercise is just as easy. I ask each partner to complete another statement, this one beginning "I appreciate that . . ." But in response to the "I appreciate . . ." statement, I ask the receiving partner to say simply, "Thank you."

People are relieved that there are not pat sentences to remember as a response to "I appreciate . . ." But you will be surprised at how quickly you will memorize the three "I resent . . ." responses. This consciousness-raising exercise has changed wild-eyed, destructive couples into ones who can be compassionate and empathic with each other.

You may be surprised to know that the "I resent . . ." part brings more solace than the "I appreciate . . ." part. Actually, and sadly, many couples have trouble coming up with three things to appreciate. And, in fact, about 40 percent of my troubled couples can think of no appreciation statements. This is, in itself, a diagnostic tool for the relationship.

Two possibilities can account for the lack of appreciation statements. One is that the couple is so furious and so frustrated with each other that it is impossible to get beyond the scars for even a moment to begin to remember the good parts of the relationship. The second possibility is that one or both of the partners have never learned how to make positive statements. Couples who have been starving for reinforcement from each other will break into tears at the first words of appreciation. In fact, this little exercise alone can offer them too much false hope because it feels so good to be appreciated at last that a couple may naively think that all their problems are solved.

The reason the "I resent . . ." part of the exercise seems to bring such peace to the couple is that the partners sigh with relief upon hearing resentments they've suspected for a long time. And they cry out, "Oh, I'm not crazy after all. I have suspected you felt like this for years."

The reassuring part of this process is that your partner may have been telling you this resentment with his body language and nonverbal style for years, while denying you the actual words of resentment. When you hear the truth, you will be amazed at how good it feels, even when the words are harsh or incriminating.

The magic in this exchange is in the response statements. A couple cannot get into their old debates, trying feverishly to win "game points" about an old and tired subject. In this exercise you will simply share your feelings. Your partner will not even have a chance to respond to your feelings with ideas of his own on the subject (unless he wants to use his own "I resent . . ." time to do so).

Let's analyze each response statement.

"Thank you for sharing that." This sets the stage. In effect, it says, "Well, I trust your good intentions in saying what you just did. I'm actually grateful that you trusted me enough to air your complaint. Moreover, your sharing this tells me that you believe I will listen to you."

With this statement we are teaching each other that a resentment statement is an act of faith. The resentment implies trust that *the relationship will survive the complaint.* It also implies that the receiving partner will be mature enough to hear his partner's truth. When a couple believes that a relationship can survive deep resentments, the battle is won. I often remind couples that their relationship has already survived multiple attacks and counterattacks, and they're still "hanging in there," albeit barely. I persuade them that sharing resentments in this form is really the beginning of an authentic relationship, of trust, and ultimately of liking each other. By saying "thank you" you are telling your partner that you have faith in his/her integrity.

"Your saying so may not change my behavior." This is the big one! You need to convey that just because your partner resents this particular behavior, this does not mean that you must change your behavior. Your partner, by stating his resentment, is not eliciting a behavioral change from you.

The important thing is that you, the receiver, may change your behavior *if you want to;* if you do not wish to change, you do not have to. Hearing your partner's resentment stated may actually motivate you to want to change. A partner, though, must not feel that the exercise automatically calls for change.

Often the motivation to alter behavior comes much later, when the receiver remembers how disturbing this behavior or attitude was to his partner. Even as he recites, "Your saying so may not change my behavior," he is contemplating the possibility that he *could* change at some time in the future.

Above all, the statement takes the heat off! Each partner knows that behavioral change is not the ultimate goal. The goal is really *information sharing* about what frustrates or grieves your partner. Even when you know how hard it would be for your husband to quit smoking, or to quit eating Cheez-Its in bed, or to quit yelling at other drivers, you will feel free in this exchange to express your resentment about these behaviors. He also can listen without worrying that you will be making him promise to quit, extracting deadlines, etc., from him.

"I'm not going to defend myself!" This is the couple-saver statement! This response prevents the discussion from escalating into an argument. By saying this, you simply admit that what you do may be frustrating to your partner, and that you *accept the possibility* that you do perpetrate this act.

Defensive statements such as, "I only do that because you are so sloppy around the house," or, "You yell so loud that sometimes I have to turn off to save my ears," really disclaim the complaint.

"But I was only doing it for your own good," or, "I certainly didn't know that this would bother you" are excuses. Sometimes when we can't make a good enough excuse for ourselves we will distract away from the complaint with, "Well, my first wife loved it when I tickled her that way!" Excuses are counterproductive. By not defending yourself, you are validating your partner's need to express his feelings about the alleged behavior.

Another common response to a resentment is the outright denial: "Oh, I never do that," or, "Well, I don't do that anymore." The denial does not acknowledge that your partner, with his own perceptions, actually experiences what he says he is feeling.

Couples sometimes go away frustrated when they first do this exercise. So may you. But it is worth the practice. It is a frustrating exercise because I ask couples to discipline themselves, instead of giving full vent to the usually painful subject areas. Our energy subjects (money, the kids, your mother, housework, drinking, weight, etc.) have become so raw to couples that at the slightest mention one or both partners will go into the *persuade position*. Now, actually, this persuade position will get you nowhere. Yet, couples will talk for days and nights on end, each hoping his partner will hear the truth and change his/her mind on the subject. In my office, couples lobby for their positions hoping that I will act as referee and declare one of them right!

The fact is that your partner may not be able to hear anything! A sci-tech may be too busy preparing his next argument in the never-ending debate. Another reaction your partner may have, if he is not compiling retaliatory statements, is one of *stark terror* when a delicate subject is introduced: Your sci-tech mate will again turn down his hearing aid, and will retreat to take care of himself by attacking back at you, always in defense, terrorized that you will say something that he cannot emotionally handle.

The happy part is that you don't have to promise anything in this exercise. This is a feeling-sharing experience only; it is not a problem-solver, and it is not a time to make apologies or promises to improve. When you get used to the idea that you don't have to sign any contracts or pledge any new behavior, but simply have to listen to your partner's point of view, you will begin to relax, start to really hear your partner and to uncoil from the defensive position.

HOW NOT TO RESPOND

It's very hard not to intersperse solutions, ideas, and sensible decisions in the sharing-of-feelings segment of communicating. When sci-tech says, "Now, Ruth, that doesn't make any sense at all," he has invalidated her feelings. Here are examples of what not to say when your wife comes home from a meeting crying, "I feel so ashamed of myself."

Do not say:

1. "Oh, honey, that's stupid. Of course you have done nothing to be ashamed of." (This statement *denies* her feelings. It implies that she does not know what she did and does not know how she feels.)
2. "Oh, honey, let's forget all this. I will take you out to a nice lobster dinner. By the way, here's a letter from the kids." (This statement aims to *distract*. She is not ready to be tricked away from her feelings. As much as sci-tech would like to move on, he needs to wait with her and not try to change the subject.)

3. "Oh, honey, I'm going to call Betsy right now and tell
   her to stop picking on you. She's got a nerve, after all
   you've done for that organization." (This offer to help
   does not indicate that you can listen to her feelings. It
   sounds like you want to problem-solve for her and will
   not address the way she feels! Don't be her *rescuer;* be
   her listener-mate.)
4. "Oh, honey, I feel that way too sometimes. I had a terrible
   lunch with John and PCG today, and I felt that I had not
   done my homework. I think I'll go into the office early
   tomorrow morning." (No! Don't talk this way either. It
   sounds self-centered. You took one cue sentence from
   your mate and turned it into your own thing. This is a
   common response to pain: "Oh, I feel like that too; let
   me tell you about it." She doesn't want to hear about it.
   She wants to release her own pain!)
5. "Oh, honey, let's think about how to get back at that
   group. I want retribution. I'll help you figure out a way to
   make them sorry. (This statement is cultivation; you
   want to help her figure out a plan to stop the feelings.
   Instead of being with your partner with her feelings, you
   want to scheme to get her away from them.)

HOW TO RESPOND

Sci-Tech, I know you would like your wife to stop talking about
it. You'd like to get on with dinner. You even believe that talking
about things like this makes matters worse.

Sometimes it does seem to make things worse—at the moment. In the long run, it will help your partner if she can let the
feelings out *right now,* and as many feelings as she can squeeze out
of this little embarrassing binge.

So the perfect response for you is:

"Oh, honey, I can see that you really feel humiliated. It must be
awful to be feeling so regretful about what happened to you."

You see, Sci-Tech, all she really wants to know is that you can
really *hear* her; that you recognize pain when you see it, even if it
may be unfounded, based on paranoia, based on incomplete information; based on irrationality. Just let her know that you are able to
relate to her feelings for even one moment. If you try saying the

above response, I promise you that your partner will relax, sigh, look at you in amazement and relief, and will be able to move on quickly so that you can eventually make one of the rational responses you're more comfortable stating.

Partner, your sci-tech has just responded perfectly with an effective listening response! Now, don't goof it up. He finally stopped his usual methods: (1) deny; (2) distract; (3) rescue; or (4) self-center. He finally gave you an authentic "I hear you" answer.

He is wonderful. And in order to continue his wonderful new behavior you must *reinforce* it. That means you must let him know he did a good thing, and let him decide to do so again sometime.

You have two jobs to do. First, thank him for the appropriate response. Tell him how wonderful it felt to have your feelings acknowledged. Tell him that you felt a sigh of contentment that he wasn't going to argue you out of your feelings or try to dissuade you from having them. In order to shape his behavior (so that he will respond this way again), let him know that he was perfect this time.

The second job (and the hardest one) is to discipline yourself into not wanting to prolong this wonderful response. Take what you get. Don't try to eke out more! You will spoil the whole training if you try to tease him into giving more than he is prepared to give.

Yes, I know. You would like to sit down and spill out all the pain you have ever experienced about being embarrassed or goofing up on something. You would like him to hear you completely and resist showing judgment or rushing into problem-solving techniques. You would like him to whine and sigh a little with you. Well, don't try to get blood out of a turnip!

He is coming around. He is trying to listen. Now you do your part. Stay with your feelings for about twenty minutes (maximum) and then drop it. If he wants to do a little problem-solving, go along with that, or simply say, "George, I know that you want to do a little talking about how to prevent this next time. I am willing to do problem-solving soon. But not just now. I'm not quite ready. But I don't want to burden you. So let's move on, to dinner, to another topic, or to reading the paper."

The biggest problem for most sci-techs is that they want to hurry the feelings along. They are deathly afraid that their partners will want to talk all night long about an incident. They are especially sensitive if the feelings are about their problems, such as smoking, drinking, or affairs. So right in the beginning of the conversation they need absolute assurance that this talk will only last thirty minutes, one hour, or whatever. They can take almost any time limitation, just so they know there is one.

Now, if you do end a conversation prematurely because he just can't take any more, or because the time limit is up, plan on another session. Contract for another session when your partner is ready for more emotional catharsis. Ask him to continue the subject the next day or the next week. Be sure that you remind him again that you will talk only for a specific period of time each time you talk. There will be no more open-ended tirades that go on for three days. There will always be periods for time out, and there will always be possibilities for emergency extensions. The time-out period should be about as long as the emergency-extension period. Sci-tech will call for most of the time-outs. His partner will call for most of the extensions.

PROBLEM-SOLVING

Here sci-tech shines. He loves problem-solving. And he will be perfectly reasonable and fair in the process. His partner needs to spend as much energy and sensitivity on the problem-solving phase of communication as sci-tech does on the sharing-of-feelings phase.

Let me give you some guidelines about problem-solving.

1. You need to stop when you have come to a stalemate in problem-solving because the feelings involved have become too strong. Take a detour from problem-solving and go into the feelings-sharing session again. Make rules about exactly when you will get back to problem-solving.
2. Decide ahead of time which method of problem-solving you are going to use. Stay with the contract.
3. Write down the final decision. It's amazing that four hours later we can remember only the emotional barbs, and we cannot even remember the solution we battled so fiercely to achieve. Divorces are like that. I have spent hundreds of hours with couples who hammer out decisions about custody (second Wednesdays and first and third weekends) or property-settlement figures, and then six months later they cannot even remember the details

of the hard-earned decisions (was it six thousand dollars or eight thousand?). They remember the pain and the arguments for and against, but not the final decision.

4. Decide on consequences if the contract is not met.
5. Plan on an evaluation meeting in the future. Sometimes the most mature decisions are not practical because the partners make moves to change right in the middle of a long-term contract.

THE ONE-THIRD, ONE-THIRD, ONE-THIRD METHOD

One-third of the time we will do it completely his way.
One-third of the time we will do it completely her way.
One-third of the time we will compromise creatively.

Let me give you an example. My husband is a night owl. When we met he could stay up until three in the morning. But I am an early bird. I love to get up at five o'clock to work, and even earlier to go on trips. Of course, getting to bed and getting up immediately posed a problem for us. If I got up early in the morning I was a bit groggy by 8:00 P.M., by 10:00 P.M. I was a dud, and by midnight I was asleep on the couch. By the same token, in the morning, when I was my most adorable, wanting to communicate, be physical, and start the day with singing, Don was snoring away. For the first six months we were together, we both just coped. After all, that was the phase-one period anyway, and we were both eager to cooperate and conciliate. But as time wore on, I grew sleepier and sleepier and Don was lonelier and lonelier in the late-evening hours. We could not really go to bed at the same time and enjoy it. When I would say, "Don, it's eight-thirty. Let's go to bed now," he would freak out. "It's the middle of the afternoon!" he'd bellow. Well, here is our compromise:

One-third of the time we go to bed late, usually on Friday and Saturday nights, and get up late. I can't sleep as late as Don does, so I get up earlier, do my chores or writing, and then crawl back into bed with him around eleven o'clock or bring him breakfast in bed. Now, to stay up late on weekends, I make myself take a nap during the day so I will be fresh in the evenings. It works out wonderfully.

One-third of the time we go to bed early, usually on Tuesday and Wednesday evenings at nine-thirty or ten o'clock, and get up early. Don is actually getting to like that because he is now able to get up earlier to go to work on Wednesday and Thursday mornings. And, of course, I love getting that good rest in the middle of the week.

The last third of the week is Sunday and Thursday nights. On those nights we retire early to our bedroom suite. Don sits in his recliner and reads or listens to the stereo. I start out reading, which usually doesn't last long. Sometimes I sit up with him and we talk about the week's happenings. I am usually in bed and asleep long before Don is, but we have at least started out together. We have each sacrificed a little too. Don has to read in our bedroom (instead of in the living room). And I have to try to go to sleep in the bedroom with the light or the stereo on.

Now, I didn't talk about that seventh day or night, Monday night. We use that as an open night. We actually go to a class together that night, so that is usually a good, close time for us. It is a class on couples, so we get time to be together there. If we come home and want to be together, then we do. Most of the time, Don stays up later and watches TV, and I go running off to bed so that I can get up early for clients on Tuesday morning.

Now, most sci-techs don't understand the need for sacrifice or compromise. Why should we both be unhappy one-third or two-thirds of the time? Get ready; here is the answer: for the sake of the relationship. If you are going to be on a team, you have to play as a team. That means sometimes you have to share, sometimes you have to indulge, and sometimes you have to put your needs aside—in the interest of fostering a team approach. If Don spent five nights a week going to bed alone (or seven, which would be more accurate), and I spent five or seven mornings getting up alone, we would not be building a support team, or a chance for nurturing, for exchanges, or for new behavior to develop.

Since most couples spend their days apart, I believe that having some evening time together is very important. Many couples do go to bed separately every night. The problem is that this eliminates the time of letting down, letting go, and of appraising the day. I firmly believe that couples should end their day together most of the time.

THE ONE DOZEN OPTIONS LIST

Decide what the problem is. Let's suppose the problem is that Lisa hates going to Toby's annual Christmas party. He owns the company, is proud of it and of Lisa, and he really likes having Lisa there. But she hates parties, doesn't enjoy his colleagues, and is, in fact, scarred by a few Christmas parties when Toby either ignored her or was even rude to her.

Check with each other to see if you need to exchange some feelings on this subject. If so, recess and go to the sharing-feelings phase again.

Then make a list of twelve options. Each of you sit down and make a list, out loud. Also, write them on the same paper. First, Lisa puts down a solution, then Toby puts one down.

Example:

1. (From Lisa) Eliminate the Christmas party altogether. Give everyone bonuses instead.
2. (From Toby) Lisa attends because she is the wife of the company president, no matter how much she hates it.
3. (From Lisa) Have the party at our house. In this way, I can have some control over what happens.
4. (From Toby) Have the party at our house, but have it catered so that I won't have to hear Lisa's complaining and crying for weeks before and after.
5. (From Lisa) Have it at the restaurant, but have Toby make a speech about how wonderful I am, and have him stick to me like glue all evening.
6. (From Toby) No, have me mention in my state-of-the-company talk how nice it is to have a supportive wife, and make sure that I dance with her first, last, and most of the time. I will introduce her to new people, talk to her when I can, and sit next to her at dinner.

Do you see how Toby and Lisa are each beginning to give in order to come up with the perfect solution? It is important to have lots of room for options, so that they can be creative and really brainstorm without feeling tied into any of the solutions just because it was brought up. I've used this exercise in my practice over three hundred times; I always explain all the rules first, then I write down the lists as couples call out the solutions to me. It works!

7. (From Lisa) Toby and I go out to early cocktails first at the same restaurant. We have about an hour to just be together alone. At this time, Toby tells me his worries and joys about the company. Then he tells me all the ways I've been cooperating and how much he loves me! (No worries about me tonight.)

8. (From Toby) That's good. I like that. I would even add that if I don't have to worry about Lisa all through the company party, I will promise to take her out for breakfast when we are through. Alone!

9. (From Lisa) We invite another couple that we are both fond of, so that I will have someone to talk to if Toby gets embroiled in company politics.

10. (From Toby) We invite one of the company couples that Lisa could tolerate over to dinner a week or so before the party so that Lisa could feel more simpatico with someone else at the party.

11. (From Lisa) We leave the next morning for a two-day trip of my choice, to be spent alone and not talking business.

12. (From Toby) Lisa goes on a trip with me before the party, so she is really feeling full enough to share and give me this time with my company.

The next step is very important. Each partner alternately crosses off the options, one at a time. Of course, Toby will probably cross off Lisa's first solution. She may immediately cross off Toby's tenth solution. The very exercise of demonstrating the power to veto a suggestion by your partner is good work for the relationship.

Keep crossing options off until there are three solutions left. Read them aloud to each other. All solutions left may be benign. The perfect one may have been crossed out in the effort to be strategic. Don't worry about that. Now is the time to caucus. Look at what is left. Look at whose turn it is. It really doesn't matter who started first. You will be amazed that all three remaining options would be suitable to both of you. At this time you may want just to discuss the viability of what is left and choose one solution together.

If you need to cross off until you get to the final solution, do that. Acknowledge that you have both agreed to this solution.

The last step is to define the parameters around the solution. Let's suppose that option 11 won—"We leave the next morning for a two-day trip of my choice, to be spent alone and not talking business." In particular, the couple did not mention in this option what the party would be like. I'm assuming Lisa would be thoroughly cooperative, but there are some parameters that they had better discuss. Suppose Lisa gets so upset at the party that she does not want to go on the trip the next day. What then? What if Lisa wants to cry and yell at Toby the first two hours of the trip the next day? Will Toby be prepared for that?

Problem-solving techniques are really quite simple, and they do produce amazing results. Try one or two. Adopt your own.

If you find that you or your partner is sabotaging each method I suggest, you can assume that you are keeping up the fever so that someone will notice and call the doctor!

UNDERSTANDING YOUR PARTNER

Take off the blinders, the rose-colored glasses, and put your partner under the microscope. Learn *why* he is the way he is. In this way you can predict his behavior under certain conditions.

Plan for crises in your life. And plan that your partner's most bizarre qualities will be exaggerated one-hundredfold whenever a crisis arises. Stress conditions bring out the maniacal tendencies of an otherwise gentle person. When pushed to the wall, some of us resort to primitive behavior. So you will have to dissect the crisis behavior of your partner. Expect that primal responses will surface whenever the tension is too great for him to handle.

Learn to spot the danger signs that warn that stress is building. If your scientist partner tends to go underground with his feelings, watch for the beginning stages of this behavior. He will become more quiet than usual and will demonstrate some going-away tactics. Look at the content of his life. Is his business going badly? Is it tax time? Is he up for review? Is he having to tell his mother she can't move in with you? What is happening in his life to contribute to worry or concern?

If he cannot share worries easily, he is going to begin to accumulate the information and store it down inside himself. Eventually the "stuffed feelings" fill up the hole he keeps for worries. Then the boil-over point occurs.

But this type of sci-tech does not boil. He gets more rigid. He begins to stop coping with information and just tries to stop the flow. He stops by hiding. He hides the feelings from himself and especially from you. He cannot tolerate coming close to the feelings. Hints about "let's talk about your problems, honey" will simply frighten him. Instead, gently and methodically point out the facts: "Bill, I've noticed that you are more quiet than usual. This is the time of year that the engineering project seems to take a big dip. I am getting a little concerned that you and I are not finding a way to talk together. I notice you seem to be watching more TV. I also notice you are going to bed earlier, sleeping more, and not laughing at all. These could be signs that you are under stress and that you are taking all the worries of your life into your own system, and soon you may get to that place that is so scary to me—that place where I feel shut out by you. What can I do to help?"

THE "WHY" QUESTIONS EXERCISE

If you are a sci-tech and your partner displays confusing characteristics to you, you will have to do some work to understand her. Let's imagine that you think your partner goes overboard in preparing for company. She seems almost crazy about it. You have tried to harass her and ridicule her out of it, but it has not helped at all.

Here's a solution: Try to understand her obsession for preparing for company. A simple "why" question session will help. Be sure, though, that you both discuss the *rules* of this "why" session first:

1. Partner must answer every question with some sort of reaction. He/she cannot say, "I don't know." Respond with at least a feeling, or an observation like, "Gee, that was a stupid question." "It feels warm in here right now" is better than no response.
2. Each answer then forms the next question. "Well, why was that such a stupid question?"
3. Husband asks each question. Wife responds. Write down the questions. Each answer, started by "Why . . . ?" will become the next question, so writing the questions is enough.
4. You will eventually get into a circle asking the same questions in different ways. Don't worry about that. There is always a way out of the loop.
5. Just keep asking questions.
6. Husband cannot offer anything in the way of reactions except the next question.

You will gain lots of insight from every question session if the two of you can abide by these simple rules. Here's how the questions would go with our obsessive party-giver:

HUSBAND: Honey, why do you have to work so hard to have everything perfect when guests come?

WIFE: Because I don't want to be embarrassed with a mess when they arrive.

HUSBAND: Why don't you want to be embarrassed with a mess when they arrive?

WIFE: Because I like to present a lovely image when company walks into our house.

HUSBAND: Why do you like to present a lovely image when company walks into our house?

WIFE: Because I want them to think well of us.

HUSBAND: Why do you want them to think well of us?

WIFE: Because I want them to like us.

HUSBAND: Why do you want them to like us?

WIFE: Oh, that's foolish. You know why. I want people to think we are good, interesting folks. I don't want them to think we are trash.

HUSBAND: Why would they think we are trash?

WIFE: Because if things are all cluttered and grimy, they will consider us trash.

HUSBAND: Why will they consider us trash if things are cluttered and grimy?

WIFE: Because my mother was trash and she kept things cluttered and grimy!

HUSBAND: Why was your mother trash?

WIFE: Because she came from the wrong side of the tracks and my father always reminded us all that she presented a dirty side because she didn't know better.

HUSBAND: Why didn't your mother know better?

WIFE: Because her mother kept house that way and didn't teach her otherwise. She didn't know better either.

HUSBAND: Why didn't her mother know better?

WIFE: Because she didn't have a father like I did who would remind my mother of what trash she was, because he did know better and he was ashamed of our house.

HUSBAND: Why did your father have to do the reminding?

WIFE: Because he knew the difference. And so do I. I am not like my mother!

HUSBAND: Why are you not like your mother?

WIFE: Because I know what it takes not to be trash. I clean up and prepare because I don't have a man (you) to remind me, and because I don't need a man to remind me, and because I know better.

HUSBAND: Could you just know better and not do anything about the house? Would knowing what trash is make the difference?

WIFE: Yes. Say, maybe I don't really have to do as much when I know the minimum standards, and I could never even come close to being called trashy!

In this question session the husband discovered the root of the special cleaning ritual. He learned that his wife had closely associated preparing for company with her degree of social appropriateness.

If his partner is very sensitive, he may discover that she had been severely traumatized by her own father's recriminations that her mother was trash.

The point is not to deduce that the conclusions drawn by the wife were from faulty reasoning. The point is to *understand* that she did make those deductions, and, to this end, she was struck by them.

The husband has two choices of action at this point:

1. He can try to help his wife undo her programming, giving her logical reasons why there is no chance of her creating "trashdom."
2. He can assist his wife in keeping the house immaculate when company is due.

Neither solution is therapeutic!

1. Asking your wife to be sensible about a primal message will take months, maybe years. She will not hear the message from you. She may even need outside people to help her sort through the myths and the conclusions she made so long ago. ("I'm not going to be like Mom. I don't need a man to tell me if I'm being trash or not.")
2. Cooperating with the supercleaning is playing into the neurosis. Unless the partner has some form of that neurosis in his own psyche, he probably will sabotage the cleanup effort anyway. Learning that his wife has a partic-

ular neurosis about housecleaning for guests is one thing. Learning that it has a strong foundation about her worth (trash or not) is quite another thing. Even if this worry has no sound foundation, even if she is the princess of entertainment, this woman was traumatized by her worry over appearing elegant. Her husband can cooperate by knowing it is important to her to have things neat.

A second segment of the neurosis has to do with the wife's recalling that her father always chastised her mother into preparing for guests. A husband of her own who does not seem interested in the preparations for company actually adds to her stress! Without a man to seem worried, to be concerned with appearances, she has the full burden.

Solution: When the husband can understand his wife's background material about entertaining, he can begin to show some small concern. Then the wife can relax a little. A combination of her knowing that she would never be trashy and her husband's frequent confirmations of this will start this wife on the road to health. Additionally, her husband needs to help her out in preparing for company so that she can begin to let up on her obsessive behavior.

PRACTICE

When we get new skills we are clumsy with them. It takes practice to jog smoothly without hurting your body and to gain speed at the same time. It also takes practice to give or receive compliments or to share feelings. All too often an impatient spouse gives up on the partner before he/she has the moves perfected.

For example, when someone who has never before safely expressed his anger out loud suddenly begins to do so, he will be very klutzy at it! He will yell at you in inappropriate places, in front of your mother, your boss, or the kids. He will "dump" anger stored up for years when you least expect it. Or he will pick on small items, this and that, not discriminating about which deserve his attendant feelings of anger. He will spit and sput and act very self-indulgent until he has mastered appropriate displays of anger.

Or, when the partner learns to be assertive, without enough practice, she will be "trying on" some behavior that borders on the aggressive instead of the assertive. I've heard husbands respond with, "Well then, if this is what it takes for you to be more initiating, I don't need it. You've turned into a bitch!"

The truth is that the wife is still learning to take care of herself. She needs to try on her wings. And sci-tech needs to be forgiving and lenient in those beginning stages of assertiveness training.

We get freaky, though, ready to bolt at the slightest change in behavior! I suggest to clients that they plan in the beginning for the pendulum to swing in the opposite behavioral direction. As the new behavior gets more comfortable, the partner will use it more cautiously and will eventually come to mid-center on the pendulum swing. In the meantime, the other partner needs the confidence to withstand some bizarre reactions from the partner who is learning.

Don't abandon the ship! Prepare each other for changes, and contract for indulgence. When husband or wife gets promoted, or when wife or husband goes to therapy or to any new class, or when there is a chance for growth in any capacity on either side, watch out!

Sometimes a mentor appears for one or the other and new behaviors frighten partners. Learn to prepare both of you for the change. Alcoholics who give up drinking, or obese people who diet, often report that the change was harder on the partner than it was on them. Yes, the partner is unnerved, caught off guard by the change. Even if the change is a positive one, if your partner is not actively involved (lost weight, or stopped drinking too), the reaction to the pleasure and confidence of his/her mate is sometimes disconcerting. The partner who is growing, of course, is disappointed that his mate is not tickled with his new behavior. Again, it takes *preplanning* to assist each of you in attending and anticipating the changes in your system. If one person shifts in any direction over any issue, there will be a shift in the system. Get ready for it, anticipate feelings of being threatened, and contract for concomitant coping behavior for your partner.

COMFORT STYLES

When I was a child, my parents had a beautiful bedroom with twin beds across the middle of the room. My mother had a pink satin comforter on her bed and my father had a green one. On Sunday mornings my little brother and I would run in and jump into one of my parents' beds. My father would read us the funnies. I remember the lovely, secure feeling of being under the satin comforter, with all of us in the room, laughing and playing in the beds.

My mother would sometimes bring breakfast in bed to all of us. It seems like we stayed in there for hours. It was almost the only time I saw my dad relaxed, with nothing to do, and with no one from outside, none of his business contacts, disturbing our reverie.

Now, my husband had a very different experience of being in bed with his family on Sunday mornings. It never happened! His family scurried about on Sundays, preparing for church. They would have been very disturbed about having such frivolous Sunday-morning romps.

Don learned to comfort himself by going down into the basement to build things with electronic equipment. He loved to be in the quiet basement to invent, read, and explore batteries, radio transmitters, and so on. He enjoyed being out of the main line of family talk. He took good care of himself down there. Sometimes he brought cookies and milk into his little basement hideaway. His parents never disturbed him by using the washing machine while Don was in his seclusion.

Each of us learned how to be comforted. Or we learned what does not feel comfortable to us. When I ask people to visualize a scene of comfort from their past, they usually can come up with something so sweet, so soft, so soothing that their bodies even begin to relax when they start to relate their description. With biofeedback equipment we can see dramatic changes in a person when he/she thinks comforting thoughts.

Now, let's suppose I'm feeling a little blue, kind of down in the dumps. I really don't know what I want, but I feel a need for some primal comforting. Then, I like to lie in bed for hours on end, preferably in the morning, and preferably with the Sunday funnies scattered about. I even like my children all gathered about. I recall my fondest memories of my own children snuggled up against their father and me, all six of us in bed at once. Someone would always be slightly damp, lying there in our bed, and eventually one of the older children would tattle on the little one, and pillow fights or noisy sibling exchanges would drive us all from bed.

Recently, though, when I suggested having the kids come sit on our bed one Easter morning, Don thought I'd gone nuts. Our eight kids—we each have four—range in age from 21 to 29!

And when my husband goes down to our basement (wouldn't you know he would find a California house with a basement?) to horse around with electronic equipment, even though he has a 24,000-square-foot factory of electronic equipment, I know that he needs some soothing.

Please don't judge what feels like comfort to your partner. I knew a man who liked having the bottom of his feet scratched. Many of us enjoy long walks together, while others want to go to the movies with family or friends. We are seeking the emotional anchors that pleased us as kids.

Ask your partner exactly what feels good to him/her. Then ask what words, if any, go with this perfect interlude. Learn to create those moods for your partner when you want to give a special gift.

When I do communication classes, I ask each person to demonstrate physically and then to say sentences that would most comfort her. You might be amazed at the range of comfort moves people want. When we get over the initial embarrassment of asking for what we want, there is nothing sweeter than having a willing partner who *wants* to please us.

Getting comforted is acquired behavior. So if your mate has never acquired the behavior of having someone physically or emotionally comfort him, of course, he will not feel eased by such behavior now. How many times have I seen a mate stroking his partner's arm, nearly rubbing the skin off, imagining that his partner is being comforted. When a crying partner lies on our chest we often pat, pat, pat, on the back, as if to burp the tears out of our loved one's body!

If your mate is not at ease with touching and soothing caresses, don't give up on him. Remember that this is acquired learning. Whoever said that you need to acquire this in childhood? Many an adult learns to feel and enjoy physical touching *eventually*. It does not have to be sexual touching to feel good.

Teach your partner what you need. Practice this. Take your time. Give yourselves permission to ask for what you need. Promise each other that these requests are actually essential to the marriage.

MAKE A FUSS! IT'S CHEAPER THAN DIVORCE

Martyrs go about ignoring their own needs, and eventually, after the resentment builds up, they find a way to retaliate, usually through the back door. This is called passive-aggressive behavior in psychological terms. Some of us just call it chicken!

The "chicken" wife is too frightened to speak up about the unmade bed or the kid who rocks chairs, or the tools on the porch, or the lipstick stains on her husband's collar. So she makes the bed herself, buys new linoleum each year for the kitchen, trips over the tools, and quietly ignores the lipstick stains.

And, inside, she stuffs down the anger until one fine day, when her partner least expects it, she lashes out, just before the boss is to arrive for dinner or as they are boarding a plane for an anniversary trip.

This is why I advocate talking about something as soon as it occurs. Otherwise, you may retaliate, by withholding sexually and, oh yes, by forgetting—you know, just little things, like forgetting to take your husband's briefcase to the airport, or leaving the flowers for your mother-in-law in the ladies' room, or forgetting to send the income-tax check on time when you know your partner is phobic about late returns.

Take the time and energy *now* to address problems. It will cost you less now than later!

WHY COMPLEMENTARY COUPLES WORK SO WELL

Together you can be a wonderful team if you will just relax and let the complementary traits begin to work together. You are a great team! You have a whole package of styles that are invaluable in a relationship team. You have pragmatism. You have idealism. You have zest, lust, caution, tenderness, and objectivity—all in the same partnership! You can learn to delegate to each other. "Paul, you are really better about this than I am. Why don't you call the real-estate agent now?"

Weaving your styles will take a magical and deft touch. It is like matching up the bull and the china shop. You will each have to change your style a little. What works with other friends and loved ones will not work with him. What works for him with some colleagues and friends will not work with you!

My husband and I learned that I am often very unconscious about material things. I have learned that he is very very unconscious about emotional things. And now we have learned to raise each other's consciousness a little. It is a slow lift. And discouraging. And vital . . . vital to our relationship. Vital to yours. Belief in the possibility that you could be a complementary team, an exciting, interesting, capable, productive, and profitable partnership, will push you into the work ahead . . . and the pleasure. . . .

4

Right Brain/Left Brain

THE TWO COMPUTER BRAIN MODELS

At birth we are handed out a particular brain model. Every model has full-function capacity, with complete potential for right-brain use and left-brain use. But as we grow up, experience the world, and learn from our parents' modeling and proclivities, we often develop one side of the brain more than the other side.

Generally, we keep favoring our use of one side of our brain until we become known as a right-brainer or a left-brainer.

Most engineers and scientists favor the left brain. Since our brains are our computer, we can even say they have a left-brain computer. Now, to function fully, to handle all the thinking forms necessary in our lives, lefties seem to pick a right-brain computer partner to finish up the work their own computers aren't doing. Each computer brain seems to have a "dedicated" specialty. Together, the two brains can solve any problem, soothe any situation, or create any system. The trouble is, though, that the two computer brain models can't talk to each other! Their computer languages are different.

So the right-brain/left-brain relationships are like the American astronauts who try to problem-solve with the Russian cosmonauts. These space scientists must have an interpreter in order to communicate! It's hard to create world defense, world health, or world peace without a translator. And it is hard to create a party, raise kids, or manage a budget without a translator.

Yes, we are really that different. What makes the problem an insidious one is that we do have some language compatibility. We can dialogue about most rudimentary things. But it is our emotional reactions and our styles of problem-solving that differentiate us. And when the scar tissue begins to form between our differences, and the early wish to cooperate disappears, we end up with a right-brainer who does not understand his partner and a left-brainer who does not comprehend her partner!

We have no built-in translator system, no converter that makes us *system-compatible*. No one tells us how to work together or how to use each other's talents or skills. That is what I intend to do in this chapter—tell you how to work together. I will translate your computer brain models to you and I will convince you that your differences can be an asset to your team!

Let me show you my version of the two brain types:

Left Hemisphere	*Right Hemisphere*
Focal	Diffuse
Lineal	Nonlineal
Intellectual	Intuitive
Explicit	Tacit
Propositional	Appositional
Sequential	Simultaneous
Active	Receptive

Although sci-techs appear to be left-brain models, they have, of course, the capacity to use both sides of their brains. With all due exceptions, please consider the above hypothesis about your relationship even if you both sometimes cross over. In truth, I work in my left hemisphere a good deal of the time (or how could I complete this book?), but emotionally, in areas of communication between my scientist husband and me, I represent the right-brain model, while he represents the left-brain model. Let's look a little deeper.

LEFT-BRAIN MODEL	RIGHT-BRAIN MODEL

Focal: He focuses on one thing at a time; he does not divert his attention. If he is assembling a Christmas bicycle, he will not stop to console you because you miss your uncle Paul. "Let's get this bike done!" he yells.

Diffuse: She turns, deflects, twists, disperses, and even distorts. She can disseminate and move on; she is capable of doing many things at once. She has learned to handle what is at hand! She is a generalist who juggles it all.

Lineal: Sequentially performs tasks or approaches problems in series. Ordinal, requires an order about tasks, even feelings. Is baffled by disorderly effect. Does not work out of order.

Nonlineal: Can start in the middle or at any point in the sequence. Does not need order or structure to comfortably perform the task. Can be disgruntled over partner's planning requirements.

Intellectual: A philomath, a lover of learning, he will seek knowledge, want to understand. (This is why he makes a good candidate for a partnership; he is willing to *learn* about differences.) Putting it all into practice is harder!

Intuitive: Uses involuntary impulses to second-sight a situation. Acts on hunches without proven experiential data. Has a precognitive instinct that is not in the realm of her partner's library of facts.

Explicit: Has a straightforward approach; can be accused of being blunt, tactless, brusque. His unequivocal style is transparent, but does not yield to the deft touch sometimes needed in delicate situations.

Tacit: Without having to say it, has a capacity for understanding. Does not have to see it in writing or hear it from an authority to accept the information. An implied figurative reference is enough. Often baffles and aggravates her partner, who wants "the facts, ma'am."

Propositional: Takes a stand; has an opinion. Does not like the gray shades of the issue. Makes a premise and moves forward "as if."

Appositional: Can compose, building and arranging one thing next to another. Connects; joins. Allows for similarities and overlaps. Enjoys the gray parts of the issue.

LEFT-BRAIN MODEL	RIGHT-BRAIN MODEL
Sequential: Pragmatically, and in succession, proceeds to a logical deduction. Without interruption, uses information in a logical series to draw conclusions. Does not do two things at once.	*Simultaneous:* Can do concurrent tasks and, moreover, can empathize with concurrent emotions (Dad is disappointed and Lucy is fearful), and can synchronize coexisting poles that frighten, confuse, or infuriate partner.
Active: Observes, operates, initiates, and does not spend as much time receiving information. Inclination to influence and judge rather than reflect.	*Receptive:* Pliant and open-minded (unless closed down to anything partner suggests because she has given up on his judgment), usually this brain is available for new data; does not require past program or imprint to consider.
Orientation: The left brain depends on the recall of facts in the same way that it stores them. The most reliable method for recall is memorization of previous examples; has difficulty with new situations for which he has no former source of reference or orientation.	*Creative:* Can take a holistic approach to reasoning because metaphors and visual thinking are available. No anxiety about orientation, can be comfortable with confusion, frustration, and uncertainty.

Engineers and scientists can be creative! Their jobs, in fact, require the ability to design. Read below the parable printed in 1932 by the president of the Society of Professional Engineers.

THE ENGINEER—A PARABLE*

One day three men, a lawyer, a doctor, and an engineer, appeared before Saint Peter as he stood guarding the Pearly Gates.

*By D. B. Steineam, president of the New York State Society of Professional Engineers, and past president of the American Association for Engineers. Reprinted from *The American Engineer*, January 1932.

The first man to step forward was the lawyer. With confidence and assurance, he proceeded to deliver an eloquent address which left Saint Peter dazed and bewildered. Before the venerable saint could recover, the lawyer quickly handed him a *writ of mandamus*, pushed him aside, and strode through the open portals.

Next came the doctor. With impressive, dignified bearing, he introduced himself: "I am Dr. Brown."

Saint Peter received him cordially. "I feel I know you, Dr. Brown. Many who preceded you said you sent them here. Welcome to our city!"

The engineer, modest and diffident, had been standing in the background. He now stepped forward. "I am looking for a job," he said.

Saint Peter wearily shook his head. "I am sorry," he replied, "we have no work here for you. If you want a job you can go to Hell."

This response sounded familiar to the engineer and made him feel more at home. "Very well," he said. "I have had Hell all my life and I guess I can stand it better than the others."

Saint Peter was puzzled. "Look here, young man, what are you?"

"I am an engineer," was the reply.

"Oh yes," said Saint Peter. "Do you belong to the Locomotive Brotherhood?"

"No, I'm sorry," the engineer responded apologetically. "I am a different kind of engineer."

"I do not understand," said Saint Peter. "What on earth do you do?"

The engineer recalled a definition and calmly replied, "I apply mathematical principles to the control of natural forces."

This sounded meaningless to Saint Peter, and his temper got the best of him. "Young man," he said, "you can go to Hell with your mathematical principles and try your hand at some of the natural forces there!"

"That suits me," responded the engineer; "I am always glad to go where there is a tough job to tackle." Whereupon he departed for the Nether Regions.

And it came to pass that strange reports began to reach Saint Peter. The celestial denizens, who had amused themselves in the past by looking down upon the less fortunate creatures in the Inferno, commenced asking for transfers to that other domain. The sounds of agony and suffering were stilled. Many new arrivals, after seeing both places, selected the Nether Regions for their permanent abode. Puzzled, Saint Peter sent messengers to visit Hell and to report back to him. They returned, all excited, and reported to Saint Peter.

"That engineer you sent down there," said the messenger, "has completely transformed the place so that you would not know it now. He has harnessed the Fiery Furnaces for light and power. He has cooled the entire place with artificial refrigeration. He has drained the Lakes of Brimstone and has filled the air with cool perfumed breezes. He has flung bridges across the Bottomless Abyss and has bored tunnels through the Obsidian Cliffs. He has erected paved streets, gardens, parks and playgrounds, lakes, rivers, and beautiful waterfalls. That engineer you sent down there has gone through Hell and made of it a realm of happiness, peace, and industry.

Yes, our sci-techs are creative. It is only in emotionally laden crisis situations that we suffer the consequences of the more rigid and conservative approach to thinking assigned to the sci-tech personality.

HOW A LEFT-BRAINER GOOFED

A pilot, Max, was baffled by his wife's jealousy about a flight attendant who always managed to schedule flights with Max. His wife, Lorraine, was terribly threatened by this beautiful young woman, who had even telephoned her to say she had designs on her husband.

Max stiffened at the news of this call, but was secretly rather flattered. He did not, however, want to engage in an affair with this stewardess, nor did he find her as attractive as his wife feared.

When an opportunity to be on a special commission arose, Max learned that the flight attendant had been appointed to the same commission. His wife begged and screamed to have the other woman removed from the committee. Max had the power to do this. But what should he do?

Max could understand the problem only from his own perspective:

1. "I want to be on that commission."
2. "I have no interest in the flight attendant."
3. "I do not like asking for special favors [to have the woman removed from the committee]."
4. "I do not want to imply to anyone that my wife is jealous."
5. "And I do not want to indicate that my wife has any strong influence over my career decisions."

With limited reasoning applied, Max did not include the marital implications of this dilemma. Finally, what persuaded him to act were the following conclusions he made in my office:

1. "I'm having to pay to go to a therapist just to talk about this silly problem. I would rather spend the money on something else."
2. "My wife and I are spending countless hours arguing about this and I would rather spend the time doing other things. Thus, this problem is wasting my time."
3. "The discomfort of getting that woman off the committee does not outweigh the problems at home."
4. "I do not like conflict and this will settle it all."

And so our pilot soothed his wife. He acted on the problem. But he never addressed his wife's feelings about the problem. This often happens when men have affairs. "Well, it's over, isn't it? Why do we still have to talk about it?"

Sci-techs assume that the end of the behavior means the end of the emotions regarding the behavior. This faulty logic causes pain for both partners.

Back to Max, the pilot. It really doesn't matter if his wife's preoccupation with the stewardess was reasonable or not. Perhaps this was a recurring problem, and his wife had so much history with such situations that this was the last straw. Or perhaps this was their first threatening issue because her husband had always been monogamous. It does not matter what the history or the truth was. It only matters that the wife *has the feelings, they are real to her, and her feelings need attention.* This is difficult to get the typical sci-tech to address. He continues to argue the logic of the feelings:

1. "It doesn't make any sense."
2. "She has nothing to be nervous about."
3. "She is being childish or silly about all this."

All of the preceding is true. And she still has those feelings! And the feelings still need to be addressed. Here is what the husband can say:

1. "Now, honey, I know you have strong feelings about this."
2. "I want to help you get over them."
3. "Even though it is hard for me to understand your sensitivity to this, I am willing to accept that it is a horrible problem for you."
4. "I am learning that your insecure feelings about me don't have to be based on fact; they can be based on your own anxiety. On either basis, real or anxiety, these feelings must be devastating to you."
5. "I am sorry you have to go through all this."

You see, in this case, the husband did not do any defending of himself, of the truth, or of the logic of the situation. He simply assumed that his wife's anxious state, built on neurosis, or an expanded obsession, was still a burden to her. To that end, he was willing to help. It is strange to me that husbands and wives will put up with all sorts of phobias until the partner's phobia affects their own behavior. The urge to defend is so strong that we rush to absolve ourselves instead of rushing to assist our partners.

Now, my perfect sci-tech will interrupt me at about this time with, "But, Ms. Hollands, am I not just indulging her with this nonsense? Actually, am I not encouraging this neurosis or anxiety and making it worse by giving it validity?"

The answer is "no." Acknowledging fear in your partner does not presume that you believe the fear is worthwhile, accurate, meaningful, or the truth. It does mean that you believe your partner has the phobia. No amount of denying that fear will make it go away. It is like consoling a child who awakens from a nightmare. No amount of showing him that there are no tigers in the room will stop the "but I saw them here just a moment ago." You console your child, you may attempt logic, but mostly you try to reassure him that you are close by and available.

Tell your partner that you do believe she saw the tigers, that they are not there now, and that you want to be close by and available.

SPLIT-BRAIN THEORIES

The human brain is so organized that two potentially independent mental systems exist side by side. When a surgeon separates these brain parts with a knife, each side still has the capacity to learn, emote, think, and act. But, with the forebrain commissures still intact, these potentially independent neural spheres work cooperatively to maintain a mental union.

Our scientific description of split-brain theory changes every ten years. The era of popularity of the right-brain/left-brain theory will soon end. I think we are embarking now toward the integral brain again. It does not matter to me which era we are in. The only concern I have is that we come to some peace about the possibility of the concept that certain people seem to demonstrate attributed right-brain thinking, while other people (often their partners) seem to demonstrate attributed left-brain thinking.

ENGINEERING SCHOOLS/PARTNERING SCHOOLS

Most engineering schools understand the left-brain mentality of their students. Advanced degrees are conferred upon students who are most successful at left-brain operations. Subsequently, the best of them become educators of the engineering curricula.

The scientific curricula are dominated by courses that solidify serial problem-solving methods and search for the right answers.

The left-brained person tends to concentrate on verbal and symbolic logical reasoning, and the right-brained person seems to use visual and spatial holistic reasoning. A left-brainer will say in class, "I don't know what you want," or, "Give me an example." In an emotional entanglement, the same sci-tech will say, "I don't know what you want," or, "Give me an example."

If only the mate or lover of a sci-tech could be as patient with sci-tech's needs for examples as the engineering professor is. The professor understands that the sci-tech brain needs that sense of orientation to begin to apply principles. Wives can wish on, forever, that their husbands would not need the examples! But they do. Don't judge sci-tech for his lack of creativity in loving you. And don't judge your partner for her lack of order in running her life.

Each of you at birth seems to have been granted your beginner's tool kit. The husband may have gotten a lot of lineal thinking, absolutes, and logic in his kit. His partner may have received strong doses of intuition, spontaneity, and simultaneous responding in her kit. But you can teach each other some new tools. The possibilities for interaction, problem-solving, and being an effective listener are endless. You will need to believe that the communication advantages are worth the effort it will take to teach each other new tools. You will also have to believe that the relationship merits all the practice time it will take to develop these new tools.

LATERALIZATION: USING BOTH SIDES

The ideal couple will use both sides of their brains alternately. Don't worry; we don't expect you to be an ideal couple! If your partner is a sci-tech and you are not, you are going to be very different in your approach to feelings and problem-solving; thus, your reactions to those differences won't be ideal!

But once in a while you can each use both sides of your brain. This is called lateralization of the thought processes between the two hemispheres. The physiological and psychological lateralization of your reactions allows for the shift from a singular dependence on the left brain, with its focus on the correct answer, to the inclusion of the nonlinear right brain, with its attendant capacity for syntheses and holistic approaches to situations.

We have disappointing research data that shows that engineering students whose grades in the first undergraduate years are excellent do not correlate with the original thinkers who later lend themselves to mastery in new frontiers of science. It is difficult to be a good student of structure who works within the letter of the law and, at the same time, to generate the cross-brain work that provides a big-picture mentality.

Many of the elements of communication assets seem to be located in the right-brain hemisphere. The ability to brainstorm, to foresee, and to intuit during judgment all seem more readily available to right-brainers. If that same person can cross over to a structured order for thinking, for diagramming outcomes, and for sequential planning, lateralization is possible. When the left-brainer conceives the whole picture, creatively using a holistic approach, lateralization is again possible.

So, teach each other how to use your computer brains. Sci-tech, teach yourself how to translate you to your partner. Partner, teach yourself how to translate sci-tech to you in case he never becomes good at it. And by all means, translate you to sci-tech.

Here are some of the tools.

To get it across to left-brainer:

1. Communicate by using left-brain models. Use concrete examples, procedural diagrams. Demonstrate with actual case histories, use linear approaches, drawings, maps, or schedules. Talk his language!
2. Don't overwhelm him with emotional content. He can take only so much feeling. Remind him that you will translate your feelings to him on his terms, if he will take some time out to attend to your emotions now. Bargain!
3. Put boundaries and time limits on anything that may be uncomfortable for left-brainer. He can tolerate strong emotion if he feels that it is for only a limited amount of time.
4. Remember to teach by example. Do not assume that your partner will know what you want for your birthday, know how to apologize, or even know how to make love to you. Be explicit, be patient, and *beware* that your partner does not like to be found wrong or have his faults exposed to others.
5. Teach sci-tech that he does not have to be responsible for your feelings. Many times there is nothing he need do but listen to your feelings. He cannot make you blue, sad, or angry. You have a choice with those emotions. The fix-it mentality of a sci-tech may want to repair your emotional damage by explicit action. Let him know that *compassionate understanding* will be the best medicine he can offer.

To get it across to right-brainer:

1. Communicate by using right-brain models. Use holistic, abstract designs. Talk in the language of feelings, empathy, and sensuality.
2. Don't overwhelm her with the facts! Go easy on the logic and the rational conclusions; she can take only so much methodical information. Tell her that you will try to listen to her feelings and that you will try to tell her yours (even though they are not very available to you), but that you would also like her to promise to take some time to go over the sensible approach to an issue when she is

ready for it. (You will be surprised at how sensible your partner can be if she has a chance first to emote some of her feeling reactions.) Try saying, "I feel disappointed, sad, happy, excited. . . ."

3. A method to prevent left-brain responses is to eliminate the word *that*. *Whenever we say "that," we conceptualize our feelings instead of expressing them!* Look at the difference between:
"I feel that you are too permissive with the kids,"
and:
"I feel hurt about the kids."

4. Remember to teach by example. Don't assume that your partner knows you love her, that you are sensually aroused, or that you are sorry. Memorize love poems if you have to, but try sometimes to think and feel as if you were a poet! Be patient, don't be too practical, and *beware* that your partner has emotional nerve endings much closer to the surface than you may have.

ELASTIC, PLASTIC BRAIN

Don't think of the brain as carved in cerebral granite; think of it as elastic or plastic material, which is pliable, adaptable, and able to switch from the left-brain disk to the right-brain floppy disk. Yes, we have a strong proclivity to react in one stance or another, but we also have the capacity to use, improve, and change directions.

The late Swiss psychologist Jean Piaget hypothesized that we develop our intelligence potential in a maturational process. This unfolding of innate biological talents takes its time to bring us to intellectual maturity. New thinking has emerged. And in Bucharest, Dr. Feuerstein has developed ideas about the nature of intelligence and the awakening of dormant mental powers that are being tested all over the world. In fact, we are on the brink of learning, finally, about how we learn.

Our complicated brain has spirited away data about itself, has kept us for so long in primal darkness about how we think, feel, move, and react, that the secrets to our functionability are only now becoming available to us. Until we are sure, though, let's just assume that we can make changes in how we learn, react, and feel, and that in a complementary partnership we each need to learn how to do this switching.

Much of the problem in communication between loved ones is not that each is unmotivated to convey information, but rather that one or more of the partners is actually deprived of communication skills. Adults with impulsive reflexes often jump to conclusions because they do not have the emotional security to give the benefit of the doubt to the partner's accusations. As soon as Richard hears, "Well, Richard, last night you left the room when everyone was waiting for you to react," he will go into an involuntary state of paranoia that he is going to be blamed for the failure of the evening. He does not wait to hear, "But I know that the situation was too upsetting for you to address at that moment, and I'm relieved that you had the opportunity to get away and digest the situation for a brief period."

Even if Richard does hear the conclusion of the statement, he may be so deeply self-centered that he is unable to respond with a real listening ear. Richard cannot give his partner the benefit of the doubt. This happens all the time in dysfunctional couples. They hear only beginnings of complaints; there is no chance for complete transactions.

For those of you who are new to the elastic/plastic concept, consider starting to raise your consciousness with this little exercise. When your partner starts something that you feel will be hard on you, stay in the conversation by saying to yourself or, better, out loud to your partner: "I am going to trust that our relationship can tolerate this conversation. It may feel scary now. I may wish that this were over or that I could run, but I won't. I will trust your good intentions and my own ability to convert something sticky into a possibility for growth for both of us."

Another statement that helps both parties is this: "I know that this may be hard on you. I wish that I were an easier partner for you. I am sorry that you have to go through this with me now."

These statements are magic. I promise you good results if you can say them automatically.

Allow for some *crossover time* for your poor overworked left-brain. Even a nonintellectual woman can begin to take over the more serious aspects of the couple's life if she chooses to give her mate a break. It is sad that so many women wait until they are widows to discover or to demonstrate that they have an enormous capacity to assume responsibility.

The reason that many women do not assume the left-brain tasks while the husband is alive is because they are wary of their husband's criticism. If you can both decide that the wife will not do the bookkeeping or the taxes or the vacation planning in exactly the same way as the husband does, she can try her hand at new work in an unrestrained fashion. Fear of judgment can actually inhibit creativity!

LEARNING TO LEARN

Our poor little three-pound brains (1,375 grams) have ten trillion bits, ten billion switching units, ten thousand memory picture elements, and an average data processing rate that still surpasses the fastest microcomputer we can build.

This little monster must be very cleverly wired and amazingly packaged to allow us to love, laugh, recall, and defend ourselves all in one instance!

Sci-techs love research, empirical data, and any substantiating facts that they can gather on a subject. If I were going to write this book strictly for their benefit, I would pack the pages with footnotes and reference material. I was determined, though, that this book would come from my own experience, and because I am trying to appeal especially to the mate of sci-tech, I will risk not substantiating everything I say. Let me warn you, though, dear partners, that you will fare much better with your man if you can tell him the increase in electricity rates, the square footage of the house that interests you, the horsepower of the car, and the interest rate for the loan you want. Never say simply, "I think we should do this." Showing that you have drawn your conclusions from vital statistics will make much more of an impression on your man.

I enjoy consulting with sci-techs, because they are good students. If I can speak their language and give them rationales for their efforts, they will try anything.

PARTNERS TALK MORE

Yes, we partners seem to be more verbal. My husband thinks I have an answer for everything. In fact, I used to spit out my response even before he got his statement out of his mouth. Finally, after many frustrating arguments in which he would lose the desire to debate with me, he came up with the ideal plan. I use it constantly. He asked me to:

"Close your mouth when I say something. Keep it closed for at least thirty seconds. Then I will assume that you are digesting what I am saying. Even if you are not, and your little mighty brain is already formulating your answer, keep quiet so that I may at least hear my own statement and can digest it myself."

It was such a simple request. So simple to do. And it worked so well. My silence implied to Don that I was contemplating what he said instead of dismissing it too quickly. Don seemed more relaxed. This gave him more time to hear or even respond to my answer.

Probably Don needed the time more than I did. I am quicker to assimilate verbal data. After all, I listen to people all day long. Don, on the other hand, reads much more than I do, looks at graphs, drafting boards, and engineering designs all day long, and is often silent for hours on end. Although Don is highly intelligent, he still needs this process time to cope emotionally with my responses. This is why a discussion of the brain is so complicated. Like our physical health, our emotional life affects our reactions to data. I suspect that one day we will have little X-ray machines following our reactions in our brains. We will watch our partners' computers working out their responses to us. Then the phrase *does not compute* will be more evident than what we experience now. Now we can easily confuse each other with the message of "I think I understand you" coupled with a response that indicates something else.

EMOTIONAL RESPONSES

In an experiment by Stuart Dimond, a psychologist from University College, in Wales, special contact lenses were employed to show films to the right or left hemisphere only. Subjects were asked to rate a variety of films in terms of emotional content. The results demonstrated a significant tendency for the right-hemisphere samples to view the world as more unpleasant, hostile, and emotionally devastating than did the left-hemisphere group. Dr. Dimond's psychologists also found that when both hemispheres were working, the emotional responses were closer to that of the left hemisphere only.

The negativity of the right hemisphere is apparently strongly tempered, then, by our easygoing left hemisphere in our daily lives. This will be no surprise to the partner who is married to a real left-brainer who seems to have no emotional response to deeply touching moments. The detached personality may be sublimely enmeshed in his left hemisphere, where the emotional impact of the right brain is not available to him.

Putting aside the physiological reasons for a left-brainer to be emotionally detached, I have counseled thousands of husband clients who were sci-techs deprived of emotional content as they were growing up. They had learned to cover their feelings, disappointments, and hurts at an early age so well that the search for that deep hurt is not available to them now.

"Don't be a baby. Don't cry. Grow up," all helped persuade the little boy to grow into a man unable to address his feelings. Learning the techniques of showing feelings now will be hard for him. Having those feelings again will not feel good, either. They will hurt him, depress him, convey ill will or discomfort or uneasiness. Why would he want to feel that awful loneliness again when he has so masterfully learned to hide it? Why would he want to learn to show anger when it has heretofore gotten him in trouble? Why would he want to experience his grief over lost loved ones when he has neatly tucked the pain out of the way?

Why? Because he needs to be able to convey himself so that his partner can make contact with him! So that she can feel him, know that he breathes, has a heart, and can experience a wide range of feelings that she can share with him. In this way she can feel his love, test the depth of his feelings for her, and can safely display her own happiness, disappointment, grief, or ecstasy.

And now why should the partner of a sci-tech learn to discipline herself, to put away some of her emotion, and to reach out to others to dissipate some of her pain? Why should she divest herself of some of the energy she would want to invest in her mate?

Why? Because she needs to show her partner that she wants to cooperate with him. If he is to show her love and acceptance and demonstrate the depth of his commitment to her, she must learn discipline so that she can communicate on a level that brings him satisfaction instead of confusion or threats.

Some sci-techs yearn for the ability to try on technical theories at home. They would love to explore scientific information with their wives, to share the newest gadgets, and to feel that their mates could be partners to them in the ways that feed their intellectual or scientific pursuits. A scientist who intellectually starves at home is just as lost as the wife who starves for the emotional connection she needs.

So learn to speak your partner's language. Take a computer class, and don't feel overwhelmed by his electrical-engineering degree or his twenty years of experience. Our technological world is moving so fast these days that an informed newcomer can catch up in some high-technology frontiers very quickly. Since the rapidly expanding video, computer, and semiconductor businesses are all only about ten years old, you have a chance to jump into the information era.

You can also do other things. You can attend a lecture about future technology with your husband, you can read a science fiction book, and you can begin to feel comfortable with the rush of scientific progress. Just as so many wives learned about football, you can learn about the science of our world. It won't hurt; it is no more complicated, really, than football, and your partner deserves a woman who has at least a working knowledge of things that interest him.

What can sci-tech do to learn? Read psychology books, like this one, that address the problems of relationships and communication. And you can go to classes and therapy sessions. For some sci-techs, going to therapy sessions is just as painful as for their partners to go to scientific lectures. But I ask you to consider doing it. It's something like the engine additive STP advertisement that reminds us: "You can pay now, or you can pay later!" If you don't pay attention to each other now, you may pay later.

The "after" is when you discover that your wife has a lover, or that she is asking you to move out, or that she is asking you for a divorce. Or she may ask you to live your own life in the home separately, while she lives her own life in your home without any emotional or physical union. Thousands of couples live this way—too frightened to make a move!

These frightened men eventually come to my office. They feverishly call, they beg, cry, and scream to get their wives back. They try everything. They promise everything! "I'll even go to group therapy or marriage encounter," they shout. "I'll do anything." But sometimes the "anything" is too late. "Nothing" will do. Nothing will fix the relationship. When the last die is cast, it is too late to attend to their partners' needs. Wake up now, my friends, while you may still have a chance. Learn about being together. Learn about your relationships with your partners. Stop lobbying for your positions. Be open to your partners' needs. The right brain and the left brain can live happily ever after.

"Jack Sprat could eat no fat. His wife could eat no lean. And so between them both, you see, they picked the platter clean!" And they didn't argue about which was better, the fat or the lean! And they didn't try to persuade the other to change his/her eating habits!

5

The Sci-Tech Woman

IS SHE DIFFERENT?

Is a sci-tech woman different from a sci-tech man? In what ways are they alike? Are their relationships as difficult as those of male sci-techs? Why were women slow to enter the scientific and technical fields? Can the potential sci-tech woman be spotted in the early years as the man can be predicted? Let me take up some of these questions now.

In many ways sci-techs *are* alike, no matter their sex or their sexual preference. The syndrome discussed in this book is prompted by a very primal thinking reaction. Say that something dreadful or exciting happens. What is her reaction? Does she *think* or *feel* first? Some social scientists will argue that you can't distinguish between thinking and feeling at the initial stage of impact. Let us, then, for the sake of argument, talk about the *manifestation* of a thought or a feeling. It is this expressed manifestation that I am talking about when I distinguish between feeling and thinking. And in my experience, at seminars at Hewlett-Packard, IBM, AT&T, and the like, the sci-tech woman responds in the same style as her male counterpart might.

At home, in an interactional situation, she also responds in the way her male sci-tech may choose. Their initial responses, then, are often similar. The *consequences* of their responses differ, though, because, in general, the woman sci-tech has acquired some extra people skills that her technical brother has not.

This leads to the ways the two sexes are different. I believe that women have been inculcated with some extraordinary relationship and communication skills. Little girls play house, school, and other interactional games much more comfortably than boys do. Little girls play pretend with more regularity. They imagine themselves in different lands, with different ages, families, and occupations. Although boys play war, cowboys, or space cadets, they do not exercise their imaginations about relationships and families as frequently as the girls do. In school, girls are often assigned the nurturing roles in classrooms. They are taught about service and peacemaking and peacekeeping early in their academic careers. In general, girls talk sooner and more than boys do. And they seem never to stop; the men don't catch up. And they seem not even to want to!

LITTLE GIRLS WHO GROW UP . . .

So, if the inculcation provides some general people skills to all prospective women, by the time they have added their technical training they are still far ahead of their male counterparts in the field of interrelating. I can't predict what they will be like when more and more mothers work and when the technology is introduced by mothers earlier into the homes.

I imagine that the sex gap will begin to close as the predicted increase in two-parent-working homes becomes as prevalent in the rest of the United States as it has already become in California. I do know that when I talk to people in Boston, where they have their own silicon area, and in Boca Raton, Florida, and Houston, Texas (other Silicon Valley look-alikes), many of the women seem still to be staying at home. The dual-career couple is not as popular in other areas of the United States, but the statistics are growing. Nevertheless, today's woman seems to learn to share feelings more easily, to listen reflectively better, to show empathy to others more readily, and, in general, to have more interrelationship skills.

The sci-tech woman does have some problems in the workplace. She often is not as assertive as her more emotionally driven sister workers. She has difficulty with leadership and sometimes seems to cower from directing others. Yet she is wonderfully cooperative when taking directions from others. The sci-tech woman does not initiate at work as easily as does the more emotionally based woman.

She is burdened with having to make sense out of everything, and thus is not about to stick her neck out if there is not a rational explanation or argument for her position. Having to be logical can inhibit her ability to demand what she needs from her mate, company, or colleagues. The sci-tech woman is accommodating and a people pleaser, her attitude emanating from shyness as much as from her rational thinking style.

Why is the sci-tech woman often reserved or shy? Perhaps because she had a basic interest in science while so many of her peer girl friends did not. This can inhibit the young woman who wonders why she is so different from her friends. Another reason for the social reserve is that she may have learned to escape (as the men in the sciences and engineering fields do), to hide from the more complicated and sometimes painful interactional communications. The scientific method is predictable. There are no surprises, unlike the unpredictable responses found with people. The sci-tech woman wants a stable, structured environment. Her workmates and loved ones do not always provide this quality of interaction.

Like her male sci-tech counterpart, the woman in the technical field has had consistent reinforcement from her work environment that being on time, being right, and adhering to the rules are important. In the office, our sci-tech woman is not going to cause a major flurry. Her personality is cooperative, she will play by the rules, and generally she will not create anxiety in others.

In her personal relationships, she will yearn for the same predictability and logical underpinnings. The problems created depend on the kind of partner she chooses.

She may choose another sci-tech. Or she may choose a more emotional partner.

CHOOSING ANOTHER SCI-TECH FOR A PARTNER

Our woman sci-tech may choose a man who is like her because she is too reserved to want to attract a more emotional man. The two sci-techs often do end up together, perhaps by default, because each of them hangs back until there are just the two of them left. I am not hinting that the sci-tech woman is not attractive. She is as lovely as any of her sisters, but she is sometimes reserved and shy, less comfortable with social situations than is the more dramatic and emotional woman. When she chooses a man who has the same instincts, whose behavior has also been shaped by his career, their relationship will be very orderly in emotional appearance. Rarely do they have outbursts, uproars are low roars, and the household is fairly stable. Of the two sci-techs, she is often the assertive one, even if her skills are limited.

After the initial prehoneymoon stage when everything is wonderful, these two sci-techs may begin to encounter what will prove to be the major problem of their relationship: *initiating!* Gestures of initiation will be the biggest issue in this quiet partnership. Neither is fully equipped to suggest ideas, to make the move, to demand change or action from his/her partner. Each partner waits for the other to make the move. These moves are about issues of:

Communicating: "I'm not sure he wants to; or that I can."
Sexual advances: "What if I look dumb or behave stupidly?"
Apologies: "I feel silly or awkward."
Sharing feelings: "I'm not good at this."
Suggestions for activities: "Will he really want to do this?"

Sci-tech couples come into my office after long waiting periods. They wait a long time to buy a house, change jobs, have a baby, or even to talk about their problems. They are not as likely to talk about their individual sexual desires either, so they may come in because sex is infrequent, misunderstood, and not very satisfying. This basic reserve causes large reservoirs of resentment inside such a couple. Their problem then is repressed anger, often alleviated by obsessive habits like overeating, compulsive exercise, or alcoholism. This internalized anger must have an outlet somewhere.

The two-tech couple is very organized, of course. Their house is generally neat, their bills are paid, and their life is quite without chaos. They are not the accident-prone, hysteric family with one tragedy after another. In fact, sometimes life is so quiet in the two-tech household that they begin to bore each other to death. Of course, they can't talk about it, nor can one insist that the other get off his duff and do anything about it. So it is the lackluster existence that finally arouses this couple.

Generally, it is the sci-tech woman who yells "ouch." She wants more enthusiasm, more attention, more action. She may not know how to get it, but she really does want it. And she will begin the research project of how to put more spunk into her life. She does not give up, either. She has all the fortitude and stick-to-itiveness of her male counterpart, but add to that the verbal skills that she will use to talk her mate into coming to classes or counseling or reading a particular book, and she has a start on the problem.

In the work arena, sci-tech women seem to have a little harder time getting what they want. Because they have difficulty with intimacy, at work they are more liable to hold back than at home. So only after taking some special supervision courses, or when a particularly sensitive boss squeezes out her feelings, will she get most of her needs met.

The sci-tech woman is also a perfectionist, like the male scientist, and will have some difficulty working with someone who is too creative or impulsive. She is exacting and detail oriented and will be very comfortable if structure is presumed. She is a dependable worker who will stay on track. She circumscribes her life with the scientific formula. Only when a boss or loved one surprises her with a sideswipe will our sci-tech momentarily lose her cool.

When she becomes upset, however, she still will not create a major emotional uproar. Being cautious about scenes, she will choose to respond in a reserved manner, often making her point in a composed but firm way.

Sarcasm is a tool used frequently by the sci-tech woman. It is easier than saying something directly. The barb is generally meant to sting, but she seems unable to deliver the sting straight to the target.

She is very good at putting things in writing. She is usually one of the "Action Line" letter writers. She also likes to write disgruntled letters to the editor or complaint letters to organizations. It is much easier to put it in writing than to face the problems head to head with another person. She is not cowardly; she is simply not in the practice of saying things in an assertive manner. She has taken the passive path, and trying on new behavior is frightening and sometimes, without the needed practice, deadly.

Two sci-techs who marry or fall in love or work together can usually adopt a living/loving/working style that is efficient for both of them until or unless the system is interrupted by a new element: a child, relatives, new employees, another person in the environment. Then there are more decisions to address, more judgment calls to make, and a host of subtle and overt choices because the field of influence now incorporates more than the two of them. So the battle lines get drawn. He wants the kids to go back to Iowa for the summer; she wants them to stay here and go to computer camp. Each member of the couple is unequipped to be a salesperson for his/her choice, and neither is prepared for the full-scale negotiating that may now be necessary.

They usually can't fight well, either. With little experience in fighting or in showing emotion, when confronted, both tend to take flight rather than fight. Both partners will be frightened about the intensity of the emotion, and they both will probably abandon the ship midstream, giving in or running away. If our sci-tech woman gives in, she will ultimately resent her partner, but giving in at the time seems easier than staying there and battling for her position. The problem with this choice of action is that eventually the resentment builds up and usually has no appropriate outlet, so she explodes without cause, or, worse, runs away permanently. When two martyrs get together they both end up doing what they hate, not getting what they need, and feeling guilty at the same time. This deadly combination does not feel very good; no wonder they will try to stay away from fights at the next opportunity.

WHEN SHE CHOOSES A MORE EMOTIONAL PARTNER

Like the sci-tech man, the woman scientist or engineer may feel some holes in her personality. Most of us look for someone whom we can love who will fill those cavities for us. These choices may be unconscious and subtle. "I never thought about how outgoing he was before we got married," she frets now, "until I later discovered that the poor man never wants to be alone for one moment."

Looking for our complements is a good idea. The problem is that we often find too much of a good thing, or the good thing becomes too much of a good thing when we have a large dose of it. Then we accentuate the negative. "He gets so upset about his family; I never knew any man could rant and rave so about his seventy-five-year-old father. My husband is really such a baby." What was our strength to our partner in the beginning becomes our weakness as time prevails upon the union. "It's not funny anymore" is the phrase I hear in my office. "I used to think it was cute when he did that; now I think it's ridiculous!"

When we marry or work with our opposites, we still have some options. We can complain and feel victimized, or we can set about to integrate the differences, or we can negotiate behavioral change!

Sylvia, director of research for TTR Company, was thrilled with her outgoing, playful lover, Rob. But after several years of marriage and of Rob's tricks, toys, and childlike behavior, Sylvia was fed up. Rob now seemed simply foolish and immature. And Sylvia felt like a grouch and an old prude. All Rob could do was create a loud fuss and call her a "stale bore," and all she could do was call Rob an immature baby who never made sense. Pulling out all the stops, Sylvia proved, via her perfect logic, that Rob had been irresponsible and that she should file for divorce. Rob's reaction was hurt and panic, and, of course, he responded with the very histrionics about which Sylvia had been complaining.

The problems unique to the Silicon Syndrome woman sci-tech and her mate are that she may eventually not be as interested in sexuality as her male sci-tech counterpart, who usually remains very eager to express himself in that way. It's possible that she is not able to initiate, cannot express herself easily in sexual experiences, and will not want her partner to make overtures to her unless he creates a "foreplay" atmosphere before the couple attempts to be together.

Why does this woman sometimes lose her interest in sexual encounters with her emotional man? Since she is not assertive, after the initial stage of getting together when partners are sensitive to every little nuance of desire in each other, she will not be able to express easily her needs to her mate. She may be feeling amorous or interested, but her partner is not mind-reading and misses her needs altogether. Unless she can come right out and ask for what she wants, and she often can't, this couple will miss an opportunity for affectional bonding.

She begins to build up a storehouse of resentments about this apparently insensitive man who can't intuit exactly what she wants. It is hard to feel sensually interested in a partner when old hurts get in front of the sensual or sexual interests. *A unique difference between men and women is that men can be sexual or make love even when they are mad at their partners. Women find this very difficult to do.* Now, I will probably have many of the exceptions call me about this, but, in general, men can compartmentalize sex better than women can!

Last, our sci-tech woman begins to lose confidence in herself because her partner complains about her style. "She is so cold, so unemotional, wants everything just right first. Unless the dishes are all done, the kids are snoring, and I am freshly shaved, she isn't interested." Of course, this is all exaggeration, but it comes close to what the husband may be feeling. When she loses her self-esteem about her approach style, the relationship is in big trouble. The more edgy she feels about her approach style, the more awkward her attempts. This creates a phobia that will not allow her to relax at all. "I am not good at this; I'm not sexy enough. I have to do it better this time. He just doesn't find me interesting enough." All these anxieties create so much fear that she will be unable to present her sensuality or her desires. This vicious circle can be broken with encouragement from her spouse, or from some internal confidence-building in our sci-tech.

There are many sci-tech women who are totally confident and who have wonderful sex and affectionate lives with their mates. In this book, however, I have time and space to address only the *problems* of the Silicon Syndrome partnership.

To conclude this section, let me tell you that sci-techs of both sexes, and in homosexual relationships as well, seem to have an added surge of passion available to them in sexual encounters. The sci-techs may not be able to tell you how passionately they feel about you, but, given ample foreplay, they are able to show it. This can surely be a surprise to the unsuspecting mate who is used to the reserved and unemotional partner in most other arenas. What a welcome surprise that the partner who is usually demure in most emotional settings can turn "tiger" when it comes to sex. But this added surge usually comes after things have gotten started. I still contend that the "getting started" is harder for the sci-tech, who, in general, doesn't take risks easily. These sexual ambiguities can confuse and disarm partners who have come to expect predictability in these sci-techs.

PROBLEMS OF SELF-EXPRESSION FOR SOME SCI-TECH WOMEN

Sci-tech women have little trouble expressing themselves when the topic is technical or concerns something with which they are intimately involved. They are on shaky ground, though, when the subject is a new one, or particularly when it is one in which they are called upon to share their innermost emotions.

Here are some hints for safe self-expression:
• *Try out your feelings in no-risk situations.* Share them with your baby, your baby-sitter, or your gas-station attendant. Say, "Dave, I am really in a hurry to get this gas pumped because my husband and I are having some marital difficulties just now, and we had a little fight and because of that I am late for work." Now Dave, the gas-station attendant, does not care at all about your marital difficulties. He will pass off the comment with a grain of salt. He hears all kinds of strange and hysteric things all day long. Your baby may not be able to decipher your explanations, and your baby-sitter may not care either. But what you need is practice!
• *Visualize in advance your persuasive presentations.* No matter the content, if it is going to be difficult for you, practice first in your head. Then fantasize the whole experiment. You will tell the boss

exactly what you need and he will understand and offer you a promotion. Always visualize the successful interchange. Your anxieties will take care of the unsuccessful ones for you anyway! Practicing to yourself will give you the "run through" experience that makes for perfection.

• *Delivery style: Start with being dramatic.* This simply means extending your feelings. S-t-r-e-t-c-h your emotions so that your body moves are bigger and your voice is bigger too. Don't worry about blowing people away. Generally you are so low-key in delivery that even with exaggeration, you still will not appear outrageous. Most sci-techs, male or female, are terribly afraid of feeling ridiculous. They will inhibit any creativity because they think they will look or sound foolish. Mirror or video work is great for reality-testing this new behavior.

• *Meet resistance with anticipated response.* Think out ahead of time: Will the audience enjoy my talk or are they sleepy after lunch, or is my topic too clinical? Will my husband want to talk about his overeating right now? Will my friend at this time be ready for the hint about her boisterous manner? Anticipating these reactions doesn't make them go away. But it does prepare you. Surprises catch us off guard and snap shut the synapses, prohibiting us from thinking or responding clearly.

• *Allow for silence.* Silence is deadly to the withdrawn or shy person. You imagine that the other person is gathering his armor, stacking the defense, and getting ready to shoot the cannon. You do not imagine that the other person *may* be just as uncomfortable with the delay as you are. Let your silences work for you. If your partner is uncomfortable, that is okay. You do not have to be an articulate debater. You simply have to be grounded enough, and calm enough, to be able to present your feelings. The silence can be just enough "white space" to equip you for sharing your next set of feelings—if you can let the silence work for you instead of scaring you.

THE EXECUTIVE SCI-TECH WOMAN

There are many high-powered, high-tech women whom this book will not address. You may be a sci-tech who has acquired enough skills for expressing your emotions that you will not have any of the problems of the described syndrome. I am not going to address the inequities of the sci-tech woman in the man's sci-tech world. I agree that these women have not yet been paid or been assigned responsibilities commensurate with their talents, but I have faith that their marvelous combination of skills will one day be recognized in the world. That women can be technically organized and still have the basic communication skills to manage people is a bonus in itself.

THE BASIC DIFFERENCE BETWEEN ALL MEN AND ALL WOMEN

I have discovered in doing group therapy for the past ten years that there is a difference in content material between men's groups and women's groups. There is a similar difference between my male and my female individual patients. And the difference shows when three or four women gather in almost any setting, as opposed to when three or four men gather. The difference is that *when women meet without men, they talk about men a majority of the time*. But when men meet in any setting, they *do not talk about women the majority of the time*. From this we can conclude that women have a greater need to discuss the issues about men than the men do about females. Or we can decide that men are so complicated to women that they must talk to other women about them to gain some understanding. My husband calls us an "alien culture." Another hypothesis is that men don't talk about women as much because they don't feel that discussing the dilemma with others will bring any new understanding.

My own theory is simply that women are more comfortable talking about relationships in general, and that they trust that other women will enjoy, or at least understand, the explorations of men as they discuss them. I think men are uncomfortable in discussions about the opposite sex, and that they are even more uncomfortable displaying vulnerability in the presence of another person.

An interesting phenomenon arises, then, when the situation later reverses itself. If a man feels his wife or woman is abandoning him, he becomes much more unstable and emotionally unfit than does a woman who is left by her partner. If the man really wants the relationship, he will be frantic to reconnect. We may conclude, then, that although women may more consistently talk about their men when they are not with them, it is the male population that becomes emotionally vulnerable when abandonment issues arise. Funny animals, we males and females. Eve does most of the talking and emoting, but Adam goes dependent if she tries to leave him.

THE SCI-TECH WOMAN WHO DOES NOT FIT
IN THE CORPORATE WORLD

There are a few women who are technically minded, who use the scientific method to respond, and who generally think before they feel, but who do not fit well in the corporate, high-tech, fast-paced world. You may be one of them, or you may know or love one of them.

In her struggle to grow up, this sci-tech woman missed some basic nurturing or self-confidence building. I am not saying that her parents were not wonderful people who tried to do their best for her. Many of us as parents make every effort for a particular child and still do them a disservice. So our sci-tech woman may be without the emotional resources to handle the tough-mindedness of the business mentality.

I have this kind of woman in my office every day. She usually ends up in the personnel department, no matter her technical beginnings, because she has as a cause the case of human dignity, consciousness-raising for her company, and a great desire to create a peaceful environment for her organization. She is not competitive, will not join the race—in fact, she hates the race, and is thus out of her element in the man-eat-man or woman-eat-woman system.

Her personality traits are often submissive, although she can rise on her soapbox if there is a cause she believes in. In a stance of righteous indignation she will abandon the "corporate" rather than try to integrate her humanity and sensitivity with their aggressiveness. Her style is to flee, to look for other arenas where her talents can be better used. She *often* retreats to jobs beneath her talents because she gives up trying to teach her values to the corporate world.

My statement to this woman is that the corporation does need you. Be patient as they (the corporate unconscious) grow, shift, and change. The profit motive will get in the way sometimes. The fear of allowing for humanity and showing feelings will disenchant some of your superiors and decision-makers.

When I consult with top-level executive officers, I do not use the word *afraid* in my exercises with them. They are afraid of the word, so I steer away from such references. I do use *concern* or get them to use "I have reservations about," which is easier to say. It is difficult for the executive who was taught as a child to be brave and not to show fear or to speak of anxiety in an open and revealing way. His vulnerability is overwhelming.

I could tell this woman to find a "softer" job. She can move to the soft sciences, or to the humanities, where she will not have to face the defenses of the male or the society that cherishes aggression and competition.

I won't tell her to do that. I will say the same thing I say to disgruntled wives who find their husbands so difficult or to secretaries who find their bosses so hard-nosed.

Translate that *tough-fragile*. Be patient. Don't expect immediate results. Use his talents to complement your own. And teach. And teach. And teach. You have an educational challenge that can enhance your own life, my life, and the world at large. Accept it.

6

Sci-Tech Couples and Sex

SEXUAL COMMUNICATION

"I think you are supposed to be doing something now, Claude."

Sci-tech men can be a little slow getting started. And a little slow in the middle parts, and a little slow in the end. Other than that, they are perfect!

Now, don't get me wrong. Their partners aren't so perfect either. It is difficult for any two human beings to be together physically and have it be all right for both of them. Sci-techs come in all sexual forms. They are rabbits, robots, and robbers. They are also rockets, rams, and reindeer. They actually fit every category that all other human males fit. But, in this chapter, I will concentrate on some of the characteristics highly prevalent in sci-tech partnerships.

In order to put back the romance, we will have to learn about the form of communication that being sexual takes. First, of course, we will have to learn about our partners—their needs, their fantasies, and their fears.

The sexual act is a form of communication. Of course, there are many forms of communication. Some couples communicate best on the tennis court. They simply feel at home together on the court. No couple in the country club can beat them at doubles.

Other couples communicate at the bridge table. When the two sit down, you can almost hear the sigh of contentment and the feeling of being at home.

Being at home with someone else is what Al Pesso, Psychomotor founder and my brilliant teacher, calls the "soul connection." It is when two people feel like one. You've had friends who say or think the same thing that you say or think at the exact moment! The soul connection is that synchronized experience that happens at the same time for both people.

In perfect communication, both partners are on the same wavelength. It feels divine. Two people who meet and go to bed that same night can have a peak experience. It can be exciting, exhilarating, fascinating, and probably cannot be repeated.

The soul connection requires much more. It falls into synchronization only with a stable, more secure relationship, one in which each member accepts the partner unconditionally, and, further, is highly motivated to prove this acceptance to the partner.

Sci-tech men have some difficulty allowing themselves the uninhibited pleasure of being entirely available to their sexuality.

Before we define those inhibitors, let's talk about the difference between "sexuality" and "sensuality." The dictionary addresses "sexuality" in terms of a sexual organ. Many people also think of sex as an orgasmic conclusion, one that eventuates in a physical release. To be sure, that is a fine conclusion, but there is more. "Sensuality" is the ability to experience all senses, to know and to feel and to accept all sensations that manifest themselves both physically and emotionally. In my mind, "sexuality" and "sensuality" can be used interchangeably. Since this text is not a lexicographic dissertation, but a practical manual to help couples understand each other, let's use the two words interchangeably! Putting back the romance calls for understanding your partner and yourself, and for putting together a soothing plan that will not sacrifice either of you and will use the best that each of you can bring to a sexual/sensual relationship. But first . . .

THE SEXUAL INHIBITORS

THE ENLARGED BRAIN

The genius's mind works overtime. It usually does not stop when he gets ready for bed. Or it stops completely! Therefore, he may need a little help from his partner to remind him of what to do, what she needs from him, and even what it is he likes! This absent-minded professor will sometimes have a very low libido. He has used it up on other things, or he has really never developed a great interest in the subject.

Basically he is sensitive, usually from having been laughed at or teased when he was an adolescent (professors at age 15 are not too popular), and he will use this sensitivity on his partner when she can get his attention. The only problem I foresee is if he suddenly has a passage into a midlife trauma or a new-woman crisis, and may discover belatedly his sexuality with a partner other than his wife. His mate can handle this if she can keep her ego intact and can place the blame on a latent sexual need and not on him, who is, in fact, quite innocent about his own transgressions. Neither partner understands the game very well.

His wife will try to perk her husband up whenever he slips back into his head and loses emotional contact with her. A patient woman with lots of energy, she will spend countless necessary hours teaching him, helping him to notice her, and continuing to inspire him. The only stumbling block is when he has a latent passage into an adolescentlike sexuality. But she can survive all this with understanding.

This sci-tech has a brain that figuratively swallows his body. His head is so full of wonderful technology that it serves him well. It is so powerful that the heady man underuses the rest of his body.

His brain gets him out of all kinds of trouble; it is used in all the tight spots of his life, except the bedroom. In this place, his body is called upon to perform, to be charming, to move and titillate, and to express the passion that only his brain has expressed until this point. This man's body is slow to engage, weak and shallow (in terms of expression), and is very noncommunicative when called upon to show affection.

His enlarged brain overworks most of the time. It is hard for him to shut off his brain and just allow his body to respond spontaneously.

Now, I know that even in sex the brain must function. We are never without our nervous system telling our body what to do or telling our body what it likes and doesn't like. So we can't shut off the brain entirely. But we can begin to push out thoughts, to close the screen to the niggling little phrases of problems that keep us from being body-present. Turning off your brain is like turning off your eyes. When you close them, you can hear better, feel more, and actually experience massage and other pleasures more fully. By turning off your brain, you are putting out worries and issues and allowing yourself to hear better, to feel more, and actually to experience what your heart and body are experiencing.

But Big Brain has a hard time stopping the thoughts. His

partner will have to work very hard to help him be available to his body. Here are some methods for doing this:

1. Ask your partner to share his thoughts, his brain teasers, any ideas that keep him from being available to you now.
2. Tell him that you want him to close down his brain for just a little while, and remind him that he will be able to return to thinking in an hour or two.
3. Suggest turning down the lights and the music (sensual and soft, of course), and ask to help him remove his shoes, tie, etc.
4. With more caution, slowly help your partner to relax. You are really going to ask him to go into a hypnotic state. But don't, for heaven's sake, tell him that. That would scare him to death! Yet, you are indeed going to ask him to go into a slightly altered state (and, of course, he can return to consciousness immediately; he never really loses consciousness). The altered state is one in which he will be relaxed enough to begin to close out the nagging thoughts of work, or even the other kinds of thoughts such as, "This is silly, what am I doing here, trying to act like James Bond?"
5. When your partner seems to be out of his head and into his body, proceed. . . .

THE SERIOUS MIND

This sci-tech is as dependable as clockwork. He does not vary his methods, his approach, his sexual techniques, or his pajamas. He will be faithful, nondemanding, monogamous, and ever available. Who could ask for anything more?

No one, if he/she has an unpredictable mate to make things lively, drag in new incense, candles, and bedroom surprises that manage to keep the relationship just a little off center so that neither partner falls asleep before the party begins.

She has to control her impulses so that she won't scare him, and he has to learn to put a little variety into his lovemaking, especially when she is out of ideas.

This sci-tech has a brain and a body that have been equipped for serious functioning. He never learned to play; he does not know how to be silly, to giggle, or to horse around. Even when he is passionate, it is about wanting you too much, actually even being addicted, and certainly, about sex, being very serious about needing release. He will go to whatever extremes to get that release, being the practical type. He can even act childlike sometimes, pretending fun if it will bring the orgasm or the sexual fulfillment that he wants.

But really having fun is not possible for him. He was probably born serious. Being in that womb and just staying alive was serious business! As he grew up, he may have learned that Mother or Dad wasn't too happy to have him around. In fact, having a baby was a big burden to his parents. He learned early that life was hard, you have to work very hard; it's no bowl of cherries out there!

A serious-minded fellow often picks a lighter spirit for a partner. And sometimes that light spirit is so light that Mr. Serious has to stay on his toes just to keep them both out of hot water. He doesn't allow himself to laugh, usually because he has created a chaotic partnership, or because, out of frustration, his partner has jumped into fun and games just to get some comic relief.

Here are some methods to get Mr. Silicon Syndrome to begin to play at life:

1. Tell your partner that you will take on part of the burdens. "John, I'm going to discipline the boys for the next two weeks," or, "How about my doing the finances for a while?" (It is important that you demonstrate confidence, so be sure that you add something like, "I know that I have not had a long history of financial stability, but I am ready to make a major transformation in my approach to our finances.")

2. Teach your partner how to play without ridiculing him or making him feel too foolish. Tell him about the difference between childish (acting like a child) and childlike (doing things a child would do while still maintaining adulthood). Try this: "Phil, I know that this will feel a little silly to you, but it is important to me to see you being playful sometimes, so let's just nuzzle each other like puppies for a while. You can be a big Saint Bernard, and I will be a little cocker spaniel."

3. Being playful takes practice, lots of practice! Don't expect him to be able to have fun for too long. After a brief period of time, return to a more serious matter, so that he can assume a more comfortable position.

WHAT HAS ALL THIS TO DO WITH SEX?

A serious-minded, large-brained man does not even begin to feel sexual until he is ready to give up his thoughts. That readiness state requires that he shed some of the responsibility of having to think and of having to be in control. Giving up control is the hardest thing in the world. A good example I can give to mother/wives is the feeling you experienced when you first left your child at nursery school or kindergarten. You were lost and empty and without mooring. The engineer/scientist is lost without the use of his ability to be logical and rational.

A couple who can be together with comfortable, sensual charm that pleases both of them is lucky. They can assume, persuade, titillate, and inform each other with their actions. When this form of communication is not available, couples wonder, "Am I doing the right thing?" "Does he want me to make the next move?" "What is she wanting from me now?" He imagines, "I think I should be doing something right now." If he could just let his partner know that he is in doubt about what to do, both could relax!

THE NEED TO SLOW DOWN

Sometimes the sci-tech is the high-strung, hyperactive type who is always in gear, running about, doing something, thinking something, planning something. He is a performer—in all areas! In the professional world he ends up in administration, usually as a manager or supervisor. He has so much energy that he can't stay in his own field of expertise; he has to be suggesting, urging, or motivating someone at all times. So he gets promoted.

He uses his high energy to get things done. He will also want to get things done at home, in bed, with you. He is passionate for release, response, and schedule. He will complain if you are not together often enough. He is quick to remind you about what night tonight is, and, frankly, he is not too subtle in his approach to being physical together.

Methods for slowing him down:

1. Teach him about tunnel vision. Tell him that you want him to set aside all other matters in his life. He will need help in learning how to focus. And he will need a lot of help in learning how to focus on *you*. Talk to him about

eye contact, about body language, and about the words of affection that will pull you in his direction.

2. When you have fine-tuned him to be available to you, for this one moment, for this one interaction, you will next want to teach him to stop analyzing or criticizing. He must stop the technical observations that are a complete turn-off to most of us. "Did you? How was it? What did you like best?" are important questions, ones that need addressing at some point, but he needs to learn the proper timing for such questions. Teach him that for now you want simply a sweet and delicate interplay between the two of you. Later you can dissect the union!

3. Ask him to begin to experience the sense of your being together. Teach him that the destination is not nearly as exciting as the journey. This will be the hardest thing for him to understand. As a results man, the bottom line is the outcome. Tell him how the kisses, the sweet caresses, the gentle whispers, even the pauses, silent and solemn, can feel wonderful. Slow the old boy down!

GOOD SEX, LOUSY RELATIONSHIP

Many of us are confused if we have a good relationship and a poor sexual life. This is accounted for because being sexual is a learned behavior. Even people who love each other may never have learned how to demonstrate their physical reactions.

More confusing is a lousy relationship in which the sex life is wonderful. Disappointed couples come to me when they realize that the only thing they have in their relationship is the ability to express their sexuality together. That is not enough. Because it feels so good, though, it complicates matters for a couple who don't understand their mixed reactions to each other.

If you can have only a limited number of success patterns between you, good sex is one of the better assets to have. But don't delude yourself into thinking that good sex can cure all the ills in your relationship. It can postpone some problems; it can't save the marriage!

Many couples on the brink of separation will report the best sexual relationship in their couple history. And they worry that once they actually do split up, they will never be able to live without the great physical life they have had together. But herein lies the surprise! For when the relationship is truly over, the sex dies too. Oh, there may be a few last gasps (and grasps), but couples who do separate generally discover that they don't miss each other sexually at all. With the absence of the old incumbent problems of the ailing relationship, a new contentment sets in, the kind of contentment that only sex brought before. If there aren't so many arguments, there aren't so many calls for making up.

Once again, I want to point out that if you *are* saying goodbye, you may experience the best sex life you've ever had. Watch out for this because it can really throw you off base. The truth is that the profound and painful parting, the pathos of the ending, actually brings forth *emotion* about each other. This strong emotion (from pain, not love) is confusing because it generates excitement in the partnership. Our bodies are confounded by double messages: "I hate this guy; why am I eager for his touch?" You can really be perplexed by the enormity of your sexual reactions. In most cases, I warn couples in advance about the possibility of this startling reaction. I also warn about drawing any inferences about the health of the relationship because sexual energy is high. It is like making love on the night of a funeral. There is emotion; where to spend it is confusing!

Nevertheless, an adequate sex life can do much to keep a sci-tech marriage alive. When the sci-tech is quiet emotionally and does not give the verbal feedback his partner craves, if he is sexually assertive, even exciting sometimes, it can save an otherwise dry relationship.

It is surprising and wonderful that many engineer/scientists can actually allow themselves to be playful, passionate, and initiating in this one area of their lives. If they can then learn to transfer this skill to social interactions, to emotional conversations, to being psychologically sensitive to their partners, there is a chance for a completely fulfilling relationship.

WHAT IT TAKES TO MAINTAIN A GOOD SEXUAL RELATIONSHIP

The major prerequisite to a good sex life is high *self-esteem*. Having esteem for your individual sexuality and being able to feel that you deserve good treatment will enhance your physical life together.

Oh, there are people with terrible self-esteem who use their sexuality as a means of getting love and affection. They don't actually believe that they deserve good treatment, and so to get any treatment at all they have maneuvered ways to receive love through sexual favors. People with very active sex lives do sometimes suffer from a very low ego. The ego needs to be raised before any work on the sexual alliances can be addressed. These people say to me, "I just don't know why I do it. I find myself in these same situations over and over again."

The second prerequisite to a good sex life is *information*. I am continually amazed at how little sophisticated people know about their bodies, about their partners, and about techniques to enhance sexual relationships. Try something as simple as the information below:

- You can be sexual without touching sexual organs.
- You can be sexual while touching sexual organs.
- You can be independent while being sexual.
- Talking about your sexual needs does not have to spoil things!

Communicating your sensual feelings can be accomplished in many ways. You can touch with your feelings and you can touch with your words. Engineers do love to talk about the technical aspects of their lives; they often have difficulty talking about the sexual sides of their lives.

One of my client couples went away for a luxurious anniversary weekend. The morning after the anniversary night they strolled into a scrumptious champagne brunch, compliments of the hotel. Martha, delighted with their night before and wishing somehow to prolong it, said happily into Harold's ear, "Let's talk about last night, honey. I'll tell you what I liked best, and you tell me what you liked best."

Now, Harold, intent on eyeing the luxurious bruncheon table, retorted quite unromantically, "What, at breakfast?"

This couple could have found a way to elongate their sexual communication. Obviously, breakfast was not the way. If Martha had cheerfully said, "Okay, then, maybe later, huh, honey?" instead of being devastated and hurt (which for her took away all of the prior night!), they may have found a way to soothe each other.

To check out your sexual-relationship possibilities, go over the list below for review.

DID YOU KNOW THAT . . .

1. Most men don't know that women enjoy being sexually assertive when given permission to be so.

2. Most women don't realize that men enjoy being sexually passive when given permission to be so.
3. Most people still think that masturbation is a lower form of sexuality, as opposed to intercourse.
4. Many men did not masturbate as youths. Even more women did not.
5. Sex therapists project that only 30 percent of women are able to have orgasms with a penis inserted in their vagina. I believe that 50 percent of the people don't know this. And I believe that 80 percent of the people who know this continue to hope it isn't so.
6. The penis does not work on command. Neither does the clitoris. The brain is the most important sexual organ in both sexes.
7. Most first encounters are clumsy, embarrassing, and often cause a delayed-stress syndrome later.
8. Premature ejaculation can often be altered by relaxation techniques, by analysis of parental and religious prohibitions, and by reeducation of the penis by physical techniques.
9. Most people are uncomfortable with street-language words for sex.
10. Most people are uncomfortable with clinical sexual language for sex.
11. Lots of couples make up their own love words for their sex.
12. Many people feel bored with their sex lives.
13. Most people talk more about their dog or cat or their income-tax forms than they do about their sex lives.

ABOUT AFFAIRS

Affairs happen when marriages suffer. We reach outside when we are not getting our needs met from within. Overcoming the affair may be the hardest task you will ever have, whether you are the wife, the husband, or the lover. Affairs are symptoms of dysfunctional marriages. Knowing this doesn't help much when it happens to you.

I'm not talking about the pathological need to continue to find new relationships. And I'm not talking about philanderers, nymphomaniacs, or womanizers who need different partners in order to breathe.

I am talking about the *once in a lifetime* interlude that can scare the heck out of all concerned! There are a few accidental interludes that do occur in very good marriages, but 99 percent of the time an affair occurs when there is trouble in the marriage; usually big trouble!

Most people think it will never happen to them. It is like death. It happens in other families, not our own. Until it happens . . .

I've had clients who swear to me that their mate would never or could never have an affair. They remind me that the husband has never spent one night away from the house in eleven years. I remind them of the affair that went on for sixteen years, during the lunch hours, track meets, and afterschool events of the school in which the two lovers taught.

I am not trying to scare you, but I want you to be alert to the possibility that even the most shy, introverted, and emotionally clumsy partner can stumble into a hot romance. When the tether is jiggled a little, we learn quickly. Don't be complacent and rule out the possibility of an affair for your mate, no matter the age, social graces, appearance, or apparent disinterest in the opposite sex, or sex at all.

Don't kindle your paranoia, either. If you choose to make a career out of suspecting your mate, you may be wasting your time and emotional energy.

Let's talk first about the affair itself. The new relationship can be enchanting. So delightful. So exciting. So filled with stolen moments. Often one person is the more reluctant party, afraid, resistant, hesitant. But it is awfully hard to resist someone's adoration of you. Nothing is more flattering, more titillating than someone who wants you even when you belong to another.

Affairs do not always culminate in sexual encounters. Sometimes the experience of being with someone who listens, who wants to be with you, and who seems to appreciate your existence is enough.

But usually, after the first hint, it doesn't take long to get the flame going. The first flutter of air brings oxygen into the romance. After that, watch out. It takes little encouragement to turn it into a full bonfire.

We can get a lot of mileage out of an affair. Moments of love can be stretched out with long phone conversations. Soft moments can be prolonged by reliving the experience. Talking about the rendezvous to your lover, your friends, or any one who will listen is nearly as much fun as the original experience.

Scientists who never talked to their wives, especially about their sex lives, suddenly find themselves in the most delicious exploration of their sexual discoveries. When I hear how wonderful they feel about being able to tell the new lady "everything," I always wish that they had been able to talk to their wives in that way. Those same sexual conversations might have been possible earlier with their mates, if only . . .

It has been said that the titillation of an affair can breathe new life into an old marriage. But this is a hard way to introduce excitement into a union. Yes, sometimes there is a temporary improvement in the marriage when one partner is getting new satisfaction elsewhere. Paradoxically, the sex life even improves considerably at home for a while. I still think this is a circuitous route for getting some life into a sickly relationship.

If your marriage is failing, instead of an affair, try something like this: "You know, honey, our marriage is so bad and so stale right now that I *feel* like I would like to start an affair. In fact, I am already attracted to someone at the office, so I know that we are on dangerous ground. Please help me get us back together again. I don't want to follow this temptation."

There are really no rules about affairs. It would be easy for all concerned if there were. In the state of California, we have "no fault" dissolutions so that a victim spouse cannot even claim vindication in the courts. I have seen women who twenty years later still carry poison because of husbands who left them for other women. Of course, women do not have the only license for vindictive behavior. Many men cannot let go of the anger toward a mate who left them for someone else.

The transgressor is only partly at fault. That is the hard part for the person who feels rejected and abandoned to grasp. Yet, until each member of the team is willing to look at the precursers to this interlude, there is no chance for permanent reconciliation.

The victim often has difficulty taking any responsibility for the deterioration of the marriage. Yet, if you don't eventually take your share of responsibility, the marriage is doomed, even if the affair ends. Here are some questions to ask yourself:

1. Was I available?
2. Did I read the signs of estrangement?
3. Have I been distracted?
4. Did I ignore or reject my mate?
5. Have I done my share sexually?

6. Did my partner feel love from me? Respect? Comfort?
7. Have I known, lately, what my partner has been wanting from life? From me?
8. Have I made efforts at relationship renewal?
9. Have I provided openings for my mate to talk to me?
10. Have I deliberately or unconsciously turned my face from the truth?

The engineer/scientist personality is not that of the prototypic person who seeks an affair. I do not think affairs come naturally to our scientist. He would not generally take this course as a relief from a marriage. Working long hours, turning to television, reading, exercise, or alcohol are more usual escape routes for the sci-tech personality.

I am not saying that sci-techs don't have affairs. They do. But they have them with more trepidation than does the romanticist or the hysteric male, or even the salesman. Characteristically, the sci-tech does not easily fit an extra relationship into his structured life.

When the exceptions strike, however, and they do, our sci-tech is usually overwhelmed by being in love with a second woman.

The sci-tech in an affair will surprise himself with how deeply moved he can be. The enormity of the possibilities that such a liaison can provide is staggering. Being a human being, and usually coming from a dry relationship, the sci-tech will be immensely excited and pleased by a new and scintillating relationship.

It can be so overwhelming that hypertension, general anxiety, and many other psychosomatic illnesses prevail on the poor sci-tech, thus preventing him from completely enjoying the new liaison. Often the sci-tech is like a schoolboy in love, and he can completely ignore his usual business practices because of this out-of-the-ordinary experience. This adds to the tension.

Wives of the sci-tech also reach outside the marriage. And sci-tech women can have affairs too. In fact, women are beginning to have affairs in the same way that businessmen used to have them. In California, more divorces are initiated by women than by men. And more women tell me about affairs they have initiated than do men. A woman of the eighties is no longer as shy about making initiating gestures toward men.

Take the discontented and discouraged woman who learns to be assertive. Now add an era of instant sanctions, and we have a woman who is probably an easier candidate for an affair than is her husband who seems to be a bit more conservative.

But no matter the sex, the sci-tech who falls out of a dry relationship into the arms of a passionate, giving lover can become completely addicted to the new relationship.

The male sci-tech is usually bowled over by the idea of being infatuated again. He is often immensely pleased with the new and exciting relationship. He becomes temporarily hysteric in temperament. He can't make decisions, and he becomes giddy, anxious, and completely and hopelessly hooked on the new person. Fortunately, this is usually a temporary condition. . . .

Trying to handle, no less love, two women at one time will ultimately be a sci-tech's undoing. He can lose sleep, job, money, erections, and his own self-esteem over such a predicament.

Generally a sci-tech will be relieved when the affair is over. He can also be very relieved when his wife's affair ends. He may not even comprehend the possibility of her unfaithfulness, so she often has to shake him with the hurtful truth. A sci-tech does not equip himself to handle the devastation of his wife's infidelity. Like a child without resource, he aimlessly broods, often afraid to talk to anyone about what his wife is doing.

Sometimes the sci-tech leaves his wife and ends up marrying and living successfully with the new and more compatible woman. Sometimes he just stays addicted and pathetic, at the whim and mercy of his lover.

And sometimes he returns to his wife. This is the hard part. Then the couple will need a reconciliation phase, to recuperate and renew their trust, love, and communication skills. Sometimes when the man comes home, because of obligations and family guilt, or even company pressures, he is home no more than an hour and a half before he feels that he made a mistake to return.

I try to persuade both partners that the return must always be conditional, depending on the length and breadth of the affair and the emotional balance left between husband and wife. It's hard to talk reconciliation conditions to the woman who felt abandoned and now receives her husband back into her home and heart. Often if the return is premature, there will be a second leaving. That is always more painful than the first one.

If both parties can just believe that the return sometimes takes a few tries, they will not be so distressed by the stuttering return. To leave took courage. To return, to start trying new boundaries, to release resentments, to create a new and profound relationship, perhaps for the first time, is rough. Very rough. Very frightening for all concerned.

The odds for marital recovery after an affair are the same as those following any tragedy or mishap that occurs in a marriage. People get divorced when a child dies. People get divorced when a partner inherits money or gets a promotion. Anything can get a marriage into dangerous waters. An affair does not have to sink your couple-ship!

What recovery takes, though, is maturity—lots of maturity—to reinstate the trusting relationship. Sometimes both parties have to do a lot of soul-searching. The person who has reached out of the marriage will have to build a faith bridge again, convincing by performance, not by promises, that he will be faithful. And the injured party may need to share the anger and tremendous hurt. This person may need to work through the primal issue of abandonment.

Life after the affair takes guts. Each member of the team has work to do. The person who temporarily left the marriage may have to say goodbye to the relationship that pulled him away. He may mourn that relationship for a long time. Sometimes that takes years. It is a quiet grief. A "why did it have to end?" or "why can't I love two people?" grief. And the injured member has to forgive and forget the transgression. Sometimes that takes years. It is a quiet grief too. A "why did it have to happen?" or "why can't I be enough?" grief.

And sometimes the grief is not too quiet. Sometimes it is downright noisy! The victim may yell and kick and scream and want to hear every detail of the partner's liaisons. The compulsive person who will not allow self-discipline can hang on to being the abused party forever. There is a fine line between telling and keeping information from the spouse when the affair is finally brought to the surface. Frankly, I think those decisions depend entirely on the maturity of both members of the marriage.

Often we give up too soon. We are afraid to hurt each other again, afraid of the conflict, of the consequences of reconciliation. A couple may give up a long marriage simply because they are battle-weary. Yet that last stand may win the war; it may bring peace. Try it. Try one more time. It is possible to go back. It is hard. It is humiliating or scary, or both. But we heal. . . .

Mending the remnants after an affair is possible. The repair work is tricky, often fraught with new territory never before touched in the relationship. When egos and jealousy and rejection complicate an already delicate balance, it is hard to make the adjustment.

You will not be the same again. That is all right. You will also never be 25 again. Or naturally blond. Or in the fourth grade. Don't mourn the preaffair mentality. You are wiser now. But not necessarily more cynical, either. It is possible to have an affair interrupt your life and survive it. Survive it very well. With new wisdom, new skills to communicate, and an important hurdle that you both stepped over together—perhaps not simultaneously, but together.

THE ONE-THIRD SYSTEM IN SEX

Because it is likely that the sci-tech and his partner have some sexual problems, I suggest that you contract for your sex life in the same way that you do for other areas of your life.

> One-third of the time do things her way.
> One-third of the time do things his way.
> One-third of the time do things in a compromise (his/her) fashion.

The sci-tech does not usually believe in compromise. He wants to have things purely his way some of the time. But basically he is a very accommodating fellow, really wants to please, and is happy when his partner can also be satisfied.

It is funny how few couples learn, on their own, the notion of the one-third method of being sexual. We try to be idealistic and imagine that we can actually please each other just because we have good intentions. Sorry, no. That does not work!

An important complication to the idealized approach is that we imagine that we know what will please our partner, or, worse, we imagine that our partner knows what will please us! Sorry again.

So the intelligent couple will sit down and talk about ideal scenarios for each partner.

One-third of the time:

For Lucy: A long romantic dinner, both partners in formal clothes, music in the background, children out of sight, with John reciting poetry or humming lightly between bites. Eventually John will share verbally his most intimate desires for her and will carry her off to their bedroom, whereupon he will share again some new insights about how much he loves Lucy.

One-third of the time:

For John: Lucy will meet him at the door, nude, will feed him, dance seductively (no singing), and will lead him off to the bedroom. Lucy will then proceed to do to John all his heart's desires, never resting, never looking inhibited, and always seeming to be excited by John's body.

One-third of the time:

John and Lucy compromise: John and Lucy go to a sophisticatedly erotic movie, stroll home quietly, make love to each other on the couch, and, finally, have cornflakes and bananas in the kitchen and go to bed and watch the late news.

SILICON COUPLES AND SEX

The above suggestions may be extreme, and they are certainly not explicit enough (it is important that you talk to each other precisely about what sexual methods you most enjoy, what you are not too fond of, and what could make it more palatable for you). Just as you have made certain decisions about how the holidays should be handled, you need to make certain decisions about how you want to be together physically.

Giving your sexuality is like giving other gifts. About sex, we need to think of giving gifts to each other. "No, Bob, I am not really interested tonight, but I would like to be there for you anyway. I love you and I would like to give you the gift of my attention, even if the idea does not wholly excite me tonight."

Let's go back to some of the couples we dealt with earlier and see how they cope with their sex lives.

THE CAUTIOUS AND THE RISK TAKER

Experimentation will not be part of the repertoire, unless the risk taker takes the time to convince her cautious husband that trying some new things may be good for their relationship. While she's doing her sales pitch, she needs also to convince him that if he does try something new, he may feel a little uncomfortable, but he must not let himself worry about feeling foolish.

She loves to try new things. She thrives on excitement, so he will have to learn to surprise her with his own innovations once in a while, just to keep her interested. She shouldn't expect the innovations to be about sex, though. She will be lucky if he gives her some suggestive nighties; that's as close as he may get to experimenting!

THE ASSERTIVE AND THE PASSIVE

Surrendering is difficult for a man who lives to have things under control at all times. He is always fearful that he will be called on to handle something beyond his capabilities; he shrinks from demands by his partner. No fear, though, because his partner is herself so afraid that she is not about to test his tolerance level.

This couple desperately needs to learn the art of alternating responsibility. If she can convince him that men enjoy playing the passive role sometimes, and that she would actually like to be seductive and assertive with him once in a while, the possibilities are enormous. Both members will be hesitant in new roles, and it will take some real trust to begin some healthy new patterns for this stuck couple. She needs lots of courage to take on her sci-tech. If she can convince him that it is like hypnosis (one can always return to a conscious state at any time during the trance), she may be able to persuade him to surrender control. He's probably hypertensive and, health-wise, will eventually be prescribed relaxation techniques anyway!

THE HIGH PROFILE AND THE LOW PROFILE

Since he can do anything in his professional life, he will want to believe that he can do anything in his personal life. This can be very confusing if his body refuses to cooperate. He needs a spouse who can understand his need for a satisfying image, even if it is in the bathroom mirror. I am not saying he is conceited or self-centered. He is self-concerned, and he does need to feel that he is powerful and can handle anything that stands in his way. Heaven help him if he discovers his wife having an affair, because it will be very hard for him to adjust to her reaching out to anyone else when he is so readily available or wants to be. Even if he is terribly distracted with work, his intention is to be all things to his mate.

Sexually speaking, she does not cause waves. She does not want the spotlight. Rather, she is content for sci-tech to steal every show and is happy just to be his woman. She realizes that he has some ego bruises and is not as powerful in all areas as he might wish to be, and she is just as delicate with his sexual ego as she is in other areas of his life.

Although many corporate people use up much of their libido in sublimation forms, creating and pulling off big mergers and seducing General Motors, they still need to feel potent and desirable on the home front. Low Profile understands this, is careful not to hurt her partner, and actually appreciates the great responsibility he is willing to assume in every area of their life together.

THE DATA SEEKER AND THE BEHAVIORIST

This researcher will always be looking for the perfect orgasm. He will read a lot of books in pursuit of the ideal love experience. He gathers data with vigor. He especially enjoys data collections about things and scientific systems. He finds humans, and particularly women, a little confusing. He just can't predict their behavior.

His behaviorist wife will save him because she will bring in the big picture. "Honey, I know that those positions are very tempting, but they really won't work given the size of our bedroom." The psychologist in her will remind him of the overall goal—sexual communication. She realizes his hunger for information, and she will have to work herself into his research picture. Because she understands human nature and his nature so well, she will be able to shape her mate's behavior with a little basic, "When you finish that, darling, let's try this. *Reader's Digest* published a report that seventy-six percent of women . . ."

THE DEPENDABLE AND THE FLAMBOYANT

He would not be able to think of the magical antics that she uses to tickle his fancy. For some reason, perhaps his unconscious desire for mental health, he can tolerate bizarre and almost foolish behavior in his mate. This makes for a very interesting sex life for our unique couple. He makes no overt moves; she wiggles constantly. She is never the same. He is never different. He really needs his wife to spark up an otherwise pretty dull routine.

He needs to add his own surprises once in a while so that she won't die from her own antics. She also needs the rest now and then and will expect him to try introducing an exercise into their sex lives. To outsiders this couple may seem outrageously different. Inside, and with themselves, they complement each other perfectly!

THE RATIONAL AND THE HYSTERIC

He doesn't know that feelings don't have to make any sense. That is why he has a hard time being wildly emotional when he is sexually aroused. He tries, though! He might even let out a little "gulp" now and then. His stilted behavior keeps him from being playful.

Thank goodness, he usually picks as his mate someone who is not afraid to laugh at herself, who is kind about laughing with him and not at him, and who will introduce him to the joys of a giggle now and then. She will remind him about their human condition. She will laugh about it, teaching him to expose parts of himself . . . safely!

THE INDIVIDUALIST AND THE JOINER

This individual-contributor type will have a hard time in the teamsmanship of lovemaking. A solo person who does things better on his own, he absolutely needs someone who is not afraid to push him and let him know that she is there too.

She can teach him to collaborate, a skill he no doubt needs at work and at play. She will be the social type who can introduce him to the joys of people. If she has enough confidence, she will also introduce her loner to the joys of sex (for two). Her goal will be to teach him about mutually satisfying methods, not just sequential moves designed to please one at a time!

DISAPPOINTMENT WITH SEX

Look at your life and think about any disappointments you have about your sex life. Don't cloud your recall with the good points, but stay with the ways you have been disappointed. It may be difficult to admit that your sex life falls short of your hopes and dreams. Would you have imagined that you would be making love only once a month? Would you have believed that you could feel so bored, tired, or dispassionate after so little time or after so long a time?

George doesn't kiss you the way he used to. Martha rushes off to sleep without even a brush against your lips. Margie always wears her nightgown to bed now; worse, a flannel one! Malcolm snores louder and sleeps longer. He gazes less deeply into your eyes. In fact, you seem never even to make eye contact! You don't cuddle together on the couch, pet in the car, or spend long weekends in the bedroom.

Most couples eventually experience some disappointment about their sex lives. Don't be discouraged if you do not feel the glow that warmed your relationship in the beginning. After a couple has settled into the second era of their partnership (the length of the first era depends on the individual couple; for some it takes years, others months), there will be another era in which you begin to establish the *comfortable phase*. In this mellow phase, you can take great joy in the security of knowing that the relationship is a profound one, one you do not want to trade for the excitement of those earlier days.

But the settling-in period is a little scary. Insecure or uninformed couples wonder if something is wrong because "we just don't do those silly little things as often." Even after a few weeks, a torrid relationship can lose some momentum and become a little more humdrum.

It is quite all right to miss some things in a relationship. But it is very important to talk about the things you do miss, or to worry out loud that you have begun to take each other for granted. A sci-tech actually looks forward to the peace and security of a stable relationship. He is not as likely to complain about being bored as his partner is. He wants the structure and surety of the familiar. It is helpful to his psyche to know that things are going to stay the same; he does not enjoy change.

So be sure to talk about your needs. Tell each other about small disappointments, and talk about those early, passionate moments. I call the first era the free-ride time. Everything was wonderful. Each of you could do no wrong. You were eagerly stimulated by each other's every move. Simultaneous orgasms were abundant. (Funny how later they sometimes disappear altogether—quite normal, by the way.)

We can be reluctant to talk about what really makes us sad about our sex lives. Lilly bursts into tears when she realizes that Burt never tickles her when she reads the newspaper now. Burt feels hurt that Lilly doesn't massage his feet anymore. This doesn't mean that Burt must start tickling or that Lilly ought to start the foot massages again; but it does mean that both Lilly and Burt should talk about their respective losses, perhaps as a healthy evolution to new ways to please each other.

Don't just groan, though. When you are listing the sins of omission, be sure to recall the good things that are happening in your relationship. Assessing your improvements is important, too. As you make changes, there will be subtractions and additions to your repertoire. Share with each other the new behaviors you do like, even if they are not as passionate as the earlier techniques of being together.

ABOUT HURTS

The second area worth mourning is the past hurts we've inflicted on each other. Some hurts were accidents; some were unconscious; some were deliberate. All hurt!

It is hard to make love to someone who has just yelled at your mother or forgotten your anniversary or thrown out your favorite fishing jacket.

Because the scars are often very deep and very painful, some of you will say, "Let well enough alone. Why bring it up now?"

Well, sometimes "alone" is not "well enough." It is actually therapeutic to tell each other about a hurtful event or period in your life, especially if your partner was involved. The letting go or releasing of the feelings can cleanse you so that you are really available to each other again. Sometimes it takes more energy to hold the feelings in than to let them be relieved!

After thirty-seven years of marriage, Heather discovered that she had never really forgiven Simon for the affair he had had some twenty-five years earlier. At the time it occurred, Heather was too hurt, surprised, and confused to talk about it. Later she became too frightened to talk about it. Simon passed up all opportunities to bare his soul. Neither mentioned the interlude for twenty-five years! Yet Heather quietly grieved on, persecuting Simon—in so many ways. Sexually, Heather withheld her love.

Their sex life had disintegrated to the point where Simon made sexual gestures about once a month, and Heather either rejected the overtures or stoically pacified Simon. She also rejected many of Simon's philosophies, and she would degrade Simon in front of the children. Neither partner quite understood why. Of course, the children were confused.

One day in my office, in the presence of Simon, Heather spilled out all of her pain, the twenty-five years of stored hatred, of unspoken disappointment, of disrespect for Simon, of a bruised ego of her own.

Instead of denying, or defending himself, or confronting her for bringing up dead wood, I warned Simon to try some new responses, like, "I know, Heather. I know."

With such a response, Heather was really able to look at Simon, through her tears, and to hear that he too had some sad feelings about the whole problem. When she began to consider Simon, at last, instead of experiencing only her own pain and disillusionment, she was finally able to tell him that she was forgiving him. There were still some things she wanted to say, needed to hear from Simon. Simon, instead of trying to rush out of the conversation, began to look at this as healing for Heather, and took his time to listen, comfort, and finally to share some of his own pain, the guilt, embarrassment, and fear. Twenty-five years later, this couple sat in my office shedding tears as though the affair had happened yesterday.

Simon at last had a chance to grieve. He grieved the loss of Heather, of the trust that she had withheld all those years, of the faithful Heather who had turned cynic so early in their relationship and who had closed down a part of her so many years ago. Many sessions later (when Heather was emotionally strong), Simon even got to tell her of the way the other woman had so sacrificially sent him back to his wife. "And all those years I've been hating her instead of knowing that she had a hand in your returning to me," Heather said with compassion after all the tormented years of wishing the other woman were dead.

Here's another example of grieving and sex. Felix had physically beaten up Juanita for the first five years of their marriage. A long time after he had stopped the behavior, they came in for counseling. They had never discussed that earlier period, but Juanita continued to bear the emotional scars. Felix, an honorable man who had great responsibility at one of our local atomic laboratories, had loathed himself for those temper displays. A disciplined man in work and play, he really never forgave himself for the lack of discipline he had displayed in the early days of trying to understand living with Juanita. He felt intense sorrow for the humiliation he had caused his wife.

Finally, ten years after the beatings had ceased, when Felix was a model husband cherishing Juanita in every way, they were finally ready to share the pain and agony of the torrents of emotion that had scarred them both.

Their presenting problem was their son, Nicholas. Only by accident did we stumble on Felix's past behavior, although I had seen some terrible grief in the pain in Felix's eyes. The problem with Nicholas was minor, but Felix's phobia that he might lose his temper and hit Nicholas in the way he had abused his wife was major.

Felix and Juanita openly grieved over those past events. And then they began to heal. No longer harboring the hurtful memories, Juanita could open herself to being a sexual being again, to being gentle and trusting with Felix, to feeling playful with him at last.

This couple's sexual problem was Juanita's frigidity with Felix. She could no longer surrender to a man who had mistreated her, and there had been no process for mending the hurts. With patience on Felix's part, the couple began to mend.

One last couple—Jack and Rose. Their presenting problem was Jack's impotence. He had difficulty staying aroused and even more difficulty wanting to consider sex. This low sexual arousal was brought on by deep secrets and resentments manifested sexually by Jack. For many years Rose, who feared exposing the information to Jack, had known the whereabouts of Jack's child. The child's mother, Jack's first lover, had given him up for adoption. When Jack learned that Rose had withheld this information, he was irate, but he could not safely discharge his anger on Rose without implicating himself in the affair. So each lived with the awful secret they kept from the other, using all their sexual energy to hold back the truth and the anger each felt. This form of withholding carried over to Jack's sexual life.

When Jack was fired from his fifth job, the couple came for help. In therapy, Jack discovered the connection between losing his job and losing his son. Jack had been grieving for his son. To compound things, Jack had been grieving for Rose's misplaced loyalty, which he dismissed when he learned that Rose had not told him the truth.

When Jack allowed himself to grieve the loss of the son and the loss of Rose's loyalty, he began to mend. Rose's good intentions in making the decision to withold information were not the issue. All that really mattered was Jack's translation of the events. After the grieving period, Jack could begin to be rational in his approach to things, and he even began to forgive Rose. Eventually he was able to thank her for her behavior. Then each partner felt free again, and Jack began to surrender himself sexually at last. Sexual and emotional "exposure" and withholding had complicated this relationship.

We often translate actions, our own or our loved ones', in ways that hurt us. If we can't talk about our translations, we can't begin to settle our differences. Sci-techs hold on to their pain, their hurts, their own realities. They do not open themselves to other interpretations. Partners do the same thing. We are all most biased about our own rational translations, no matter how much they may ultimately hurt our relationship communication.

Look into your heart to see if anything needs mending in your relationship. Talking about old mates, lovers, old sexual assaults, or incestuous experiences can be immensely healing when you are not trying to defend yourself or trying to make the other person wrong. A reconnecting process can start with a soul-searching discussion of past pain.

EMOTIONAL FOREPLAY

Everybody understands physical foreplay. Emotional foreplay requires much more explanation. It really means preparing yourself and your partner for that delicate physical human condition of ultimate connection. You will have to learn just what each of you needs to begin that readying process.

Some of you will want to begin the seduction subtleties about four hours before the final physical act. You will want your partner to begin talking to you sweetly or touching you in loving ways the moment you see each other. Dinner can be a very sensuous experience, each of you savoring the expressions of the other person, and allowing a teasing atmosphere to prevail.

Talk about sexual expectations can be very arousing to some people. It is important that you begin to discover what feels, sounds, and looks inviting to your partner. Sharing the turn-on signals is important to a relationship.

Don't keep 'em guessing. Please! It can be fun in some instances, but I have heard too many surprise endings to believe that we are good at guessing what our partners want.

Emotional foreplay sometimes requires an exchange of anger before you can begin the journey toward love. Getting something off your chest before you make love is better than trying to get it off during the lovemaking! That can result in premature ejaculations, withholding of orgasms, and some very indelicate massage techniques! Check each other out about your feelings. If one person is still stuck with feeling mad about something, it would be more helpful to ask her/him to try to share the angry feelings than to gloss over them.

ON WITH THE MUSIC

Making love can be like a symphony. Remember all the foreplay at the symphony? The light violin strokes, the bustle of the people as they take their seats, the sound of the crisp programs, and the entrance of the maestro as he triumphantly approaches the platform.

By the time the first note is sounded, you are ready. Can you compare this to the way in which you ready yourself and your partner for the state of making love?

And the symphony begins. The rest of the symphony can be a mixing of passion, quiet and gentle sounds, harmony, stirring great music. Let your lovemaking experience feel like a concert, with ebbs and tides, crescendos and light movements, all in the interest of the grand experience. Reading your partner and feeding back information are very important to your own successful concert.

AFTER THE CONCERT

Again, you may have to negotiate and perhaps compromise about what happens after you have made love. Some people want to drop off to sleep immediately, others want to talk. Still others want to get up and eat cornflakes and bananas. Many of you will want to be completely disconnected from your lover, bathing in your own saturated and satisfied body. Still others want to prolong the exquisite feelings of closeness, wrapping themselves in or around their lovers for the remainder of the time together.

Your "after concert" will depend on how well sci-tech and you communicate. Not on how well you make love! And these conclusionary moments are very important. Don't tarnish them with misunderstandings.

Do not take someone else's ending style as a reflection on you. The way your partner uses his knife or fork is no indication of the way he/she loves you. So it is with afterplay. He does not intend disrespect if he starts to snore immediately following orgasm. But you had better start talking about that if it bothers you. If you have strong wishes to assist your partner in changing any behavior, start with a careful conversation in a neutral place, not the bedroom.

Don't take your partner's habits personally. Since endings are important, make sure that you can talk about how to close your lovemaking times together. Sci-techs usually don't want to talk about their love times. They have enough difficulty verbally communicating their feelings of sexuality, so sometimes the digestion of the feelings will in itself take up all the aftertime.

Put the finishing touches on your relationship by closing your physical experience together with a combination of moves that pleases both of you. And be patient if it takes months, maybe years, to find the perfect musical scale to define your relationship. The tune will come. And the music will be a love song.

7

Sci-Tech Couples
and Money

FINANCIAL PROBLEMS

Financial problems in Silicon Syndrome couples are symptoms of incompatibility. Generally speaking, though, the problems are more those of communication about money than they are about basic value differences. Usually, you just don't know how to talk to each other about money. And you certainly don't know how to plan, negotiate, or contract about what to do with financial differences.

I will now present some of our Silicon Syndrome couples in reference to their money problems. Don't be offended if you spot your relationship. I hope that you do. The problems are really a matter of becoming aware of your polarities and then finding the methods that can bring you closer together. By the way, the amount of money in a relationship has nothing to do with the agony experienced about the subject. You can add or subtract zeros in the conversation, but the symptoms of the problems are still the same. See if you can get any insights about yourself from the following couples.

THE CAUTIOUS AND THE RISK TAKER
He does things by the numbers. Therefore, the numbers are important to him. He is ruled by rules, governed by the law of averages and by actuarial tables. Because he is so cautious, he probably will not spend with the flair that she needs now and then. So he will have to take some lessons in luxury spending just to keep her around.

The risk taker often gives way to her hysteric nature. She also gives away anything within her reach. She could happily spend all their money if her partner did not have such a foolproof system of checks and balances. This couple absolutely needs a discretionary money fund for her so she can spend a certain amount each month as she pleases. It does not matter if she works and earns her own money or not. The fund does not have to be large, but she needs some extra cash to be able to "luxuriate" in her own sense of independence. He could also use discretionary money to put into an emergency fund or into his favorite savings account. She cannot expect him ever to suggest anything frivolous if it costs money. She can put the suggestion into effect herself, however, because even he needs a change of pace now and then, and surely he will not ask for it!

THE DEPENDABLE AND THE FLAMBOYANT

He is as dependable a provider as one could ask for. He also spends and saves and organizes with the same degree of regularity. His creditors just love him. He never misses a payment, is never late, and is absolutely reliable with anyone but his wife.

She wants a change of pace! She will change banks and checkbook colors just to get a little excitement into her life. Since he is so consistent, it is up to her to do something adventurous about their financial life.

"Let's take a flyer," she says. Worse, or better (I don't know which; it will depend on his ability to adjust to change), "I've just taken a flyer. I invested half of our savings in pornographic films."

THE HIGH PROFILE AND THE LOW PROFILE

Since High Profile thinks he can do anything, he will probably want to be omnipotent with money too. Generally, he is pretty good at managing his resources. He will get into trouble only if his ego dips a little and he decides to pay the bills for everyone at lunches and weekend activities. She will remind him about this if it begins to hurt the checkbook seriously. He will want to control the finances at home too. It will be hard to share that responsibility with her. In fine complementary style, though, she does not need the image that her sci-tech does, so she doesn't mind pursuing most of his values! She also does not mind driving the VW ("I actually feel better in it," she protests), while he drives the Mercedes, of course! He may choose a "hotter" car, though, a faster, zippier one, maybe a one-of-a-kind if this one-of-a-kind man can manage that!

The passive partner does not mind watching him, listening to him, or yielding to his intense ideas about what is right or wrong. Brilliantly she finds a way to have an interest or a project for which he has no concern, and in that arena she makes all the decisions. At banquets and parties she is willing to let him have the limelight. She is even willing to let him make most of the financial decisions. If she can keep up her interest and not let him completely dominate their financial life, she will keep up his interest in her. Basically, she will have to understand his self-centeredness while she also learns to take care of her own needs. The individualist will not do that for her. She needs to plan for herself so that she does not slip into "martyr"!

THE GENIUS AND THE RELIEF

Unless finance is his field of expertise, Genius will be as absent-minded about money as he is about other things. His brain works constantly on high-level projects; it is always twisting and turning and trying out new formulas, but money may seem pretty mundane to him. Since he does not have a high level of need for "things," he will probably not have a great emotional interest in earning, spending, or managing money.

If, though, he does have a strong interest in resources, he will be a genius about money too. Lucky for his partner, because she is really a fan, not an entrepreneur. She will be happy to cheer him on, but do not wait for her to make the expert moves. Ever an optimist, though, Relief can bail out her genius if he dips too far into the reaches of his brain for a scheme that our economy is not yet prepared for!

On the sidelines, she cheers away. Although he seems completely unconscious about the mundane aspects of life, it is her constant reminder that will keep him in this world. She is the perfect mate for him because she will keep him awake, always bringing up the subject, reminding him, "Defense, defense," or, "Come on, honey, just one more!" Basically cooperative and specific about things, she can assist him when he goes into his technological cloud. When they play Monopoly, she always wins, even though he is always planning the ultimate strategy. Sounds a little like their home life too!

THE DATA SEEKER AND THE BEHAVIORIST

He can't get enough information on where to spend his money, how to make more, and how to save it. He has ledgers and forms and books on every facet of his financial life. Of course, he prepares his own income-tax forms (even does it on the side, sometimes, for others as an extra business). He enjoys predictable profits and has difficulty with anyone who thinks that money can't buy happiness. "I never saw a happy poor man," is his motto.

Thank goodness for his behaviorist wife! She will teach him that money doesn't buy everything; she will plead for the kids' allowances, and she will help him look at the strategic options when considering financial moves. She will teach him about politics and behavior modification. She will teach him that some human beings are not motivated by money, will not be impressed by it, and will not be bought off at any price. If she is smart, though (and she is), she will also acknowledge his love for research, and she will volunteer to go to seminars on investments and surprise him with a subscription to *Making Money Count* magazine.

THE RATIONAL AND THE HYSTERIC

He is very serious about his financial life. I say his financial life because she is the minor stockholder in the family's financial scheme. She is too busy getting a kick out of life to try to be a complement to him. She can be a comic relief if he ever makes a mistake in his financial wanderings. She will laugh about it, laugh it off with him, and then let him recharge until he is ready to begin again.

When he is really depressed, he will eventually see the viability of making light of things. When he is on top, though, it is harder for him to see her point. He can be very self-righteous about making and spending money and will give the hysteric a bad time if she does not make logical decisions. If she can keep her sense of humor even when he speaks from atop his ivory money tower, she will be able to keep her perspective about their relationship.

"It's only money, honey," is not a funny song for him. But she will need to keep humming this to herself when he gets on one of his tyrannical high horses!

THE INDIVIDUALIST AND THE JOINER

He is the classic bachelor who happens to be married. He still thinks, acts, spends, earns, and organizes as if he were the sole proprietor of this agency, his household. Heaven help his wife if they have children with whom to share, divide, or counsel the financial estate.

But she does not back off. She is secure enough in her own right that she is willing to push him. "I want mine too," she says. If he spends $115 every time he goes on a fishing trip, she elects to spend $115 on herself. She is not afraid of getting into his territory. It's a good thing, too, because the individualist is not one to volunteer to share anything. She takes her half. She will also have to teach him some teamsmanship, while he makes attempts to teach her about boundaries. This couple has a good chance of becoming "whole" if they can listen to each other without defending their positions too strongly.

INCOME VERSUS OUTGO

I think I have heard it all. I've heard about the $100,000-a-year executive who gets a $5 weekly allowance from his wife and takes his lunch to work in a brown bag. I've heard about the $25,000-a-year man who may be fired next week, but who feels he must buy his wife a $40,000 Mercedes-Benz.

I've heard of the wife who scrimps and saves while her husband gambles away $200 to $500 each week. I've heard of both partners in a couple overspending or both partners afraid to cash their two-year-old paychecks. I've even heard of a man who lost $5,000 because he waited more than five years to cash his check, and then it was too late!

Now I am going to introduce you to the perfect couple and the ways they divide their responsibilities, their resources, and their rewards. Each Thompson works. He is a biologist earning $45,000 a year. His name is Joe. Linda Thompson owns a small boutique, brings home about $10,000 a year, and has an initial investment of $70,000 in the business. Sci-tech Joe is interested in stability, wants to retire to a mountain cabin in ten years, and is not interested in spending their money on anything frivolous now, except for his new Jaguar.

They put all their money (accounts receivable) down on paper, divide the accounts payable, and account for unscheduled expenses, fixed expenses, luxury items, and maintenance items. Then they write down exactly how each member of the team will spend his/her money each month. Of course, Joe has the most bills assigned to him because he has the bigger income, but they plan the accounts-payable list so that each member ends up with $200 extra per month for discretionary money. That is secret money that neither member needs to report. Joe usually puts his discretionary money in a small-funds account through his company. Once each quarter he keeps about $75 and spends it on camera equipment or on software for his personal computer.

Linda spends all her discretionary money on gifts for her mother and her friends. Joe does not believe in lavishing gifts on others. It used to be uncomfortable for him when Linda spent too much on her mother, but the money Linda spends now is not an intrusion on Joe's conservative nature because he never sees it. Once in a while Linda takes Joe out to an expensive restaurant, and whenever she goes on a buying trip for the store she takes Joe, putting it all on her expense account, including such indulgences as expensive meals and motel rooms. Since Joe does not pay for this directly (her company does), they trick each other into allowing Joe to relax about the costs of those weekends. "I feel like I am a customer, being wined and dined (and made love to, oops!), and it is wonderful fun. It honestly would not feel as good if the money were coming out of our regular account, although I know that indirectly I am paying for this."

It does not matter who makes the most money in the Thompson marriage. This pair has decided that each member is doing the best that he/she can to earn what is possible for him/her right now, and the outgo should still be divided relative to their incomes.

Suppose a wife, Cynthia, has been working since she was 15 years old, has made a very good salary for the last ten years, then suddenly decides that she wants to goof off for about three years. With a sci-tech husband, all Cynthia has to do is show him the outside boundaries (three years) and promise to return to income contribution at that time. Her husband will cooperate since he understands that Cynthia will eventually bring increased financial vitality to the marriage.

Two lawyer partners are married. The wife has a baby; the husband wants paternity leave. Molly is not as infatuated with parenthood, actually is in the throes of a big career move, and she is delighted that husband Dick wants to stay home three days a week with the new baby. Dick also wants to rest a little, play tennis, and learn about babies. He is relieved that they can afford to live on their reduced income. Although Dick will make only one-fourth his former income, he will still have the same rights and privileges as he had before the paternity leave. This is clearly a contract that is democratically decided upon. Sometime in the future Molly may want the same kind of sabbatical. I'm sure that Dick will grant it!

WHEN THE WIFE HAS NEVER WORKED OUTSIDE THE HOME

I believe that you should look at your financial life just like a corporation does. The wife who stays home attending to the household, comforting her husband, attending to their children, and entertaining customers, is actually like the vice-president of domestic affairs, or the vice-president of domestic engineering, whichever title appeals to her. She is as important to the corporation as is her husband, the vice-president of outreach, who goes to the outside job each day and brings home a check at the end of the month. It's kind of strange to me that in the state of California it often takes a divorce settlement for a wife or a husband to realize that a wife, whether or not she works outside the home, is contributing to the estate's accrual of assets. Sometimes it takes the divorce for the couple to realize that half of the estate belongs to her, even if she did not work for it in the business sense.

If couples could decide that the wife earns half of everything every moment that she is in the marriage, many marriages might be saved. Instead, wives leave their marriages in disgust, because they were unable to declare their independence within their marriages. Take a look at your own roles in your financial structure today. No matter what your income contribution is, duties and privileges must be assigned.

I urge couples to look at their married estate and divide the responsibility and authority over the estate while the marriage is solid. Often this can serve to ensure the life of the marriage. Of course, some marriages cannot be saved by mere financial independence, but many could be aided by this kind of preventive information between partners long before the relationship deteriorates.

PULL, PARTNER, PULL!

With a sci-tech man having a need for perfection, control, and being right, it is sometimes difficult for his partner to wrestle away any decision-making authority. But she must! If she does not make this move toward independence, she will ultimately be a Cinderella Complex woman who waits for the knight in shining armor to rescue her from a life of financial deprivation.

So even when a woman does not work outside the home, her responsibility to the relationship is to negotiate partial control of the finances. If she is not willing to assume the *responsibility* as well as the rewards of decision-making, she will ultimately resent her husband and experience herself as the wayward child who wants what she wants regardless of whether her parents (husband) can afford it.

A sci-tech man who wants complete control sabotages the mate who wants this kind of independence. He is the same partner who says, "Oh, I have to buy my wife this new Mercedes-Benz," when he himself would like to have this kind of a car. It is easier for him to use her as the scapegoat ("my extravagant wife") than to take responsibility for his own wishes. He should try this approach: "I would really like the Mercedes-Benz; it is expensive and I could blame my wife for it; but the truth is that I want this automobile for myself."

A sci-tech man sabotages because his mate has often demonstrated no history of being able to accept the responsibility of managing finances. When the wife acts like a child about money, she often is treated like a child. She will need a training period. Even a conscientious mate who is trying very hard to accept responsibility will goof because she has not had enough practice in using this authority. Managing the books, projecting finances, and planning how to spend takes time and practice. If the mate is new at this job, allow for some adjustment period. Sometimes the new responsibility goes straight to her head and she spends foolishly and forgets the hard parts of bookkeeping. Just like the kid with his first allowance, she may spend all of the first stipend at the candy store, but eventually she will learn to disburse the allowance over longer and longer periods of time.

RESOURCE EXCHANGES

In your partnership, each of you is better than the other at some facets of your financial life. Let me describe the separate aspects of money management.

Earners. Some of us are wonderful about earning money. We can hold three jobs, earn more than anyone else in the real-estate office, or be the top performer in all the western states. The earner knows how to "turn a dollar." He/she can accumulate income very easily. Usually this person likes to work, is ambitious and energetic, and fortunately soon discovers what kind of work he will be well paid for. My husband and I are both earners. We have both worked since we were very young, have always been offered jobs wherever we've gone, and interview very well for potential bonuses and new opportunities. We enjoy earning; it is easy. For others, the notion of earning is difficult. They have always found their rewards "short" for the effort.

Spenders. A good spender enjoys the very act of purchasing, is not too distressed as the money or check leaves the hand, and rarely has buyer's remorse. The real spender loves to dispense his resources! These lucky people (I am one of them) believe in the notion of abundance. They know that there is an unlimited quantity of everything. Like the ocean, the supply is endless; new waves roll in every few minutes. With boundless energy and resourcefulness, we spenders are not worried that the piggy bank will ever be empty, because we know how to fill it again.

But pathological spenders are something else again! These are the people who spend for the sheer love of spending and have no regard for the replenishment of the piggy bank. They spend without responsibility, simply hoping that "magically" there will be enough money at the end of the month to cover all the spending they have done.

Savers. These wonderful people know where to put their resources, how to keep them safe, and how not to tap into these resources when times get shaky. They know how to save. I have never been one of these people. The best saving I ever did was when I was 14 years old and saved all my baby-sitting money in one funny little purple marble bag. I actually saved about sixty dollars in that bag, until the bills were stuffed in so tightly that the zipper was beginning to throw up dollar bills! Savers know how to keep things; they believe in the value of holding on; they usually love old things, and, conversely, they do not let go very easily of any resource they have accumulated. A good saver has many little purple marble bags! It is hard to be a good spender and a good saver at the same time!

Managers. Some people love to arrange money. They move it about in piles, or in accounts, or in money markets, or in real estate. They are great organizers of budgets and grocery lists and make great forecasters and venture capitalists. They enjoy counting money, planning for it, and talking about it. They can be good spenders, earners, and even good savers because they are willing to take the time to organize a system to utilize all aspects of their financial life.

Now, if a sci-tech saver marries a spender, they will have the most common syndrome in our society. When she says, "Honey, let's go out to dinner and the movies tonight," he thinks, "Fifty-five dollars." Period. When he can digest the expense, decide that both he and his wife deserve it and that there will be enough money in the account to cover it, he can then consider the possibility of the dinner and the movie. If he decides against it, he may really be in trouble with his wife, because she may be so starved for excitement and a change of pace that she will do almost anything to get him out of the rut. So, she pulls out all stops, manipulates, or tricks him into spending the money after all. Eventually sci-tech feels duped. And he is even more wary the next time. A tragic cycle!

Another sci-tech couple combination is the manager whose partner is the spender or the earner. In any case, if she is not interested in the theory of financial management, the process of money, business plans, or the financial inventory, she will have difficulty communicating to her partner her need to spend or her need to be emotionally rewarded. If sci-tech sees the big plan as a way that each will earn the most money he/she can, then he is going to be disappointed if she does not voluntarily enjoy contributing her assets to the big picture. She may not give a damn about the big picture; she may just want to be praised for getting a 15-percent raise! This couple will need a second look at the big picture—does it include the mate's need to spend?

If the sci-tech is a manager and his partner a saver, they will need to develop some communication techniques so that he can convince her that there is a better way to use money than to place it under the mattress! Many sci-techs are stock-market addicts. There is something intriguing about these statistics and the law of averages. This more structured and dignified form of gambling entices even the stodgiest of sci-techs to play the market for a while. The potential problem for the manager and the saver can be eliminated if he will take the time to appreciate her spending worries, her fears over money slipping away without something to show for it, and will negotiate a safe plan that can generate confidence in his more conservative mate. Often an outsider is needed to help translate one partner's phobias and obsessions to the other.

Our values are often influenced by our family priorities. When we were growing up we heard our mothers and fathers speak about "what is important," and we often incorporate those values so deeply into our souls that a disparate set of values, from differing parents, may cause strong judgments about "what is important."

Teach each other about the underpinnings of your priorities on material things, on money management, and on security issues. Then expect to negotiate when your partner has a different set of standards.

VALUES

The symptom is fighting about money. The underlying problem is differences in values. When you analyze your value differences, you must also look at your approaches to money, the history of your parents, and your own experiences with what money has done for you and to you. You may be overwhelmed by how hard it is to consolidate your feelings about your family corporate money. If your goals are disparate, based on your differences in values, you are going to have a hard time finding a way to be in synch concerning how to spend your money.

When I was on the United Way Funding Committee, I was amazed that twenty of us had twenty different ideas about how the community money should be spent. Each of us had biases and preferences about where to spend other people's money. Imagine trying to spend your own money that way!

Couples don't really get a chance to analyze where their priority spending will be each year. They don't say, "Well, we both believe that next year it will be time to beautify the outside of our house. Therefore, landscaping will be a high-priority item in our budget. It will be above vacations, wardrobe upgrading, and piano lessons for Jimmy."

Even when the ideal couples do talk that way, they do not put a firm number value on how much should be spent on landscaping. They also do not put a value on the amount that emergencies can supersede landscaping money.

The following suggestions may be helpful:

1. Sit down and make out your own value list.

Here's an example:

Ruth:	*Tom:*
The children's college	Fishing and hunting trips
My retraining fund	Building the extra room

Gifts for my parents' fiftieth anniversary

Buying a personal computer

My sister's wedding

New tires for the camper

House remodeling (new family room)

House remodeling (new family room)

You will notice that the two lists are not very similar. The only duplicate item is the remodeling of the family room. Since it is a compatible item and each person feels an immediate connection to it, this item should probably go to the top of the list for both parties.

2. Put a number value on each item on your own list. Number 1 is your highest priority, number 10 your lowest.
3. Now combine both lists, thereby giving each of you a chance to add items that may have been suggested by reading your partner's list. When Ruth sees "fishing and hunting" on Tom's list, she may want to add "entertaining and dinner parties" to her list.
4. Next, assign a priority value to each item on the combined list, again with number 1 as the highest priority. Don't let your partner see your values until each of you has completed assigning your own values. The list will look something like this:

Ruth's Value		Tom's Value	Total Value
1	Remodeling family room	1	2
3	The children's college	6	9
9	Fishing and hunting	7	16
2	Ruth's retraining fund	8	10
8	Buying a personal computer	2	10
5	Gifts for parents' anniversary	9	14
10	Sister's wedding	10	20
7	New tires for camper	5	12
6	Six dinner parties	11	17
11	New furnace	3	14
4	Furniture for family room	4	8

5. Add up the total of Ruth and Tom's priority points for each item and make a new list of priority numbers, with the smallest numbers first:

Priority Points		Priority Number	
2	Remodeling family room	1	
8	Furniture for family room	2	
9	Children's college	3	
10	Personal computer	4	tie
10	Ruth's retraining	4	
12	Camper tires	5	
14	Anniversary gifts	6	tie
14	New furnace	6	
16	Fishing/hunting trips	7	
17	Six dinner parties	8	
20	Sister's wedding	9	

6. Check the list again. You can make value changes now if you wish. Keep making changes until you are each satisfied. Most people are amazed at the outcome from such a list. At the same time, they are usually very satisfied!

7. If the list is too long, drop off the last several items up to whatever point you both agree on. There really should be only about five priority items for the year. That does not mean that Tom and Ruth may not complete all eleven items, or that they will not address even the bottom of the list. It means that the first five or so items are declared *priority-value items for the family in the year!* Because this couple has two ties, I'd suggest that they drop only the last four items. That means that the new furnace is not a stated priority item this year. They may have to buy one if their old one breaks down, or they may elect just to do some emergency repairs on it.

Sci-techs will be more cooperative about the priority list because it was deduced by the careful planning and forethought involved in this exercise. Partners, you will be amazed at how cooperative your sci-tech can be if he really believes you have applied scientific principles to the conclusions drawn.

THE ULTIMATE RESOURCE: YOU

When you are talking about your financial assets, don't forget you! Each of you is the ultimate resource and each of you can be the best investment you ever made! Sending the wife to law school, helping the husband get his MBA, or investing in that small invention of his may be your best venture. Education, retraining, and small consulting contracts all make us money. So do your talents: piano playing, crafts, and flower-arranging skills can all serve to build your financial empire.

Look at Mrs. Fields' Cookies. This young lady simply liked making tollhouse cookies. And now she is a cookie queen of international fame. Mary Kaye, owner of a multimillion-dollar cosmetics company, started rather timidly. Mrs. Fields and Mary Kaye are the final resources in their households.

Don't be afraid to spend on yourself and on each other. Just because your wife presents her prospectus in the kitchen or the bedroom does not mean that it may not be your best financial opportunity! But ask your husband or wife for references, a business plan, collateral, and marketing tactics, in the same way you would for any potential investment.

Sometimes those opportunities run away with us. Your husband or wife may gladly trade the corporation or the restaurant for a portion of you. When you resent your mate's endeavor, it is already getting late. Not too late, just late.

The Silicon Syndrome man sometimes gets caught in the rush to power, technical breakthroughs, and adventure. If his partner can look at what emotional needs are being met for him by this effort, she may be able to tolerate some of the sacrifices he asks of her.

I liken the career path for some men to the maternity path that some women take. Their maternal instincts are so strong that they spend great chunks of their lives on their children. So may a husband be called to nurture his creative instincts! His yearning for power or achievement may require that he devote great chunks of his life.

By the way, men are beginning to have strong paternal instincts too. Several men I know are on paternity leave; one is a lawyer who has taken off two days a week to tend to his new child while his wife works all five days. Another man on paternity leave took six months off to be with his new son; his wife went back to work within three weeks. I have recently talked to a lesbian couple who decided they wanted a child. These two professional women made a decision together that one of them would carry a child in her body, while the other would stay home to raise that child for the first year. What a wonderful way for a child to know two parents. One holds it in her body for nearly a year; the other holds it in her arms at home exclusively for nearly a year!

One hundred successful executives were polled, and most of them (*Fortune* 500 types) wanted three things from their professional lives:

- Achievement
- Power
- Social contact

Now, there are many successful men and women who do not want all of those items listed above, but my experience with successful people seems to bear out that combination. Can you see why a sci-tech from Silicon Valley may need his partner to round out his social skills if he is weak in that area?

Learning to read the deep longings beneath your partner's career choices will aid you in cooperating with him. "Being picked for the satellite team means everything to me" can be translated in a dozen ways. The secure mate will translate it into:

"My husband loves and wants me, but he has an overriding need at this moment that is not about relationships but is about his need to be part of the team, to be selected for excellence, and to be acknowledged for his technical excellence."

BUT WE ARE EXPENDABLE!

Some of us forget that although we are a good resource for ourselves and are worth the investment, eventually we are expendable. I often see people nearing the end of their usefulness in a particular field. They come to me near retirement age, frightened and despondent that they have nothing worthwhile that they can do for themselves. Prepare for the oncoming poor eyesight and for when your hands won't work with the same speed. Even expect that your mind will eventually play some tricks on you, slowing you down and fooling you at important junctures.

So, as you are using yourself, consider that you are using yourself up. You need, then, to spend yourself wisely, taking care of yourself as you would a fine-tuned machine, planning for the eventually more limited use of your energies and talents.

When I began teaching, my financial consultant reminded me that I could teach with the degree of energy I have now for only about five more years! I will ultimately burn out or simply grow weary from the pace. So we considered my teaching skills available to me for a stated period. That was probably the most soul-searching conclusion about my professional life that I ever made.

YOUR EMOTIONAL NET WORTH

Working out how each of you feels about money and resources takes time. If one partner is psychologically hooked on the notion that poverty is saintly and the other believes in abundance for all, you will have some cognitive dissonance to experience. Your unconscious goals will keep bumping against each other. Talking about your values and your emotional connections with wealth will save a lot of confusion and sabotage later. It may hurt to talk about this, but it may save your marriage!

WHO IS ON YOUR FINANCIAL PLANNING TEAM?

Many Silicon Syndrome couples have financial consultants or advisers. Many have stockbrokers or other wizards or wardens for their resources. But how many of you have a team in which both of you are truly represented?

My financial-planner friends tell me about the primal marriage scenes that occur in their offices. They have seen a wife go crazy because she finally realized that her husband had never been insured, or because the company mortgage was larger than the household mortgage. They have seen a husband go catatonic when he heard what his wife had done to his latest investment strategy.

Your portfolio must reflect your emotional needs as well as your financial needs. "I just can't invest in that," she moans, or, "Why do we need a hot tub when we have a Jacuzzi in the pool?" he groans. Each of us has value biases that can affect our financial life.

Only 2 percent of the people in our nation are financially independent at age 65. Twenty-three percent of the nation must work beyond age 65 to stay alive! Seventy-five percent of those over 65 are dependent on friends, agencies, or family to subsist. These statistics indicate that we are not doing very well with our planning.

Perhaps it would help to consider an emotional look-see at your planning. Sit down together and make a five-year goal plan. It does not matter how unrealistic the goal may be. Just write it down. Then each of you look for advocates for your position and your values and your assessment of the plan. These advocates may be professional financial advisers, they may be your children, or they may be the neighbors. This is only a preliminary discussion.

Now take your goals to a financial adviser whom both of you

like. Let this person assess your goal, make suggestions, offer options. You may need to shop around for this adviser. People often will spend months finding the proper gardener, barber, or hairdresser, but then settle for the first financial adviser who looks at their resources! Often this is because we are afraid to talk about money. We may like to earn it, spend it, or save it. But we may have a terrible time learning to talk about it.

Financial goals seem to be as individual as thumb prints. One partner may long for a financially independent status, while another may want to earn and spend all his life. Making decisions about what to do with your money is as important as decisions about how to earn a living.

If you don't know your net worth, call any banker and he will gladly help you determine this. This is just a start. So is your business plan or your financial plan. Take your portfolio or your passbook to the nearest consultant. And then take it to another, and another, until you have found someone who can talk your language, who can read both of you, and who will mediate for each of you. Your team is important. Bringing in another opinion is vital to your financial life. Your values will predict your investment goals. Discretionary finance decisions must be negotiated as efficiently as any decisions you will ever make!

8

The Boss, Friend, Colleague

OPERATING STYLES

"I'd like to kill him!" you mutter. It's your boss again—being a jerk about a pretty simple task. Or it's an employee being scrupulous about a minor item. Or your friend, the one who drives you mad because he/she is so priggish about noncritical issues.

Learning to work with a personality style different from your own can save your career, earn you promotions, and spare you a lot of emotional wear and tear. It *is* possible to understand your partner, colleague, or superior. It is possible to decide what motivates him, what his reward system is, and to figure out the way he interprets data. It is even possible to get his attention. The solution is simply to find the key to his *operating style.*

I will describe several worker styles so that you can pick out the kind you are and the kind your nemesis is. Then you must learn the behavior required to approach this person.

THE VISUAL PERFORMER

This person sees his work, you, and his problems. His best opportunity to learn about something is to see it in writing—to look it over with his eyes. His eyesight is his first line of input, the initial door to understanding. So if you go running into his office shouting, "Joe, guess what? We are in trouble; we lost the order," you will not get the attention that you would get by going into his office with the cancellation papers in your hand and shoving them in front of his nose!

If you feel good about something, let him see your smile, don't tell him your smile. His best comprehension tool is his vision. This visual person will talk to you in sighted terms. He will say, "I see your point." Or he will say, "Bill, look at it my way."

This person thinks in terms of visions. He can see the past, envision the future, and plan with concrete pictures in his brain. A visual thinker looks into ideas with concrete models in his television brain. He will think in pure shapes, while abstracts will bore or distract him. Give the man charts, graphs of your performance, or concrete models of the job if you want to get his attention.

For him, the telephone conversation will not be as rewarding as it may be to an auditory person. Make your visits in person whenever you need to make any serious proposals. The painting will make the point more succinctly than the poetic speech. Let him *see* his prize.

THE AUDITORY PERFORMER

Talk to him! This person needs the spoken word, not the written evaluation. You can see how complicating this can be if you are a visual person. You may spend weeks preparing a beautiful evaluation form, demonstrating in writing all of your best measurement tools, and consecrating all of your employees' assets to paper, and then you toss it on his desk with a brief, "Here it is, pal."

The auditory performer needs to have the sounds enter his ears. This is his first line of entry. Don't use the secondary method when the first door is so effective with him.

Many people want the words of love more than they want any other concrete demonstrations of affection. They want to hear the love moves.

So may your superior or your subordinate! They may want to be able to translate your concerns for them in the best way they use information. If a person is an auditory performer, skip the written word whenever you can.

The 20 percent of you in his ear is worth more than the 80 percent of you in his vision! Even if you are not good at talking to make a point, you will have to learn to speak his language.

THE KINESTHETIC PERFORMER

This person is alerted to data by body talk. Touch him and you will probably get his attention. He is sensitized to his body feelings. My husband, Don, is kinesthetic. If I want to get his attention, I have simply to reach over and touch his knee or pat his hand, and then his receptive state is available. I could talk the same movement and he would not even notice the statement.

A kinesthetic performer will be more moved by the handshake than by the letter of commendation. He will respond better to an arm around his shoulders than to a long-winded promise of loyalty or compassion.

An engineer/scientist client of mine was terribly despondent when his wife left him. As a therapeutic intervention I asked him to share his burdens with another human being, someone he knew. This robust man, a black-belt karate expert, marathon runner, and skier, who uses his body to express himself, could not think of a single soul to whom he could express his emotional pain. I pushed, hoping he would find someone he could relate to about his despair. Finally, a name surfaced—Dr. Robinson, another physicist from his laboratory. This is how my client remembered him and why: "One Christmas party, about nine years ago, when Dr. Robinson heard I was having trouble with my son about drugs, he came up to me while I was sitting at my desk. He put his hands on my shoulders and said, 'I'm sorry to hear about your son.' " It was the touch, that one symbolic touch, remembered for nine years, that allowed my client to reach out to this man for help.

If you are not a toucher yourself (many people are afraid of intimate contact), you can use some alternate means to approach your kinesthetic colleague or friend. Bring him a sandwich, something he can use his senses on, something he can feel. Bringing flowers to a kinesthetic secretary can say a thousand words. Some men, too, enjoy receiving flowers. Buy your scientist a plant, or an interesting tree, if you are a little worried about image. Get him something he can touch if you want to touch him.

PHILOSOPHICAL STYLES

THE PEACEMAKER

This pleaser personality will approach all business and personal problems motivated to avoid conflict. If this person is in your office or on your team, do not expect him to fight for a cause. He may be able to rise to the issue if the conflict is about inanimate things: "That darned winding machine failed us again." Don't expect him, though, to talk about the operator of the machine if that is really the cause. People pleasers are afraid of calling on another's inadequacies; they will go through a lot themselves before confronting you.

This "pussycat" will not be congruent and will avoid his true feelings if they might lead to conflict. Treat this pleaser with kid gloves and do not expect an adversary role from him.

THE FENCE JUMPER

One step up from the peacemaker, this jumper will vacillate from one position to another, depending on the company.

So eager to seek approval, so phobic about disfavor, the jumper will change tunes so fast that you may feel dizzy. Understanding his insecurity rather than calling him on his discrepancies will serve you better. You will need to bolster this person. Remind him that you will help him when the opposition tries to dissuade him from his position. This person needs a support team. "I'll help you out when the Smithson Company comes around again," will give Fence Jumper the needed relief. Coach him by being a model. Show him how to take a strong position on something. His experience is that strength didn't work; he needs a new teacher!

THE FIGHTER

The fighter wants to mix it up. He makes a statement by taking the other side. He will position himself so that he is on the opposite side of every philosophical fence. He does not really want to be different; he just feels in a more comfortable position (one he is more accustomed to) when he is taking the devil's-advocate role. At the other end of the spectrum from our first two positions, his behavior is just as pathological because he cannot really take an honest position of integrity if it happens to match yours. Handle the fighter with, "John, I understand that you would like us to see another point of view, and I'm grateful for your obligation to the minority position, but we really need your support on this issue."

Another approach is to acknowledge that John must fight, by reminding him: "Okay, John, we realize that you will have to take the other side in this argument, but we are going to have to disregard it because we need a team-player approach here. We have lost our enthusiasm for your dissident opinion because you are so often across the fence from us."

THE SCHOLAR

You will never get a gut opinion from this researcher. He will study, analyze, and throw data about because the information disbursement is more interesting to him than the action that must be taken.

Always use this person in the beginning stages of the project. A great market researcher, he will provide lots of data. But do not expect him to make the final decision, because just as you may be about to decide on one direction, one supplier, one move, he is likely to say, "But if we approach this survey from another vantage point, we had better look at . . ."

This scholar loves theory; he does not enjoy action. Keep him away from the man or woman of results. They will drive each other crazy.

THE PRAGMATIST

This practical person will strive for the end product; he makes a great production manager or procurement expert. He uses what is at hand, and doesn't dally with "what ifs" and "wouldn't it be wonderfuls." He is not introspective and theoretical. He wants to get the job done. "Let's cut the crap and see how many we have left and what we can do to substitute."

If you are not a results person but are in a relationship with one, you owe it to your partnership to give credit to this person who can get results. You can approach the pragmatist with arguments for the merits of analysis, but only if you can show that the analysis will offer a higher yield. Don't theorize; demonstrate with charts, figures, estimates. The results-now approach is open to what works; just show him how.

THE AUTOCRAT

The autocrat believes in rule by defined power. He enjoys a system in which someone (it does not have to be he) holds the scepter. He is most comfortable when the authority is clearly defined and there are no possibilities for democratic sway.

To be political in the office, start with an understanding that this colleague does not want to be tyrannical, but that he/she does not feel free of anxiety if there is a decentralization of authority. The structure of the decision-making lineage is more important to him than the resultant decisions. Think of a child who is more concerned with how the blocks are turned (so that the letter or picture will appear) than with whether the blocks are serving to build something. For the autocrat, the process may be more important than the destination.

THE DEMOCRAT

This boss, employee, friend, or colleague believes in the coopera tive society. The community effort thrills him; he is a cheerleader for the team approach. If you are an individual contributor who believes that committees bog down efforts and that democracy is sometimes inefficient, you will have difficulty cooperating with the participative personality of the democrat. If he is your boss, this democratic position will frustrate you if you are looking for a more authoritarian approach.

To communicate, learn the advantages of the team approach; capitalize when you can by reminding the democrat that you do understand his philosophy. Attempt to convince this team player that a division of authority between the two of you may accomplish a great deal. Each of you can be responsible for half of the job, but you must accomplish the project using different styles. You might assign tasks, oversee the job, and make final arrangements or inspections. Your democratic partner might urge everyone to volun teer for chores after first discussing which chores are really appropriate. The democrat is, in the long run, the easiest person to have in an office because when differences or crises occur, he will be cooperative about handling the difficulties by several approach methods.

ANGER ON THE JOB

When the president picks someone else, when your partner blows it, when colleagues ruin the campaign, can you express your anger?

Seventy-five percent of the people in this country cannot! We have been so well programmed to cool our anger, contain it, control it, that we are now nationally "actor-inners."

An "actor-inner," as opposed to an "actor-outer," is someone who fears the repercussions of his/her anger in front of someone else. Actor-inners suffer, though, from their inability to express appropriate anger freely. Cancer studies confirm this. A compilation of recent surveys on cancer victims indicates that the average victim does not express anger, is not assertive, and often feels powerless in the wake of external pressures. Other diseases that weaken the actor-inner are ulcers, of course, and skin diseases, colitis, cystitis, and back pains.

An actor-inner stuffs the feelings of anger down into his/her body, instead of expressing them, and then lets the body hold all of the pain of frustration, disappointment, and hurt. (We know about fat people who eat anger instead of showing it to others!) Finally, though, our bodies get fed up and begin to yell about the pain inside. At this point most people go to a doctor instead of a psychotherapist.

There is preventive work to do long before the doctor's visit. I have conducted anger workshops at IBM and Hewlett-Packard in Silicon Valley. These companies know the toll that unexpressed anger takes on their executives, and they don't want to encourage heart disease and all the other maladies that an actor-inner is subject to when he cannot express the full range of feelings.

An actor-outer is the person who flares up, usually inappropriately, whenever the fancy strikes. They are ruled by their emotions, and willfully display their feelings without regard to the consequences to others. "You board members are all up the wrong tree. You don't know how to work, and I think you are stupid fools!" the actor-outer bellows while kicking over the chair, then slams the door of the board room. This person indulges his/her feelings to the fullest extent, forgetting the resultant trauma to others.

The ideal method of expressing anger is to understand the theory of appropriate behavior. Some readers will balk at the idea that they have to make appointments to be angry. They will complain that if they can't express the feelings at the moment of impact, they are unable to dredge it up later. I suggest that it is possible to get the feelings back later. Oh, not 100 percent of the experience will return, but by re-creating the events, the dialogue, and the participants, with practice you can nurture back those feelings.

The reason you want to nurture them back is because you don't want your body to continue holding the anger, which eventually turns into a much more subtle, quieter resentment. If you can pick an appropriate person, place, and time to be angry, you will be rewarding yourself with the response you may be wishing for. If you surprise someone, take him off guard in an inappropriate manner, you will find that your listener cannot respond in ways you may want, like, "Gee, I'm sorry about that" or, "Wow, that's just awful!" Instead, your startled listener will close down in fear, run, or stutter out defenses. You do not want defenses. You want someone to *listen* to your feelings.

The way you make an appointment is to say, "Susan, I am aware that you really cut me off just now in the sales meeting. It's happened before, and this felt like the last straw to me. Now, I know we both have to attend the retirement dinner in another hour, so I don't think this is a good time to share my feelings with you. How about tomorrow? We can take a walk at break time and I will tell you about how I felt today."

Oh, that sounds too civilized and contrived? Well, it assures the possibility that Susan and Tim will get to discuss what angered Tim. If Tim said nothing now, he would be adding another straw to the already burdened stack. But if he started expressing his anger now, Susan would be too distracted about the dinner party to hear him fully. She would also be too caught off guard to be able to hear his complaints without defending herself or showing anger back. Many people, when dumped on without notice, simply stop thinking! Their synapses close in fear and they stand in a paralyzed state, not really able to take in the range of emotion you have to share.

Will Susan have to worry all night about what will happen tomorrow on the walk? Tim needs to reassure her that it is his own reaction to Susan that is bothering him, and it may not even be anything that Susan deliberately planned to hurt him. He needs to reassure Susan that it will be a time-limited conversation (the length of the break), and that his complaints are not anything that Susan should lose sleep over. He also needs to assure Susan that, indeed, this is a matter that will not seriously damage their relationship. The idea is not to upset and worry the other person, but to remind the person that you trust the relationship will survive this expression of your anger. In fact, the ideal partnership is one in which the stated rule is that you trust each other enough to be able to share your real feelings, even when they are the negative, more frightening ones. Making a contract to allow the truth of positive or negative feelings to surface between two people is an absolute guarantee of an authentic relationship.

The problem with expressing feelings is that we confuse rational thinking with emotional behavior. Anger is not a rational state. It is an emotional state, not based on logic, but based simply on the reaction our feelings take. It is similar to the feelings a child may have when his mother leaves him with a baby-sitter. The child does not care if his mother must go to work, or if the trip is, in the long run, for his own good. He cares only that his mother is leaving him, and he is mad! The way we sabotage each other's expressions of anger is to reply with, "But, Barbara, that doesn't make any sense at all!" Feelings don't have to make any sense at all.

The single most important deterrent to the expression of anger is to expect anger to be logical. Angry feelings are the inversion of hurt, or, in other words, the flip side of depression.

Anger on the job is appropriate only when all the involved parties contract for the expression of anger. Surprise attacks are harmful and delay production. Tackle the boss or the secretary with, "Dr. Peters, I would like to arrange to talk with you when all the visiting dignitaries are gone. I want you to know about some of my feelings when you yelled at me just now. I know that this is not the right time to discuss this, but later I want you to hear my reaction to your abusive language just now."

Many people are uncomfortable with their own anger. This reaction evolves from decisions we made as kids about our parents' anger. There is a difference between anger associated with violence and anger expressed in arguments. Many of us fuse violence with our memories of anger. If our father was a tyrant, we may decide that anger holds no sensible place in our interactions with others. On the other hand, if our mother always got what she wanted by screaming and kicking, we may decide that this behavior gets us what we want out of life.

Many progressive companies are using consulting seminars to present conflict-resolution packages when disagreements arise. A professional psychologist can suggest positive and creative ways for business people to resolve conflicts safely. My organization, the Growth and Leadership Consultants, offers management seminars that introduce senior-level executives to the notion that anger needs to be expressed in an atmosphere of understanding. When each member puts the other members of a team in a perspective outside of his/her own, team members begin to see varying points of view.

When you hear anger from a partner at the office, say the following to yourself:

1. "I'm grateful that this person thinks enough of our relationship to tell me the truth as he/she sees it."
2. "His saying this may not alter my behavior. These statements do not demand a change from me."
3. "I don't have to defend myself. I will hear his anger and know that it does not have to be a direct indictment of me."

Certainly anger can kill. But holding anger inside also kills. Be easy with your body. Learn appropriate ways to describe your feelings and to deal with the angry feelings of others. It could save your life, can feel very freeing, and certainly clears the air. As long as you remember that anger is not *the truth* but your own reaction to your perception of the experience, you will begin to feel the safety of showing anger on the job.

A TEST FOR "ACTOR-INNERS" OR "ANGER-STUFFERS"

If you answer "yes" to most of the following questions, it is likely that you tend to stuff anger. You are probably not always being authentic in your reactions to situations or others. Try looking for the *appropriate* time, person, and place, and then registering your legitimate anger when you really feel it. *This will save your body a lot of trouble!*

1. Do you usually duck conflict, fearful of saying what you are mad about?
2. Are you afraid to be in the presence of others when they are angry?
3. As a child, were you traumatized by inappropriate displays of anger or violence in others?
4. Do you suffer from lower-back pain, ulcers, colitis, cystitis, skin rashes, or hypertension?
5. Do you generally refrain from sharing your true feelings, fearful that you will lose control?
6. Do you shout and swear at other motorists (in the safety of your own car)?
7. Are you known as "even-tempered Tina" or "sweet Suzie"?
8. Are you overweight (stuff down your feelings)?

9. Do you fantasize what you could have said long after the discussion is over?
10. Do you daydream or dream at night about violent acts on others?
11. Are you generally not very assertive, not getting what you want most of the time?
12. Do you worry that you might lose control if you started to tell someone how you really feel?
13. Did your parents tell you "nice children don't have tantrums"?
14. Do you fear anger displays in other people even when you are not personally involved?
15. Do you feel awkward playing some of the action sports like racquet ball?
16. Do you feel you are holding things back a good deal of the time?
17. Do you start to cry or shut down when you want to be angry?
18. Is it difficult to find people to share your anger with when the source is too frightening?
19. Do you feel hurt instead of angry most of the time?
20. Are you prone to depression?

THE CARE AND FEEDING OF YOUR MENTOR

One way to prolong a professional life is to get a mentor. If you or your mate is lucky enough to have found a professional sponsor, you can give yourselves an extra ten years and countless sums of money and satisfaction. Having a mentor assists you in maximizing your potential. Sometimes, though, this benefactor is looked upon as a disloyal figure who pulls the mate away.

If your husband is the "fair-haired boy," rejoice! Not everyone gets the opportunity to be the chosen one by his superiors. It is a special place, one that can teach us countless leadership techniques and can ice his confidence cake for a lifetime!

Worrying or feeling jealous about your mate's sponsor or mentor complicates his ability to enjoy that social relationship. Mentorships do not last forever! The mentor gets tired, the protégé loses favor or goofs up, or the relationship simply runs its course.

Mentors usually have previously experienced that grand position in their own careers. They always remember "Ted Matheson, who guided me up the corporate path, teaching me, yelling at me, saving my butt." When they find their own protégé, sometimes twenty years later, the urge to extend to their own protégé is very strong. Don't get in the way of it. Even join in on it when you can. "Do you think we should invite Dr. Brown over for dinner to thank him for all he's meant to you lately?" is the helpful thing to do. Studies show that a large percentage of the real corporate kings have had mentorships along their corporate way. Use that asset like another master's degree! The aid of comfort from someone who has been there is worth a million dollars!

BOSS READING

Your boss says no to the trip to Boston. Or your boss promotes someone else to the position for which you worked so hard. Or your boss doesn't regard you as a human being, only as a machine that gets him reports or answers questions on demand. These are the complaints that would surface in the bargaining room of your organization, if you had a bargaining room! Of course, you don't. The best you can hope for is an open-door policy and a supervisor who listens well once in a while.

No, that's not the best you can hope for. You can add some boss-reading skills and you may have a better chance at getting what you want. Studies now appear to prove that a good communicator has a better survival rate, no matter what his/her competency skills are.

As industry recognizes the important tools needed for employees and implements these with classes on communication, assertiveness, and stress management, we are experiencing a new caring attitude about the human product. Business wants every employee at maximum output. To this end, the Silicon Valley corporations and other companies throughout the United States and the world offer classes on topics ranging from alcoholism to finance.

(Last year I was a keynote speaker at an IBM Executives Awards Banquet. I mischievously reminded the three-hundred-person forum that the one course IBM still neglected to offer was on sexuality!)

Figure out how the brain of your boss actually works. Understand his/her sense of logic. It does not have to match your own. You have simply to be able to predict the collection of data that your boss needs to make a decision. You also need to know what his sorting or discarding process is. Does he make snap decisions, does he deliberate, is he conservative, does he move rapidly with an on-the-spot decision? If your boss has an engineer/scientist mentality, he/she will probably look first for what is wrong with the idea. Don't let that discourage you. It simply means that he looks for flaws first. When you realize that your boss will look for flaws, and will then look for usefulness in the idea or proposal, you may be able to wait through the flaw-finding segment of the consideration. This is an important warning: Don't give up too soon!

What is the most comfortable kind of support for your boss? This understanding of your boss's nurturing requirements will help you to read his moods, his proclivities toward some employees over others, and his reaction to you when you try to be sympathetic.

The four classifications of supporters are comforter, clarifier, cultivator, and confronter. Think about your positive experiences when you have tried supporting your boss in one of these styles. But do not assess your own needs for support. That is like buying a gift for your boss that would satisfy your own needs. If you like being supported with *comfort* statements and a pat on the head, don't support your boss in that way unless you are absolutely sure that is the form his needs take. Some people feel very supported if you will help *clarify* the situation for them. They need an attentive ear who will help sort out the data. Others need support in the form of *cultivation* ("Well, we know the problem now; let's see what we can do to explore the option of going to the vice-president about this. First you will need to . . ."). Other bosses will want you to *confront* them with their issues, reactions, and problems. If it is not easy for you to confront, I suggest assertiveness training, because being able to have your boss experience your willingness to risk opinions may be invaluable to your career.

To read your boss, you must determine your ready state and his ready state for input. To check the ready state, ask yourself the following:

• Is this the *appropriate time* of the day to discuss this item? Is he/she a night person or a day person? Is 8:00 A.M. or 6:00 P.M. the time when the boss will be most susceptible to new information?

• Is this the *appropriate place* to discuss the important news? Is the conference room, the parking lot, the cafeteria, or Charlie Brown's Happy Hour the right place to talk? Any of these spots may be the appropriate place. You need to think about the right place for your boss, but also think about where you are most comfortable. (His

office, with the door closed, and a "five-minute do-not-disturb" sign may offer the most privacy and work consciousness.)
• Are you *emotionally ready* to plead your case? Are you too angry? If so, cool off a little first. Tell your story to an objective friend first (not your mate, who may be prejudiced). Are you too intimidated? If you are afraid of your boss, or of your position with him, better get some phobia or anxiety counseling before you tackle the "impossible dream."
• Are you *immediately* ready? What is your current psychological condition, even if you did plan to present your information at this precise hour? Better to postpone the talk if you just had a "rear-ender" accident on the way to work, or you woke up feeling depressed.
• Have you done your *homework*? Most talks with the boss are unproductive if you have not prepared yourself for his answers, his reactions, or his solutions. Think up every possible response that he may have to your suggestion. Write them down. Then plan your strategy to respond. Do all the research you need. Prepare several options.

And now, about the boss:

• Is he/she in an *emotionally ready* state to hear you? Is he too angry with you, with the company, or with his boss? If so, give him a cooling-off period or he won't be ready for your input. Or is he too preoccupied with his own personal problems (mate left, kids on drugs, house was reassessed to a higher tax bracket)? Or is he preoccupied with business details, the quarterly report, the sales meeting, the budget deadline?
• Is she/he *immediately ready* to hear your case? If, in fact, you have an appointment to talk about your review, and the do-not-disturb sign is on the door, but your boss looks weary, discouraged with progress in the business, or simply does not look in the mood to be with you, suggest changing the time of the meeting. Sometimes just the suggestion to change the appointment will bring the boss around to an attentive state for you.

Checking out the ready state in your boss's life is vital. This is not *manipulation*. It is using all your natural resources to present your ideas in the best possible environment. Asking for the full attention you deserve is your right. But providing for that possibility is your responsibility! Many bosses want to be attentive and responsive to your needs, but they feel torn by other tasks that call out to them, perhaps more dramatically than your needs do.

Being dramatic does not hurt. Say something like, "George, I have a very serious matter to discuss with you. It's about my immediate physical environment here. I'd like to make an appointment with you for next Tuesday afternoon, two o'clock, to discuss it."

Be cool, but be insistent. If he suggests you talk now, and you don't believe either of you is in a good, ready state, insist on postponing the meeting until the conditions are better.

Boss reading is a complex but rewarding tool. You may have to do a little reading of yourself, of course, on the road to this awareness. Reading your boss or your colleagues is worth the effort. It is a far more important tool than any other competency you may acquire for job performance. Further, this people-reading tool is a universal skill for you.

CONCLUSIONS

Problems at home and at work often take on the same characteristics. If you feel that you never get listened to, you are probably experiencing that in both places. The nonassertive person who avoids conflict at all costs will have to make the same maneuvers wherever he goes.

Finding the proper balance in your personal or professional life often means taking on some new behavior. I personally have had to learn that not everyone is comfortable with my open and optimistic style. I've actually had some folks tell me that I am too happy and upbeat most of the time. It makes them tired or depressed. The key to the balance is to accommodate when you can without compromising your own authenticity. Your integrity is part of your soul. It is hard to give up our approach to life just because we have met some people who find it hard on them. I do think, however, that really healthy people take a look at themselves now and then, and remind themselves that change is a dynamic adventure that keeps us young, interesting, and in process. When I hear, "Well, this is the way I've always been. I'm not going to change now," I worry. A lot . . .

9

The Bottom Line

THE TRUTH

I am not a lawyer who seeks The Truth. After many years of counseling, I accept that each partner will have his own truth about any given situation based on his experience and perception of the issue.

Now, you will both have The Truth about the date of your wedding. But you will each have your own truth about what kind of day it was. Like witnesses at an accident, the versions vary, depending on the angle of vision, the temperament of the observer, and the bias of the witness.

The way your partner speaks about his daughter's actions on Halloween night will be governed by his angle of observation (feeling protective, antagonistic, defensive, disgusted) and biased by his degree of eyesight and earsight!

A husband's experience of a conversation you both have with your neighbors may be entirely different from yours. You love and appreciate your neighbors (the woman reminds you of your mother, and the man has been helpful in your business as your mentor). Your husband feels threatened and insecure about this couple, and thus interprets their actions from an opposite point of view.

A wife may experience a conversation with your colleague entirely differently than you do. You respect and appreciate your colleague (he/she reminds you of your high-school counselor, your brother, or your best friend). Your wife feels threatened and insecure about this colleague.

There are always at least two truths. Yours. Your partner's. Count on both to be right!

WHEN YOUR NEUROSES BUMP HEADS

What if a woman obsessed about housecleaning was married to a man who was paranoid about women running his life? What if, for whatever reason, he could not tolerate cooperating with his wife? Or really enjoyed messy surroundings? Their neuroses would bump heads!

Here is an example of my own. I am very lenient with my children. Coming from my own neurosis, I tend to overnurture my kids. And I love to do this. But my husband, coming from his own script, believes in putting the "birds out to fly," and he is intense about letting his kids do things in their own way. Our parenting neuroses bump heads all the time. We have problems about holidays, money, housing our kids, helping them with school, and practically every other area of raising children. Luckily, we understand each other, approve of the values our partner has selected for parenting, and can actually appropriate responsibilities accordingly. Don has four of his own children, and I have four of my own. It makes it easy to legislate "our own" children. It is the spirit of cooperation, the tools you use for delegation, that will override the question of whose child it is. With children in common, divide decisions into issues. One partner can always make decisions about financial matters. Another can make decisions about education. If conflict arises, simply flip a coin to see who gets to make the final decision. Kids realize that parents don't always agree in theory. Teach them how to negotiate when values clash about them.

Let me describe another couple whose strong feelings really work in opposition. Maizie is very concerned about her checkbook, and she wants to have emergency money in a savings account at all times. Sometimes the amount she demands in the emergency account is excessive for the total amount the couple earns. But she is adamant. She cannot sleep nights unless the account stands at a specific figure. Her mate, Ricky, on the other hand, is a risk taker who has had an opportunity to indulge himself with gambling on specific ventures his company handles. Ricky is too adventurous; he puts no store in savings, is willing to bet the whole thing, and actually is not very methodical at all, even when his business experience calls for a more cautious approach. Each bends too far in one direction. How in the world does this couple begin to build a financial system without spending all their time lobbying for their positions? Both members of this team coming mid-center is the key. They may need outside help to assist them in sorting out their priorities and analyzing their approaches to spending.

TRUST EXERCISES

My husband was calculating bills while I was typing this chapter. I heard him chuckle. He handed me the source of his chuckle. It was our property-tax bill, which was addressed to Don E. Wuerflein *et al.*

Et al. Is that what I have become in this relationship? I happen to know that a lot of my money went into this beautiful house, but mortgage companies, even in such liberal states as California, like to place the name of the man first. But to call me *et al* is going too far.

Too far? What is actually too far? I guess this was not too far. We both just laughed. We know, even if the mortgage company does not, that I too am important in this house.

We both trust that I own 50 percent of the house and will make 50 percent of the decisions. And we both are the guardians not only of our home but of the things that are important to each of us. Here are five areas of trust to check yourself on:

1. Does your partner trust your power in the relationship?
2. Do you trust your independence in the relationship?
3. Do you trust the power of your partner in the relationship?
4. Does your partner trust his/her power in the relationship?
5. Do you trust your power together?

Learning to trust is like learning to walk! It takes practice. You may have had the belief that trust happens magically with the right person or right relationship. No, we learn to trust like we learn to ride a bike or to swim. *Trust is a behavior we learn; it is not a function of the trustworthiness of our partner.*

Some of us never learn to trust. Probably more of us learn to ride a bike or to swim than to trust. Yet the same prerequisites are needed as to bike or to swim: hold your breath and have faith that you can stay on the bike or afloat. Faith without anxiety causes the balance required to stay on the bike or in the water. Onward with the same faith in a relationship! Put your head up, take a deep breath, and decide that you can trust your partner. You can trust enough to keep your balance, to stay afloat!

Fifty years of case studies correlate positively adjusted people with positively nurturing childhoods. If we didn't get an opportunity to trust some open, loving parents, trust is more difficult to acquire later on.

Even if you got a good start with giving and open parents, a traumatic event in later life can damage your trust level.

A client of mine—let's call her Alice—had a wonderful childhood, but her husband died the night their first child was born. Her second husband ran off with a girl friend on the night the second child was born. Alice may have trouble trusting men for a while. That was her presenting problem to me. Lovers kept backing off. She was probably grabbing too tightly while at the same time she was phobic about abandonment. What could help?

She is in love with Adam, an engineer at an aerospace missile plant. But Alice has to learn to trust all over again. If her engineer lover is afraid to hear the depth of the pain she has encountered, Alice will not begin to believe that it is possible to trust him.

Some sci-techs are afraid to appear vulnerable, so they would not hint to Alice that they might ever have experienced such abandonment or rejection. Unless they can talk about their own vulnerability, they will not have an opportunity to meet Alice on equal ground.

Another problem for some sci-techs is that they do not want to depend on others for emotional sustenance. Cooperating in a business system that interconnects parts is bad enough. Don't ask him to have to depend on another human being for a stage of his emotional development. He is wary of needing to need. Of course, it is important to be self-sustaining. I am not talking about leaning. I am talking about the ability to rest for a while; for someone else to carry the burden; for someone else to support you, nurture you, inspire you, and to assist you with all forms of problems.

Try the following exchanges when you are ready to demonstrate real emotional trust between you and your partner.

Complete each of the following statements:

"I worry that one day you will . . ."
"I worry that one day I will . . ."
"I'm afraid that I don't . . ."
"I'm afraid that you don't . . ."
"I don't like to talk about . . ."
"I think you don't understand . . ."

Do these statements alternately. But don't push the sci-tech with too many of these exercises at once. He will be reluctant to do too much revealing, unless—and I hope this has not happened to you—he becomes desperate to communicate because he fears he is losing you. Then suddenly your previously quiet one may want to start sharing!

Here are more trust exercises for another session. Fill in the blanks, and alternate completing the sentences:

"My delicate body part(s) are . . ."
"I wish I looked like . . ."
"About my family, I wish . . ."
"I wish I could change my personality in the following way . . ."
"Please help me when . . ."
"I feel lonely when . . ."
"I need you to believe in me when I . . ."

THE TWO-PERSON BASKETBALL TEAM

Let's look at your relationship as a two-person basketball team. In order to win the game you must each have special talents. If one of you is highly guarded by two opponents, it will be up to your partner to get down to the basket to make the goal. Each of you must learn to shoot for the basket. That means each of you must be able to handle the kids, do the tax statements, and cook Thanksgiving dinner. Sure, one of you is probably better at each of these tasks; one of you is the better shooter. One of you may usually get to take the shots about finances, the kids, or holiday dinners; but when the best shooter is out with an injury, is out for a five-minute rest, or is out on fouls, the other better be able to sustain the whole job.

Being on a couple team, you must each learn how to pass to the other. You will have to understand your partner's timing, your own handicaps, and certainly your partner's handicaps. Reading each other, your body language, your temperaments, and your stress points will ease you through the game and prevent disappointments.

Some people are very good at working at being individual contributors. The engineer/scientist is especially good at working alone, formulating hypotheses, and testing the theories solo. Left under the basket, he may make points quite easily. But he will not always be left alone under the basket, and so the two of you will have to learn how to work as a team instead of tripping over each other.

As an individual contributor, a sci-tech can be responsible for major tasks. Working with another person can actually slow him down, inhibit him. Learning the cooperative stance takes time and patience. Use your talents alternately, with delicate synchronization, so that the team wins the game.

Many couples live parallel lives, fearing integration and fumbling all attempts at cooperation, and finally giving way to the isolation of "doing it your own way" or "going it alone." It isn't easy to synchronize, to read each other's body language, to think as a unit, but the rewards are exponentially gratifying. Each corporate technique can be multiplied by two because you are each doing less work and providing double the product.

But how can I trust that he can decorate the cake; that she can meet with the contractors; that he can take Paula to the doctor? *By practice!* Just as you finally trust that your kindergartener can find his way home from school alone, you begin to trust that your partner can handle the task on his/her own.

Having faith that your partner can handle your emotional hills and valleys is harder than worrying about sharing tasks. You will need to learn that "hitting below the belt" doesn't work in a relationship that calls for trust. Don't abuse delicate information. Discipline yourself when the "hurt button" is sticking out!

My first three children were close in age and they learned to play team sports at home. I'm talking about how to get enough of the ice cream, how to cut a pie into precisely even pieces, how to share the dog, how to cooperate on camping trips, how to get the house cleaned up before Mom gets home, and how to have secrets about the car and school-absence slips.

My last son was younger and learned to live alone. He is very independent and can take good care of himself. But he will have a difficult time playing on a team with another partner because he has learned how to be independent—not interdependent.

If you are both team players, you are lucky. You will already have learned about giving and taking and delegating and dividing responsibility. If, however, one of you was an only child, or if you learned to be totally self-sufficient for whatever reason, you will have to practice integrating some new techniques into your individual-contributor mentality.

Watch out for narcissistic qualities if one of you wants all the glory. "Oh, I redesigned the whole house" may actually mean that the two of you redesigned the whole house. A good narcissist will have difficulty sharing credit with a partner. Don't give up, though, if you have a nonsharer for a partner. How do you think you got to be a team player? *You learned.* By practice.

If you are both individual players, you will have some problems. You won't have the problem of feeling invaded, or the problem of someone looking over your shoulder at all times, but you will have the problem of isolation, with the inability to express needs. Those needs are so deeply buried that you may not know you have them. You will probably experience a pervasive and chronic feeling of depression or low-level anxiety, and be unable to put your finger on the pain. When these feelings overtake you, ask yourself these questions:

1. Do I feel that I have the whole responsibility?
2. How can I get someone else to share some of the job?
3. How could I divide up this work a little?
4. Do I feel lonely?
5. How can I share myself with my partner?
6. What can I say to let my partner see inside of me?
7. When was the last time that somebody else knew exactly how I felt?
8. How can I let my partner know that I feel overworked, tired, lonely, afraid, humiliated, or vulnerable?
9. How can I share my feelings without putting my partner on the defensive?
10. How can I show my responsibility for my own depression, anger, or loneliness?

Each attempt at sharing yourself will be a painful one. The pain eases, though. I want to encourage you to try letting yourself say or do some awkward things. If you feel foolish or frightened, probably it is because you are trying out something new for you, and it will not feel good in the beginning.

The jeopardy for partners who do not make up a team is that eventually they will travel in opposite directions. Without major psychological interaction over a long period of time, a couple becomes insensitive to each other and ultimately bored.

Joe and Maria, two individual contributors, separated last week and then told me, separately, that they were dumbfounded that they did not even miss each other. No surprise to me. They had dealt each other out emotionally for years anyway. There was nothing to miss.

So mix it up a little. Let yourself interact with your man or your gal. Share, probe, keep initiating, titillating, and stimulating. The price is too high not to!

Another situation arises from the nonteam couple. One partner may eventually—within a work situation, through a neighbor, or at the club or art class—run into someone who will teach her/him how to play on a team. By the time the reluctant partner wants to learn, it may be too late. Watch out for danger signals that your mate is emotionally leaving you. The warning signs are intense interest in activities away from you. Another signal is a new kind of enthusiasm that your partner appears to have until she/he looks at you. Watch the humming! Watch the new clothes, new hairdos. A client of mine sniffed out an affair her husband was having because he started using aftershave lotion again.

I don't mean to imply that the other interest will always be a lover. Heavens, no. Enthusiasm and teamsmanship can be acquired at church, at Democratic or Republican headquarters, or even at a company management seminar. I have had a number of engineer/scientist clients come to see me after they had experienced a mandatory communication workshop sponsored by their companies. Suddenly the emptiness of their marital relationships hit them.

If you are not communicating with your mate, don't wait. Your partner's new appraisal of, or escape from, your relationship is only a PTA meeting away!

INTENTION VERSUS POSITION

The most important contribution I can make to the subject of trust is the word *intention*. Your trust in your partner's intention is the vital link in trust arrangements. Sometimes his "positions" on an item may mask his intention.

His statement or action may not have seemed to assist you, but his intention was to do so. Trust the intention even when the result is clumsy—or perhaps seems hurtful.

We are all very foolish sometimes, thoughtless, inconsiderate, and unconscious. Assuming that the actions were meant to hurt you assumes that your partner is vicious instead of perhaps just tactless. Give your partner the benefit of the doubt. It will help both of you. Look at your partner as though he were an awkward 13-year-old child. Are his intentions honorable, pure, even when his actions look otherwise? Talk about trust. "Honey, I want to trust you, but this meeting sounds awfully fishy. Help me to convince myself that your intentions are good."

Our positions often hide our intentions. We want to do well, be fair, but our position on a subject may mask that intention.

TALK IT, TOUCH IT, OR SEE IT

We learn to express love differently. We receive it differently too. Usually we are not married or in love with someone who receives love in the same way we do.

When I want to be loved, I say to my husband, "Here, Donnie. Make love to me, right here in my ear."

You see, I want to *hear the words* of love. Being an auditory type, it is important to me to hear the words of his affection for me. Of course, I like the other forms, too, but it is especially nice for me to hear Don talk about his love for me.

Now, Don does not need to hear love talk. He needs to be *touched* with love. So when I want to show him my love, I physically communicate to him, with a pat, a caress, a backrub, and more. I can also communicate love to Don by deeds (writing his bills for him, watering the lawn, mending his trousers).

Some of you will need to *see* love. Some of you love to look around you and experience the vision about you. Those are the people who feel best when they can look at a beautiful mate. They will also want to straighten the pictures, their cars will be attractive, and they will want the lights on when they make love.

How does your partner like to receive love? Spend time now thinking about this. Make a list. If you cannot write down ten ways your mate enjoys being loved, you are in trouble!

As a further check, though, read your list to your partner. Remember that this is a list of your perceptions of your partner. You may be all wet. Ask your partner for the truth. You may get some important new data.

Last, ask your partner to prioritize your list so that you will know the best ways to get his/her attention. This list may be worth diamonds, new cars, your marriage!

DON'T BE DESPONDENT.   BE DETERMINED!

If you have much work to do in your relationship, don't feel depressed. This working time, remodeling and renovating your relationship, can be the most exciting, inspirational, and thrilling time of your marriage. It can be fun to talk about your relationship. It can be health-producing to cry, shout, be angry, be sad, be without hope for a while. It will hurt, scare the heck out of you, but at least you will know you are alive.

When you have a scrape or a cut, and you get a scab (I haven't had a good one since I used to fall as a child and scrape my knee—but I still remember the feeling), the scab goes through several stages. Remember the particular time of healing when the scab gets very itchy, and we are inclined to touch it a lot? We even touch it when it hurts a little! It hurts, but we keep touching it, even if it then hurts more. In fact, that hurt becomes almost exciting sometimes: a mixture of sting, familiarity, and surprise. And we keep touching!

Ultimately the scab falls off, and we can look down at the clean, soft, new, tender skin, knowing it will all blend together in a matter of months.

So it is with a relationship! When you have a fall in your relationship, you may cut or scrape yourself. Maybe it is one of those falls when a partner has had an affair, or a partner has been unfaithful in other ways—with money, with business, or with his/her time. Or the fall came when your parent died and you lost hope temporarily. Or the fall came when your child started taking dope or getting into trouble or making poor grades.

Or the fall came more slowly, without hoopla, without pathos, without exclamation marks. But one day you just looked down and you were hurting quite a lot! Or the fall came while you were reading this book, and you realized that your ideal relationship was made up of one of you giving too much. Or, while you were reading this book you realized that your relationship was made up of both of you giving too little. In any case, you have a sore! And it hurts.

Well, you know the hurt is there, and you are doing something about it. You are taking antibiotics of some kind. Or you are rubbing it with topical cream, or you are going to a psychotherapist, or a minister, or to a school psychologist, or you are doing all the exercises in all the books you can get your hands on. Or you are exploring and searching and resourcing, with all your heart, all the medicine, all the rubbing creams that any relationship can endure. And yet—oh yes, and yet—you still tend to pick, touch, or scratch at the sore.

You yell about your partner's past infidelities. You can't stop threatening or mistrusting, or checking pockets or scraps of paper on the dresser. Or you mope about in a depression about the child in the juvenile hall, or you torment and tease about the bad business deal, or you become frightened when a wave of grief for your mother sweeps over you. Or, after weeks of effective listening and compromise contracts, you just plain pick, get bitchy, call names, or feel more despondent than ever!

Do not despair. You are simply doing what the normal, natural, average person does when a past hurt starts to itch a little to remind him/her of how bad the fall was!

I knew a woman who touched the scab of her husband's affair so often that she never let the wound heal. She just kept picking away, never letting it rest, never letting the medicine (our therapy, and his dedication to her) work. Finally, I asked her how long she thought her husband would be willing to pay for his past deed. I asked her to be very concrete. I asked her if she thought he'd pay for one more year, two more years, ten more years, suffering her lack of respect, lack of trust, and continued harassment, nagging, and whining. As we talked, she realized that her husband had been pretty patient with her after all, and she concluded that she probably had only a few more months left to be the pitiful wife.

Then I asked her what she would do if she had miscalculated and had actually used up her last day, and her husband was at the end of his patience. I asked her if she could give up the picking and start trusting this very day, if she knew that this had been declared the final day. After reminding her that she was taking a real chance with even one more day, we outlined a plan in which she would begin to *act as if* she had forgiven her husband.

Wheee! That was a milestone. She did backslide a few times. But always she cautioned herself and eventually her behavior, which in the beginning was contrived, did feel legitimate to her.

Please look at your own hurts. Know that you will go back and touch them now and again. Know that they will itch and you may make them more sore for a while. But bathe yourself in the faith that if you both *want* to forget the hurt and you practice some new behavior, you can look forward to the scab falling off! And with that falling off you will look down and see the fresh, new baby skin of a relationship ready for adventure, love, and relating. The area of fidelity, or of money, business, kids, grief, etc., will be very tender for a while. The relationship skin will be sensitive and, periodically, even exciting. But one happy day that lovely, soft, clean skin will blend in with your whole relationship!

YOUR INDIVIDUAL LOSS IS ALSO A COUPLE LOSS!

If you are not getting your share, your relationship is not winning. If there are areas in which you as a person are in debt, the balance sheet for your relationship will be skewed. Don't be a victim, because a good relationship has no room for victims. Some people have the mistaken notion that if they give 76 percent of the time, the relationship will probably be fine. Well, the other partner may even cooperate by giving his/her 24 percent of the time, but one day, when you least expect it, the giver (you) will give up!

A client who was a tender servant to her old-world husband for twenty-eight years one day left him a note beside his bowl of hot soup, which she had had ready precisely at 1:10 every day for all of their marriage. The note said:

Dear Ewald:
    You will notice that all my things are gone. Do not try to find me. I have been planning this carefully for years. I've gone away to another state to live with friends. You don't know them. I left your clean shirts on top of the dresser. I did not take any of your money. I saved for many years the money I got working for Mrs. Hennesey. The house is clean. Don't forget to turn off the burner.
                                    Your wife, Hilda

Hilda had been the giving one in the relationship from the beginning. When Ewald came home she always had his slippers warmed, his meal ready, and everything in order. She had been a sexual partner to Ewald, on command, and she had suffered his drunken bouts and his gambling escapades. It is too bad that Hilda had not learned to be assertive early in the marriage, so that she could ask for things she wanted and say "no" to things she did not want.

Instead, again without assertion, she simply ran away. She

stumbled into my office months later, in the other town, when remorse had hit her and she had begun to worry about Ewald. I asked Hilda why she could not have at least told Ewald to his face that she was planning to leave him, but she protested that he would have beaten her if she had even hinted at leaving.

Hilda was a prisoner in her own home. To a lesser degree, so are many of you if you bite your tongue and do many things you detest and are not able to ask for what you want. You continue to postpone asking for what you want because you are not willing to risk the discomfort of the confrontation.

People are amazed, when eventually they do confront, to discover that the partner is not nearly the ogre they had expected. Sometimes it is a great relief for the ogre partner to have his mate finally set limits!

I want to share with you what happened during a couples workshop I conducted.

One couple revealed that they had been married twenty-three years, separated for ten months, and were now, that day, beginning to contemplate starting a reconciliation. The wife courageously revealed that she had been accumulating "resentment points" about her husband for the last five years of their marriage. The truth was that she had wanted to leave him, to try her independence, to be a single, free woman again, and the only way that she could leave so wonderful a husband was to begin to feel justified. So she had started collecting negatives about him, enough righteous-indignation marks so that she could walk out of the marriage. Having been out ten months, though, she realized that freedom really lies within yourself. She had tasted being single again, now had a basis for comparison, and realized that she had never really worked on the marriage, and that her husband was someone with whom she wanted to work.

Now, I'm sure that the husband in this case had had some real faults (he admitted so in the seminar). He had not always paid attention, and had kept himself so busy and so self-centered that he had not even spotted the signs of distress and unhappiness in his mate.

Don't be afraid to ask for new behavior from your mate. In this same workshop we learned that the most fearsome-looking person there actually could and did learn to negotiate with his wife. Granted, after hearing the former couple's story, he was motivated! Every couple at the seminar sat up and took notice because they had seen a couple on the raw edge of divorce—a couple who had not given each other a chance to understand the other, not even a chance to hear the other's complaints.

Sometimes complaints are easy to fix; sometimes it takes years to find a solution. But always the complaints are worth listening to. Have the courage to share your worries with your mate. You owe it to him/her. If he/she does not have the full information available about what hurts you, how in the world is he/she going to make the change?

Some partners come to me and say, "Well, at this point I'm not sure that I wouldn't leave him anyway, even if he began to change."

Then I ask, "Is what you are asking from your partner like asking him to take poison? Will it injure him to make this change?"

Usually the answer is "no." To which I respond, "Then go ahead and ask for the change. Maybe he will be changing for his next partner, his friends, the kids, his colleagues, but all of it will help him to live more fully in the world. Give him the gift of suggesting ways to be more available, even if you can give no guarantee that you will still be around when the change is completed. When a spouse loses a hundred pounds, even losing his mate does not detract from the lovely new body. If you are wanting a change that will enhance your partner, ask for it!"

BUT I'VE BEEN THIS WAY ALL MY LIFE . . .

Well, dear pal, it is never too late. Making a change in your lifestyle, your body, your personality, or your behavior can be the most dynamic gift you can ever give yourself. The rigid, authoritarian person who is fearful of change is usually also depressed, tight, structured, and unable to shift, risk, or be adventurous. Change is possible at 99 years of age; change is mandatory at any time before that! Mental hospitals are filled with people who, at the far end of mental health, are so rigid that they continue to do the same precise pattern of movement twenty-four hours a day. Don't let yourself get caught up in, "But I've always done it this way." Or, "That's just the way I am." To this I say, "Well, give yourself a break and try being someone new for a change." You might even like your new behavior. Maybe it will feel a little strange for a while, but, indeed, you will be moving . . . alive . . . growing!

CHARGE YOUR BATTERIES

If you are a couple experiencing a power loss, go for an overhaul! You may need a whole new battery. You may need a new system of getting or giving power. You may need to make changes about how you live together, talk together, make love together, parent together, or worship together.

If it is not a whole new battery you need, you may want simply to get the cables out and have a jump start. The cables may be a new form of communication. If you can learn to transmit information to your partner in a way that makes him *open* to receive the information, you are on your way. And if you can take in information from your partner, can at least hear the complaint, whether it is constructive or destructive, you are in the first stages of getting that jump start.

Before you decide you need a whole new car (partner), consider the benefits you've derived from this relationship. List the important facts about yourself and your relationship. Evaluate the miles you've put on together and make the relationship count for something! I've heard so many people in despair because it took so long to mend their relationship and make it work. "All the years I've wasted . . ." and I always respond with this statement: "Well, okay. So you've had a lot of time to ready yourself for the profound position of now appreciating each other, yourself, or your relationship. So it has taken twenty-two years. At last you can enjoy! The first inning will be a blur anyway; we always remember the last inning. Use it. Enjoy it. Make the next twenty-two years count. Cherish every moment!"

PUT ON YOUR MAGNIFYING GLASSES

Now that I am 50 years old, I have to wear reading glasses. Oh, I can clean my house, put on makeup, and do my nails without my glasses. But if I put on my glasses to read a recipe, or see a phone number, I can suddenly see the details more closely. And with them on, I am aware of all the spots I left on the coffee table, and where to apply the wrinkle cream.

Sometimes it horrifies me to see the truth, but I know that even though I don't see the spot on my blouse with my blurry vision, others will. So, put on your magnifying glasses and go to work. When I get up in the morning and look at myself in the magnifying mirror, I may be a little disheartened. But not permanently! I have faith that with a little dab here and a little dab there, and help from the curling iron, and wrinkle cream, etc., I will be presentable.

I'm asking for the same faith from you about your relationship.

Take a new and magnified look at yourself, begin to work on the spots, and trust that the relationship can survive the clear vision. Give yourself a good, deep look. And then look at your partner, seeing all of his inside parts, the scars, the fears. Finally, look at the two of you together, your powerless parts and your powerful parts.

When you restore an old car, you trust that several coats of paint and finishing waxes, some internal work, and maybe new upholstery will return the old Mercedes to her former glory. Give yourself the same help—with a little gentle massage, with some internal introspection, with some mechanical and emotional tools. You can fix your relationship by mending some old hurts between the two of you. The repair work can be tedious and messy. But begin your restoration project today. Your relationship may need some pushing and pulling, some energy boosts, or a complete new battery. Tell yourself that you are salvageable. More power to *you*!

Unhealthy relationships do exist. If you are a party to one, you may ultimately need the courage to get out. But don't be hasty! I am convinced that most *relationships are salvageable*. Before you write yours off and join the nearest singles' club, try using your independent power to improve your relationship rather than end it.

When assessing the possibility for renewal in your marriage, remember that it takes two to play the game. If your partner does not want to play, you have no game.

Too often the grieving partner who has finally seen the light will come running to my office, promising everything. And it is too late. "I will talk to the kids. I will stop pushing about sex. I will go to a health club. I will send roses." And it is too late.

The relationship game takes two people to play—and, sadly, only one to end. Since I see so many people who ultimately give up on their partners without warning, I have become a bit of an alarmist when I see the signs of ending. Usually it is something as simple as a last straw that ends a relationship—one last unpleasant phone call, one more ruined dinner, one last birthday forgotten, one last scene in front of the kids. Unless you are talking about things, keeping abreast of the problems, checking each other out, and giving each other progress reports, you may never know what the last straw might be. Sometimes we don't even know whether we are doing well. Ask your partner what you've done lately that he/she has liked!

Before you end the game, or give up on the game because your partner is looking faint-hearted, give each of you a last-minute chance at an evaluation. Miracles do happen. After all, you have a lot invested in your present partnership. As I tell my clients, "Make a fuss now—it's cheaper than divorce!"

ABOUT ADDICTIONS

The sci-tech personality is subject to addictions because he has such difficulty sharing his feelings. He hasn't the skills for or practice in letting his feelings out easily.

But it is hard to hold in feelings of anger or loneliness or discontent. Eventually the teapot boils over and has to whistle, hiss, or spit. When the feelings come out, it is sometimes in a terrible torrent of shouting, sometimes in resignation.

The only relief for his emotional pain is in some form of escape. The sci-tech survives because he can find some form of escape. This makes it possible for him to go on, to take the drudgery, the abuse from fellow colleagues, bosses, or families, and the responsibilities, imposed or self-imposed.

The relief comes in various shapes. Some are healthy; some are disastrous. Each person chooses his own escape or ritual.

Addictions are based on rituals. We do the same thing each time, in the same way, to return us to some form of security, even if it is a destructive habit.

Even the wives or lovers of sci-techs are subject to addictions. Their habits allow them some rest from the tedium of a sour or unproductive relationship. I can't tell you how many women I've seen who "habit" away the pain of the dreary relationship.

The forms of addictions for both males and females, sci-techs and no-techs, then, are complex. The first and most obvious one is alcoholism or drug addiction. One can drown his fears in alcohol. He simply swims away, finding solace in drink. Sometimes it also gives him courage, to be social when that skill is not in his nature, or the courage to say what he thinks when ordinarily he might be more hesitant.

Drugs can deaden pain. They can soothe the emotionally drained person and carry him away from the conflict at hand. Since most sci-techs have difficulty with conflict, they avoid it whenever possible. Often quite weak in negotiation and sales techniques, they worry that they will lose arguments, so they don't start them.

Other forms of drugs *lift* the spirits. Such an "upper" may fool us into thinking we are the life of the party. All the lifts are temporary, though.

Mood-altering substances don't work. They are only temporary substitutes for assertion, the ability to express yourself, and the healthy display of anger. Because these drugs are insidious and progressive, though, the poor victim is slowly subjugated to his habit. So the careful, perfect, conservative person will ultimately allow alcohol or drugs to take over his life. What a paradox when the man who so much wants and needs control in his life surrenders ultimate control to a drug. Without inner resources to ask for help, and with a strong veneer to protect his feelings, he can sleep for years in his habit. Functioning—oh yes, functioning—but without emotional support beyond the bottle or the drug.

Isolation is the key ingredient to most addictions. We fall in love with our addictions, closing out the outside world and all who love us. Unless family members are educated about alcoholism, this baffling disease can keep sci-tech and/or his mate from honest communication.

Other addictions are to food. Food nourishes our souls. Our physical hunger and our emotional hunger actually tease us into thinking that our stomachs are empty. The sci-tech or mate who is not being appreciated and cannot get what he wants in life will turn to food for emotional sustenance. The sugar or flour addict is in the same helpless spiral as that in which the alcoholic finds himself. They both have psychological needs unmet and no inner resources to sustain confidence. The substitute food helps for a while. But it never does the whole job.

Favorite addictions for the sci-tech are escape sleeping, reading, or television. Computer work, too, seems to be creeping up on the escape pastimes for some. The sci-tech who can closet himself away in his head through a book, or anesthetize himself with television or other pursuits, avoids conflict, connecting with others, and the criticism he hates.

He also becomes addicted to work. Not only is our sci-tech habitually at the office; he is a victim of the *process* of working. Being playful is not usually in his repertoire. He is not much for laughing or jokes. He may do the bills, the gardening, or the laundry using the same procedure as he uses at work. There is comfort in doing things in a ritualistic way. Excitement is not what he looks for. Security is his base need. And security comes through doing things over and over again.

Love addicts, like smokers and workaholics, are victims of their habits. With the low self-esteem that a love addict generally possesses, he may become hopelessly, completely enslaved by another person, and frighteningly possessive—all characteristics so unlike the constrained scientist who usually has such a rational approach to all things.

But it is often the wife of the sci-tech who becomes the love addict. She accidentally stumbles onto some dear person who can pay her compliments, who can love freely, who sends poetry and is dramatic. Leaving this attention, no matter how unsatisfactory the other qualities of the relationship, is hard on the wife who has only her "scientific-method mate" as an alternative.

Many Americans are becoming addicted to exercise. Although it is generally good for you, do you know that we are raising a crop of people debilitated with anxiety if they do not run their eight miles a day? So add the gym addict to the list of escape artists.

Smokers saying goodbye to cigarettes actually liken the experience to giving up a lover. To give up an addiction, it is vital to have something to *replace* the comforting ritual. That is why lifestyle becomes so important a part of change in alcoholism and other addictions. Find a new way of living or the old habit will tap your shoulder. Weak, tired, hungry, you will listen to the tap. "I need you," it whispers.

Addicts of all kinds need emergency kits, people to support them in the weakened moments, and a new form of living. Herein lies the problem in marriages. A partner gives up his/her addiction. The mate replies, "Good." That is all. That is not enough.

What the addict needs is complete cooperation from family members in setting up a whole new form of living together. Different friends, sports, eating, playing, and sometimes different love-making are called for. The addict's partner must be inspired to cooperate. Unfortunately, sometimes the partner is motivated to get the former addict back to the habit, out of his/her emotional way, wanting to settle for the old familiar system, no matter how bad it was!

An addict can give up habits without the assistance of a partner. But please consider enlisting your partner's help. For the addict, there is usually a co-addict, the enabler who will keep the habit alive. This is not an intentional role. Often enablers are incensed to be so labeled. Check your system out, though. Are you keeping the addiction alive, ever so subtly, ever so innocently, but ever so efficiently?

HOW TO MEND A RELATIONSHIP

When you get hurt, you need medicine: a kind word, a caress, or an apology. Too often these gestures are not possible because your partner feels he must justify his position rather than appeal to your suffering.

Couples stay stuck in their pain, each sinking farther into the black hole of estrangement because they are afraid to *make the first move*! What a waste of time, this waiting period.

Make the first move. Neither of you will remember who made the initial move, just as neither of you can accurately recall who made the move that turned over the applecart! Bite your tongue, cross your fingers, and go over to your partner with:

"Gee, Bill, you look awful. I guess we both feel pretty bad. I wish it had not happened this way. I'd like to do something to bring you around—to bring you back to me."

Mending happens when you each acknowledge that the facts are not as important as the remaining debris—the pain, the disappointment, or the loneliness. Even if your mate was a "turkey," he may have been out of control, unable to act with the maturity required of his 55 years. He may have a thousand excuses, or he may have none. It's done. *Now, what will it take for you to feel better?*

It is so easy to mend a situation if the wounded party will try to come up with something his partner can do to make him feel better. All too often we choose to brood instead, holding on to the wound, even stroking it.

When Eleanor decided that she could let go about the twenty-three years of birthdays that David had missed, the relationship began to have a chance. When she could decide what to do about those years, the relationship was sure to survive. And when she asked David to give her twenty-three presents now, to make up for all those missed birthdays, she began the final step to emotional growth for the relationship. Of course, she gave him lots of time to make up all those gifts. She gave him three years, and she even helped him decide the kinds of things that she could enjoy that were not too expensive. She gave David a chance to apologize, something concrete and specific to do to mend with her.

Give your partner a chance to get off the hook. Stop the painful mourning period and let your partner begin to pay you back or begin to show you his/her caring. It does not matter that the crime does not fit the punishment. The crime and the punishment are judged by two sets of perceptions, values, and experiences, anyway. But find a way to contract a solution for the suffering. "Well, I don't want to buy all twenty-three gifts, honey, but how about a promise that I'll buy one big one and five little ones within the next year, and that I'll never forget another birthday?"

Mending takes time, finesse, and an eagerness to get out of the dark spot. Too often we get so used to the storm that we don't even fight for the sunshine. If you are not used to taking care of yourself, much less your partner, much less your relationship, it will take much practice before you can see the emotional light of day.

A SILICON SYNDROME CONVERSATION

MARTHA: Oh, I hate you, George! I begged you not to leave on Sunday business trips anymore. We have so little time together these days, and I feel so miserable now. Why can't you leave Monday morning?

GEORGE: Oh, God. You are not going to go into that again, are you? I've told you that I have to leave this Sunday so I can present this design to Telegraphics at eleven A.M. on Monday. Please get off my case.

[George denies Martha's effort to explain her feelings. He doesn't acknowledge his prior commitment to her; he tells her that Telegraphics is more important.]

MARTHA: Well, this is it. I've finally got it. You don't love me. You refuse to do what will help me.

[Martha throws in the towel. She draws the conclusion that George does not love her. She does not give George a chance to compromise, to help her, to love her.]

GEORGE: Hell, Martha, you are always whining! No wonder I want to get away.

[George still does not let Martha know that he sees her in pain. He then adds the barb that he knows will add fuel to the fire.]

MARTHA: Oh, I'll bet you want to get away. So that you can seduce some stewardess. Leaving me with the kids and your relatives coming next week. As though you could make it with any woman! Your sex is in your briefcase— printed circuit boards, breadboards, and drawings!

[Martha accelerates the argument. Then she starts the affair accusations. Finally, she fights back her hurt and disappointments with the low blow about George's sexuality and performance style.]

GEORGE: Who could get turned on around here? You've got stuff all over the place; you're always sweaty after those slimnastics exercises, and you just don't know how to set a mood.

[George now does his emotional slapping. He is tossing back to Martha the responsibility for their dismal emotional connection. He has given up, too. It's easier to be on the offense than to hear Martha's disappointment.]

And now, the ideal conversation:

MARTHA: George, could we talk a minute about the trip to Washington? I know that you are intense about this and I want it all to go well for you.

[She gets a contract to *talk* about the problem first. She doesn't just spring it on George. Then she reminds him that she knows how important the trip is to him; she doesn't make him choose between their marriage and Telegraphics.]

GEORGE: Sure, Martha, let's talk about it. I'll bet you are disappointed that I am planning to leave on Sunday. That robs you of a whole day with me, when our time together has been so short anyway. And the kids are no fun when you have to parent them alone on a long Sunday. I want to apologize for breaking my promise.

[Smart George agrees to talk without defending himself! He immediately acknowledges Martha's disillusionment, her getting cheated of time with him, and that the kids are a hassle to manage without him.]

MARTHA: Yes, it's a bummer for me. But I know you would not have broken your contract with me if you had not considered this important. Next time, try to confirm with me about this kind of a change before you make the reservations so that I have a chance to plead my case!

[Brilliant Martha is trusting George's *intention* instead of doubting him. Then she is setting the seed for next time so that she can encourage George to remember to confer with her when he can.]

GEORGE: Okay. But for this time, what can I do to make this up to you? What about dinner on Saturday night, or maybe I could take you and the kids to the park all day Saturday? Or meet me at the airport on my return flight and we'll spend the night in the airport motel because our sex life has been a little weak for both of us lately.

[George makes an offer to conciliate. He is willing to bargain for his poor judgment. He *assumes* that Martha wants to forgive him and make amends. He offers something that might interest her. He also acknowledges that their sex life has been colorless for both of them lately, and he makes a two-for-one offer that may soothe feelings about the trip and begin to mend the situation about their sex life. No wonder he is the Silicon Wonder!]

THE BOTTOM LINE

All too often couples struggle in the last gasps of a relationship without even knowing what it would take to make things feel better. Finding out what you need is the first step in fixing the syndrome. If you are gaining weight from not expressing your feelings because your partner is tired of hearing those feelings, how about deciding to learn to share those feelings in *moderation* so that your partner is not scared off by them. If one of you is drinking too much, sleeping too much, escape reading too much, make some decisions about treatment for the symptoms, and especially about treatment for the underlying causes. If one of you is a workaholic, look at the problem together, checking out the co-addict as well as the overworker!

Many of you who read this book are lonely. You live in your own world, in the office, classroom, hospital, courtroom, or at home, alone. Your partner does not come in, can't find the way in, or you can't open the door. But you are lonely. And so is your partner. It is a hard, cold, frantic world out there. Our internal judges are always prompting and scolding us, and the external judges lecture too. How can we get relief?

Once, during a lecture in Palo Alto, I proclaimed, "Most of you are sitting here tonight thinking that the rest of Palo Alto is having a better time than you are. You will drive home looking into living rooms, imagining that most of the households are entertaining friends, or that families are sitting by the fire, singing or playing Scrabble. You are feeling alone, thinking that everybody else is relating better, having more closeness and intimacy than your family is."

The week after the lecture, I got many phone calls from my

sophisticated, high-socioeconomic families saying, "It was such a comfort to know that others feel as we do. We thought we were the only couple in Palo Alto who didn't relate well, weren't having any fun."

It is hard to maintain a solid relationship in Silicon Valley and in all the other valleys and hills of the world. Staying in intimate connection with our partners, given the emotional rhythms and the social and economic pressures that test our value differences, is the hardest job we have. I always tell couples that they can expect some sort of problem every fifty-five days! Warned of this and reminded not to fear those down spots, not to panic that this means they are not compatible, the couple begins to relax when things get hectic. The fine line is making a decision about how much pain is too much. If you want to overcome some hurdles, it will take both of you wanting to make the relationship work.

The bottom line is: Decide that you want this relationship. Decide that you deserve a good one. Decide that you will ask for changes in your partner to get the bare essentials that you need. Decide that you will bargain with him to give him the bare essentials that he needs from you. And then serve each other! Be "user friendly"; let your partner work you, test you, expect from you, and feed you emotionally.

It will be hard. It will feel funny, silly, awkward, and dumb. You may want to give up after the first try. "Those stupid exercises don't work for Jack and me," you might say. And I say, "Bull!" All or any parts of the relationship tactics can work if you will give yourselves a chance to take the first blundering steps. You cannot lose twenty pounds in one day. And you can't make your marriage over in one day. You will lose one-quarter of a pound in a day, no more, usually. The improvement rate in a soured relationship that is all battered and scarred will be about the same: one-quarter of a pound a day!

Going to Europe, buying a new car, or having a baby will not cure your relationship. Even a cruise won't do it. It will take small conversations, little negotiations, and minor adjustments to begin the knitting of the broken relationship.

The Silicon Syndrome serves to deepen the gap between you. The high-tech overload we are all exposed to deadens us to the emotional connections we may need. But the Silicon Syndrome will not kill you. It serves only to cause pain, itching, and swelling. It is not a terminal condition. The bottom line is that you can make it!

Your couple corporation is as important as the one you earn
your income from. But the rewards in your relationship don't come
as regularly as your paycheck comes from the company. And the
"shut-down periods" may be more frequent at home.

You may have spent four to eight years in a college or university learning to be a scientist or engineer, but how much "classroom"
have you had learning to be a partner?

If you are the mate of this engineer/scientist, you may be
feeling battle-weary. So is he! Turn your relationship around. You
can do this together. The bottom line depends on both of you. Are
you willing to start over, this time with new tools, shiny perception
glasses, and the knowledge that you are worth the effort? The
Silicon Syndrome is only the symptom. You are the treatment. . . .

10

Hope for Relationships Today

HARRY AND RACHEL

Rachel woke up feeling as shiny and bright as her kitchen looked, with the morning sun glistening over the beautifully remodeled serving bar. Like her kitchen, she was better than she had been in years.

She donned her favorite hot-pink jogging suit and proceeded down the road. Her husband, Harry, had already left the house, starting his own run. Harry ran his ten miles in half the time Rachel did her own tour of the neighborhood. It was wonderful to be able to have separate exercise routines. That was one of the things they had learned in counseling: they didn't have to run at the same pace. They didn't have to do anything at the same pace. In fact, they didn't have to be together every waking moment, just as long as they knew that, for most of the time, they chose to be together.

Rachel and Harry had learned a lot about their relationship. They had discovered that Harry was very independent and needed lots of room in the marriage. So Rachel disciplined herself to leave Harry alone for hours on end. She took up painting so that she could spend quiet time in his presence without taking up too much of his space.

She also learned that Harry could not show emotional vulnerability when he was sad, mad, or disappointed. It was hard for him to lean on others. She needed to proceed gently when Harry experienced emotional pain. He was not comfortable sharing his hurt feelings. She mastered approaching slowly, on a superficial level at first, so that Harry could "work up" to his feelings at his pace, not hers.

And Harry discovered that Rachel felt dry and dead if she did not have some dramatic or passionate interchange some of the time. He found out that he could indulge her need for being babied sometimes, and that he could move in closer to her and ask her for her feelings immediately upon the impact of her disaster. He learned that she didn't want a waiting period. Couldn't handle it, actually.

Both Harry and Rachel had been finding out lately that they each had some neurotic behavior, and that this was just fine. Sometimes they could help each other. And sometimes they could not. They discovered that being in a relationship does not mean being on guard, at service, 100 percent of the time. They began to feel comfortable if they met each other's needs half of the time. For the remaining half of the time, they learned to meet their own needs, not counting on the partner to help. They also discovered that there would be times when nothing could help.

Harry and Rachel had been in my practice several years before. They came steadily for about five months and then only for booster shots. I considered them one of my prize couples.

When they had originally arrived at my office three years before, they were on the brink of divorce. She was overweight and without goals; Harry was moody and depressed and without emotional nourishment. With patience and time they mastered reflective listening and eventually got to the point where they were safe and secure again in their love and in their relationship.

Then disaster struck this couple. Harry's company had grave financial difficulties. Harry, who was product-development director, took the company disruption quite personally.

Rachel simply could not identify with Harry's morose attitude. She knew that even if the company died, the stock sale they had made two years earlier had ensured their security. It was not a question of money. This company had been more of a toy for Harry . . . or so she thought.

Actually, Harry had come to identify with his products. His ego had become intertwined with his innovations and his company. Over those last months he had spent more and more time at the job.

Jill, his secretary, understood completely. She knew how important the products were, how many people depended on him, how the Japanese waited expectantly for the latest product word. She worked feverishly alongside Harry, and secretly wondered why his wife couldn't be a little more understanding.

And so the chasm began to widen. Misunderstandings snowballed and each partner spent more and more time building his/her defenses when they were together.

"I wish you could be more patient, Rach. It's only another six weeks."

And Rachel would sigh, "Well, I'm not sure that you are *ever* going to enjoy us again."

Even though both parties were highly intelligent, they started the tumble.

When we start a downward spiral, caused by internal or external stress, a sort of phobia takes over. Then we panic that things will continue to get worse. Worrying that we may never be heard again by our partner, we begin to lobby for our position, instead of listening for the other's complaint and asking what we can do to change the system a little. It is the frantic worry that we may never get better again that sets us into a new and frenetic pattern of exaggerating the problem. If only we could sit still, as a couple, and say, "Right now this feels awful. I am a mess and he is unapproachable, but our marriage will survive this. We are a permanent condition, and we each want to be together, although we are each currently quite ill at ease."

Harry and Rachel proceeded from lack of understanding to panic and then to the last stages of a relationship. Harry was spending more and more time with his secretary ("She understands me"). Rachel jumped to the "Rachel's not okay" position, and made herself impossible to be around. "I can feel myself getting nastier and nastier," she said, "but I can't seem to stop myself."

They began to argue about the house, the kids, the garden, the dentist, the water softener, Rachel's lipstick, and Harry's toenails. Nothing was working.

And then one day they decided to take the road back to health. It was a long journey. It wasn't just a matter of counseling. It was a matter of changing some attitudes, some value systems, and most of all, it was a matter of discipline. There were old habits to break, some patterns that had almost become involuntary. Both members of the team had to start anew, remembering to catch themselves when old responses nudged at them.

Rachel learned not to push Harry when he was feeling vulnerable. She also learned to negotiate for herself when the resentments built to such a level that she could feel herself pulling down inside herself. And Harry learned to listen reflectively. He learned that Rachel would not always be logical, that even his own feelings didn't always

have to make sense, and he practiced reaching down inside himself
and pulling out his feelings even when they scared him, making him
feel vulnerable and foolish about himself.

Yes, they brought their relationship back to life. They soothed
their wounds, bathed their misunderstandings, and braved their life
together again.

Now, back to yesterday morning—that sunny morning about
which I started this chapter. Rachel had finished her walk and was
proceeding to get ready for work. She is marketing manager for a
local Silicon Valley company.

About eight-fifteen the telephone rang.

"Mrs. Danforth, your husband has had an accident. Could you
come to the hospital now?"

Harry had been hit by a car. A drunk driver had been arriving
home from a party at six-thirty in the morning, just moments after
Harry had set off on his run. Eventually, someone discovered the
body on the side of the road, and an ambulance took him to the
hospital.

When I arrived in the emergency waiting room, Rachel sat
motionless, holding Harry's bloody running clothes. Harry was in
surgery already, his head and back being examined by the surgeons
who hoped for the right break: the kind of break that could be fixed,
that would not cause paralysis, that would not allow for seepage into
the brain or into the spinal cord.

This tragedy reinforced the decision this couple had made some
years before. Their marriage could survive sickness and health,
troubled misunderstandings, and the pain of learning to translate
differences.

Rachel was sure of one thing. She wanted Harry alive. She
wanted him, the marriage, with its bruises, scratches, and broken
bones. She would do whatever she had to do.

Now, those of you who haven't reached the peaceful spot that
Rachel and Harry obtained might take another look at your relationship as if one of you were on the operating table today. Sometimes a
tragedy will awaken the preciousness of your partner.

Don't wait for that kind of motivation, though. It takes too long,
it's too dangerous, and sometimes it never comes. Just the stale,
old, tortuous relationship stays around. With you. Withering your
spirits, damaging your heart.

So, if I haven't inspired you with tools and technology for trying
to improve your relationship throughout this book, let me scare you
into worrying that your time together is short—as short as that

jogging trip yesterday morning. Harry and Rachel were lucky. They had already made the changes. They had already begun to live in their relationship. They had mended the emotional bruises, learned to be patient with each other, and started the journey of understanding.

The tragedy will simply reinforce the work that this couple had already done in their relationship. Most of the work had been much less dramatic. It had been hours of hammering out negotiations, about money, the kids, their individual sexual preferences. It had been more time spent on learning to listen reflectively, not to jump to "fix" problems, but to hear them from each other, without judgment, without accusations.

Sometimes, by the way, tragedies don't work at all. So don't wait for one. If a marriage is really stressed, the extra burden of an unexpected trauma can send it tumbling over the hill. Divorces often follow family deaths or career crises. It's hard enough to survive when a relationship is strong. Don't wait for trauma to motivate your partner. Waiting is wasteful. Act now.

Why can't couples feel motivated before a tragedy strikes? Why can't we simply stop everything we are doing and say, "If I have a choice to be alive and make this relationship work, will I take the opportunity? Or will I bellyache, cry, whine, and wish for improvement, without lifting *my* finger?"

Yes, it's hard to make the first move. I wish my husband would do it. He wishes I would. You wish your lover would. He or she wishes you would.

The funny thing is that nobody remembers who makes the *first* move. They remember only who makes the *last* move. It's like a movie. The last scene lingers. (Like the last scene in this book?)

Make the first move. *Whichever* of you is reading this book:

Please remember:

You make the gesture.
You may even be rejected.
You may have to make several attempts.
Do not expect your try will restore the relationship.
You may even make some clumsy tries.
You may inadvertently delay the reconciliation.
Try again, round 2, 3, 4 . . .

Now, back to Rachel and Harry. Last night Rachel slumped in

the chair in Harry's room, sometimes sleeping, sometimes crying, sometimes praying, always worrying.

Fitfully Harry dozed, cried out in pain, and groaned and cowered when the nurse came in to check him. At last Rachel saw the dependent Harry, the needy one who could express his pain, his fear, his agony. The dependent Harry she had once wished for . . .

Harry had concussions in five places in his skull, one dangerous break at the base of his skull, and cuts over most of his body. Both of his legs were splintered. He lay very still. Very still.

The worst problem was the blood Harry continued to vomit. Was there a leakage in the brain? Would that beautiful brain ever work again? Would those once firm brown legs run at high speed again? Would he haul Christmas trees or carry groceries? Would he laugh, yell at the kids, or shout at the neighbors ever again?

Please put yourself in Harry's position. Take a look at how bad it is for you now, and see if you could rise up and do something on your own behalf. Is there something you can do? For your mate? For your life? For your relationship?

Yes, there is hope. For you. For the human condition. We can withstand a lot of agony, serious amounts of change, shocks of all kinds, and even the emotional witherings of family members.

We can survive a father who beat us, a mother who was an alcoholic, and siblings who molested us. We can survive. And we can survive the trials and tribulations of a mate who can't hear us or a lover who disappoints us.

Use the tools at hand. Classes, exercises, your friends who will give you feedback. And don't give up unless your partner gives you an unequivocal, absolute, positive, **"No, I do not want to be with you anymore, under any circumstances."**

. . . Rachel just phoned me. It is thirty-two hours after the accident.

Harry will live. The bleeding has stopped. There will be no paralysis.

My heart fluttered with relief. Another beautiful person is spared, for now.

Harry will run again, produce again, hide from Rachel again, and slip into old habits. And Rachel will probably take things personally again too. She will whine, groan, and plead. They will feel estranged. But they may never again *be* estranged. They have had the wondrous, final shock, which sometimes startles us into knowing what is important. The trauma reinforced their commitment, but the relationship got sturdy years earlier.

HOPE FOR SILICON SYNDROME MARRIAGES
ALL OVER THE WORLD

There is a future for Silicon Syndrome marriages all over the world. Recently I was interviewed by *Radio Free Europe*. The reporter said that my voice would be played in Russia and East Germany. My actual voice, in "bites," as they call them in the trade. He told me which quotes they would use. In Russia, you see, they also want to know how to pull out an emotionally detached personality and give him love. They also want to know how to mend a broken relationship and how to get your partner to love you in the way you want to experience love. The problem is not American; the problem is human.

There is relief for relationships in which one of you is a lawyer, a bricklayer, a teacher, a tennis pro, or is unemployed. We are in an era of beginning to understand families, how people interact, how they treat each other and why, and what to do when we make mistakes with each other.

We have been studying interactional behavior for only sixty years. The profession of the licensed marriage-and-family counselor is only twenty-one years old. We are babies in the field of human systems. Give us time. Give yourselves time.

Oh, I know. You can't wait. You can take only another two or three days of this. Or you only have another twenty-five years to be married, or maybe even ten years to live, or another dozen years with your partner. "Hurry up," you say.

We did without the clothes dryer and the microcomputer for a long time. We may have to do without all the answers for a while longer. In the meantime, I urge your indulgence with your relationship.

Cancer may not be cured in your lifetime. Relationships may not be either. But stay as healthy as you can anyway. Use all the preventive medicine you can.

Decide that all the answers aren't available yet. We can look at the moon, but most of us can't touch it yet. Still, we can enjoy the moonlight. . . .

Stroke your sci-tech's hand, pat your woman's forehead, and promise each other that you have a few more attempts left in your heart. Shed the grief-case, plan to teach your partner how to love you, and then wait, building in for mistakes, planning an emergency kit, and holding on to the hope that relationships do work. The simple act of holding that hope makes it possible.

CHARLES AND SHARON

My last anecdote:

Charles and Sharon attended one of my workshops recently. They were new to my practice, but their problems were not new. They are the classic Silicon Syndrome couple. Charles, 53, manager of engineering, at one of our largest Silicon Valley industries, was attending his first workshop ever. They had been to counseling before. Yes, indeed. Many times over their stormy marriage. And he hated all of it. He sat at the outside of our seminar group, near the door, ready to escape.

Sharon was a beautifully attired woman who seemed both angry and despondent at the same time. "This is my last attempt," she said. (How many times have I heard that in my office? You might think I would shrink from all that responsibility. The Court of Last Resorts . . . for marriages.)

For over twenty years Charles had been putting his career first. The decisions concerning the children were left to Sharon. Although she now worked too, she still had emotional needs from her husband, who flew all around the world, entertaining customers instead of being at home with Sharon.

Charles was morose. "I don't know how to please her. I don't drink, gamble, or chase other women. I have sent three kids through college, we have a beautiful home, and I just bought her a diamond necklace and a new Mercedes in her favorite color."

Sharon sighed, sent him a look that could kill, and whispered, "And you took the IBM account people out to dinner on our anniversary."

This couple seemed inconsolable. Sharon had collected years of resentments. And Charles felt so defensive in her presence that he yearned to stay at work, where he was understood, respected, and admired. "Yeah, I was a lousy father. I just never could relate to kids. But I never spanked them." I noted that Charles never looked anyone in the eye when he spoke. His face was gray, like his suit, and he seemed terribly uncomfortable.

Emotional scar tissue covered both of them. Charles felt unappreciated for all the effort he had made to provide for the family. He didn't think that Sharon knew the best parts of him. I think he was right. And Sharon was suffering from lack of emotional contact. She wanted a major sacrifice from Charles: some sign of love bigger than his contracts, his company, his gifts. She wanted a gentle, loving touch, a look of love.

Of course this was an impossible wish. How could someone who felt so badly about himself, no matter his protestations about his grand efforts, feel open and giving enough to share himself with his wife?

How could someone who never had a model for compassion and who was reinforced by company and profession, for his logical and scientific approach to all things, suddenly become gentle and dramatic or passionate?

Disappointment seeped out of every pore in their bodies. "I never dreamed we would end up like this." Each of them cried inside, wanting, unable to give.

I had my work cut out for me. In five hours, with fifteen other people who also had needs in that room, I had to teach this couple to hope.

I lined up all the women on one side of the room with Charles. I told them all to role-play Charles, with no lobbying for Sharon's position, even though I knew that they wanted to be on her side. Most of them had felt her despair, had experienced the loneliness, the desolation of being a single parent in a double-parent household.

Then I lined up all the men to sit on Sharon's side. I asked them to put themselves in her place, to try to imagine her responses to the marriage, to give a speech to Charles as though they were Sharon. And I warned them not to respond from Charles's point of view, though I knew how comfortable they would be on his side.

"This is the last hour of your life," I began. "You have but one speech to make. Tell your partner now that you understand her/his position, the pain, the toll this marriage has taken. And tell your partner that if you had another chance at life, if the executioner could stay your death, what you would do with this partnership."

The first man role-playing Sharon said; "Charles, I know that I have been a difficult partner for you. I don't seem to appreciate how successful you are. I concentrate only on how awful you are as a husband and father. I should remember that you had no father as a model. Yours died when you were six. And your mother was poor, very poor. I should remind myself that you believe that you have given me so very much more than she had . . . security, luxury, your presence. . . ."

"Charles, I'm sorry," another man said simply. And tears began to roll down his cheeks. He glanced at his own wife. . . .

And then each woman gave a speech to Sharon, as though *she* were Charles. And they said things like:

"Sharon, I know that I have disappointed you. God, it must be rough to feel completely in charge of the whole family, even when you are working on your own. But I had no skills for being a husband. I love my work, Sharon. But I love you too. And if you leave me, I will be like those old withered-up, bitter guys at my club, worrying about how to get their kids to come to Thanksgiving dinner. Sharon, I'm not dead yet. I can learn new tricks. I want to. Coming today is proof of that."

"Sharon, I know that I have a lot of making-up to do. I am ready to start. I'll probably slip back. Jean Hollands told us that that would be okay too. I am more familiar with my old and inconsiderate behavior, and I will be like a baby trying new stuff."

Then I asked this couple to give each other a few more months. "But I've given him over twenty years," Sharon wailed.

Yes, I knew. But I explained to Sharon that Charles was a kindergartner in relationships, and now she was expecting graduate school. That he was willing to enroll in relationship school was enough!

The group convinced Charles that the ball was in his court. It was up to him to make the first move, to start the gestures, blundering as they might be.

At the workshop I taught Charles how to say, "I love you, *baby*!" passionately. I made him stand up and shout it and flail his arms. And he did it. I knew he would. His marriage was at stake.

And we encouraged Charles to say, "I know I've been a turkey. Please give me another chance."

And we taught Sharon to give up soaking in the twenty-odd bad years. Resentments are a waste, poison, I screamed at her. All she has is today.

And you, dear reader, have the same day. . . .

I reminded both Sharon and Charles that Sharon, too, would slip. She has been holding resentments so long that her involuntary reflex is to doubt Charles, to distrust his motives. So sometimes Sharon will sabotage Charles's best attempts.

If you are a Silicon Syndrome couple or a Canadian couple, or a couple of Texans, start to forgive yourselves for your divisive love, for your unique comfort- and decision-making needs. It is hard to love another human being. . . . "He just doesn't act like me." But there is hope. Find it. Put it in your pocket. That gesture alone will start you on your journey.

And the trip—the rocky, bumpy, desolate, exciting trip—is, after all, the only alternative to being alone.